The TRAVELLERS GUIDE to CUMBRIA'S WESTERN LAKES & COAST.

THE MOST COMPREHENSIVE GUIDE-BOOK
EVER TO THE WEST COAST OF CUMBRIA.

RegentLane Publishers & Printers

have other non-fiction book titles available

- *Towns & Villages of the Lake District and Cumbria*
- *Towns & Villages of Yorkshire*
- *Towns & Villages of Peak District & Derbyshire*
- *Towns & Villages of Lancashire*
- *Kendal & South Lakeland Guide*
- *Northern Murders & Manslaughters*
- *Made to Measure*
- *Granton–Memories of a Wartime Farmer*
- *Ready for Easter*
- *Venus and Her Men*
- *The Brass Bandmaster*
- *Guidelines on Brass Band Sponsorship*
- *Murder Most 'Orrid*
- *Two Wheels on a Tin Road*

A wide range of fiction titles also available
In case of difficulty, contact the publishers.

01229 770465

TRAVELLER'S GUIDE

to

Cumbria's Western Lakes & Coast.

compiled, edited and written

by

Alan Bryant.

We gratefully acknowledge the support of the firms whose advertisements appear in these pages. As a reciprocal gesture we have pleasure in drawing the attention of our readers to their announcements at the end of the book. It is necessary however for it to be made clear that whilst every care has been taken in compiling this publication and the statements it contains, the publishers can accept no responsibility for any inaccuracies or for the products or services advertised.

© Alan Bryant 1997. First published 1997.

All rights reserved. No part of this publication may be reproduced, stored in a retrieval system, or transmitted in any part or by any means without prior permission in writing of RegentLane Ltd.

This book is sold subject to the condition that it shall not, by way of trade or otherwise be lent, re-sold, hired out or otherwise circulated without the publisher's prior consent in any form of binding or cover other than that in which it is published and without a similar condition being imposed on the subsequent purchaser.

Published, printed and distributed by RegentLane Ltd.
Devonshire Road Industrial Estate. Millom. Cumbria.

ISBN 1. 900821 35. 4.

Author's Foreward

Walking and generally exploring our beautiful Lake District has never been as popular as it is today. The honeypots of such scenically attractive places like Tarn Hows, Windermere, Bassenthwaite, and Keswick all bring their thousands of admirers every year... and especially on sunny weekends.

However it is this very beauty that might one day be their downfall for all of them, and many others, for they are in danger of being spoilt by over use. Too many visitors to a place of special interest or beauty can by their volume quite unintentionally destroy the fragile environment of that beauty spot. Footpaths are widened all too easily with over-use, and attractive flowers are often trampled under foot by the most caring and well meaning visitors.

The Western Lakes & coastline of Cumbria is one of those areas which is becoming better known year after year, not least due to the efforts of those worthy individuals who man our tourist information centres...but it is totally unlike the central lakes. For starters it does not have the same mass of visitors year after year, and it is for that very reason, as well as its delightful coastline and lesser known towns and villages, each with their own story to tell, that is bringing back people to it each year, to discover yet another lesser known spot.

An example of this is Wastwater and Wasdale Head...For some reason or other the lower reaches of Wasdale have tended to have been ignored by walkers and climbers usually more intent on reaching their mecca beyond Wasdale Head...certainly the majestic giants which range round the upper dale....England's highest point on Scafell Pike, Great Gable and Kirk Fell...all make this the most spectacular mountain scenery in England. Wastwater lake at its foot is 200 feet above sea level, and some 260 feet deep in the middle, over three miles long and a half a mile wide. Thrilling and awe-inspiring is the journey along its rock-strewn shore, winding in and out like a serpent and up and down like a switch-back, whilst gaunt bare mountains rise sharply all around. This spot is always a wild magnificent scene with magical colour as the seasons come and go.

This is an area where not long ago it was the custom around Wasdale to drive cattle through the smoke of Beltane fires on May Day. This Celtic festival was meant to rid the beasts of evil influences lingering from winter darkness. Another custom , also now abandoned, was that of leaving a new born child's finger nails and hair uncut , or not washing its arms before it was six months old. This, the local people believed, would prevent it from becoming a thief. It was not recorded if the outlaw, Prentibjorn, was treated this way, but he was a wrongdoer and ended his life on a gallows by Sty Head Tarn, beyond the head of Wasdale.

Not a long way away will be found the Duddon Valley, which has to be one of the least appreciated valleys of the Lake District, as it is often only used as an escape road by motorists who having "stormed" Wrynose and Hardknott Pass...usually in a queue of slow moving traffic; turn left at Cockley Beck Bridge and drive quickly down the Duddon in search of teas and gift shops.....But what are they missing?

The Duddon cuts its way south from Pike O'Blisco, the southerly outlier of the Bowfell massif: to the west is the graceful symmetry of Harter Fell and the wild expanse of the Ulpha Fells. To the east, the venerable giants of Dow Crag and

Coniston Old Man top an area of jumbled crags and remote combes. There are no large lakes in this area, but there are certainly dozens of tarns, the longest of them being the partly man-made Seathwaite Tarn.

Of all the tarns around the Duddon, perhaps tiny Stickle Tarn is the best. High up on the Dunnerdale Fells and protected by the crags of Stickle Pike, it can only be reached by a somewhat difficult scramble from the back road between Hall Dunnerdale and Broughton.

The valley bottom is undoubtedly Duddon's best feature, crags force the road to meander in a manner designed to delay those in a hurry, but to please those with time to spare. The true valley bottom is given over to grazing and hayfields, and what little is left has been kept as semi-natural woodland. In spring and summer a pageant of wild flowers bloom in their season, including wood anemones, violets, primroses and bluebells as well as rarer flowers.

Not to be overlooked is our west coast which is colourful and full of character, and despite the impact of hundreds of years of habitation and in some instances (albeit small) spread of holiday-site development there remain many miles of unspoilt coastline where the natural beauties of seascape and wildlife can be enjoyed ...often in rare solitude...

This, of necessity is but a brief introduction to our delightful west coast. For years now my own visitors have thanked me for introducing them to a part of Cumbria of which they knew little...There are so many delightful villages...and just a sprinkling of towns, together with the deepest lake, the highest hill, the steepest pass, along with a number of attractions...that this book can really only skim the surface in order to keep it at a price that all can afford. There are so many other books that write in detail on specific areas for those who want to delve even further into an area's history or archaelogy.

Alan Bryant. West Cumbria. 1997.

KEY TO MAP SYMBOLS USED

🏰	Castle or Historic House
✝	Church
🚶	Walking or Hiking
▲	Camping or Caravan site
🚤	Launching Facilities
🐦	Bird Sanctuary
🦌	Other Nature Reserve
⛳	Golf Course
⚓	Boating Facilities
🏫	School
🍺	Inn or Public House
🏠	Holiday Accommodation
✿	Garden Centre or Nursery
⊕	Travel Agent
✦	Arts or Crafts
●	Sports Facilities
i	Information Services
☕	Cafe or Restaurant
▢	Theatre or Cinema
📖	Printing & Publishing Services
⚱	Attraction or heritage Centre
🛒	Food or Drink Supplier
⛽	Motor Services

CONTENTS.

Title Page.	3
Foreword.	4
Map Symbols	5
Contents.	6
Lakes & Coast Map	8
Areas	9
Dunnerdale Area	**11**
Map of Dunnerdale Area	12, 13
The Duddon Valley	14
The Coast and Beaches	15
Bootle	16
Broughton-in-Furness	16
Haverigg	18
Millom	20
Seathwaite	24
Silecroft	25
Thwaites	28
Ulpha	29
Whicham Valley	30
Information	31-37
Eskdale Area	39
Map of Eskdale Area	40, 41
Esk Valley	42
Eskdale Coast	43
Boot	44
Corney	45
Eskdale Green	45
Ravenglass	47
Waberthwaite	50
Information	51-55
Wasdale Area	**57**
Map of Wasdale Area	58, 59
Irt Valley	60
Coast & Beaches	61
Drigg & Holmrook	62
Gosforth	63
Irton & Santon	65
Seascale	66
Wasdale & Head	67
Information	69-72
Ennerdale Area	**73**
Map of Ennerdale Area	74, 75
Ennerdale	76
Ennerdale Coast	77
Beckermet	78
Calderbridge	79
Cleator & Cleator Moor	80
Egremont	81
St Bees	83
Woodend	85
Information	87-95
Whitehaven District	**97**
Map of Whitehaven District	98, 99
Moresby	100
Whitehaven	101
Information	105-113
Workington & Solway Coast	**117**
Map Of Solway Coast	118, 119
Solway Coast and its beaches	120
Abbeytown	122
Aspatria	123
Bridekirk	123
Camerton	125
Causewayhead	125
Crosscanonby	125
Flimby	125
Maryport	126
Seaton	128
Silloth	128
Westnewton	129
Westward	129
Workington	130
Information	133
Cockermouth & District	**153**
Map of Cockermouth District	154–155
Bothel	156
Brigham	156
Buttermere	157
Cockermouth	158
Dean	163
Embleton	163
Gt & Lt Broughton	164
Lamplugh	166
Lorton	167
Papcastle	167
Information	169–180
Events	**181–196**
Advertisers' Announcements	**197–200**

ADVERTISERS' INDEX

Abbey Travel	20	Lamberlea Garden Centre	78
Arts & Crafts	65	Lamplugh Tip	166
Beach Shop & Cafe	84	Lutwidge Arms Hotel	63
Billy Bowman's Music Shop	159	Manor Arms	17
British Nuclear Fuels	Inside Front	Maryport Aquaria	127
Bower House Inn	46	Mealo House Caravan Park	126
Brockwood Hall	26	Millom Palladium	21
Broughton Crags Hotel	165	Millom Recreation Centre	22
Carlisle Castle	201	Muncaster Castle	48
Copeland Sports Management	Back	New Bookshop	159
Craft Shop, Santon Bridge	66	Newfield Inn	24
Cum West Exhibition	Inside Back	Oldbury Contract Services	19
Cumberland Toy & Model Museum	160	Port Haverigg Holiday Village	18
Dent Aeriated Water	80	Printing House Museum	159
Emma's Pantry	21	Ravenglass & Eskdale Railway	49
Ennerdale Country House Hotel	81	Regentlane Ltd	23
Eskdale Outdoor Shop	45	Rosehill Theatre	103
Fellview Caravans	79	St Bees School	85
Florence Mine Heritage Centre	82	Screes Hotel	68
French Connection Restaurant	83	Silecroft Caravan Park	28
Gosforth Pottery	64	Spindle Crafts	62
Holly House Hotel	49	The Stables B&B	16
J W Jacques & Co	79	Ulpha Post Office & Crafts	29
John Bull Inn	28	Walkmill Garden Centre	68
Karen Foster, Artist	25	Walls Caravan Park	47
Kellet Country Guest House	27	Waltham Nursery	21
King George IV Inn	46	Whicham Old Rectory GH	25
Lakeland Sheep & Wool Centre	161		

Travellers' Guide to Cumbria's Western Lakes & Coast

CUMBRIA'S WESTERN LAKES & COAST.

Within the relevant sections will be found the following (south to north)

DUNNERDALE

the towns and villages of Bootle, Broughton in Furness, Haverigg, Millom, Seathwaite, Silecroft, Thwaites, Ulpha, Whicham Valley

and the lake of Devoke Water.

ESKDALE

the towns and villages of Boot, Corney, Eskdale Green, Ravenglass, Waberthwaite

and the lake of Burnmoor Tarn.

WASDALE

the towns & villages of Calder Bridge, Drigg, Gosforth, Irton, Seascale

and the lake of Wastwater.

ENNERDALE

the towns & villages of Beckermet, Briscoe, Cleator, Cleator Moor, Egremont, Ennerdale Bridge, St Bees and Woodend.

WHITEHAVEN & DISTRICT

the towns & villages of Whitehaven & Moresby.

COCKERMOUTH & DISTRICT (including Lorton Vale)

including the towns & villages of Brigham, Cockermouth, Dean, Dovenby, Embleton, Great Broughton, Lamplugh, Lorton, Papcastle and the lakes and communities of Buttermere, Crummock Water and Loweswater.

WORKINGTON & THE SOLWAY COAST.

including the towns & villages of Abbey Town, Allonby, Asby, Aspatria, Bridekirk, Bromfield, Camerton, Crosscanonby, Flimby, Maryport, Plumbland, Seaton, Silloth, West Newton, Workington.

RegentLane Publishers & Printers

are a refreshing new concept in quick-printing.

RING NOW FOR A QUOTATION

01229 770444

FAX: **01229 770339**

CUMBRIA'S WESTERN LAKES & COAST.

DUNNERDALE.

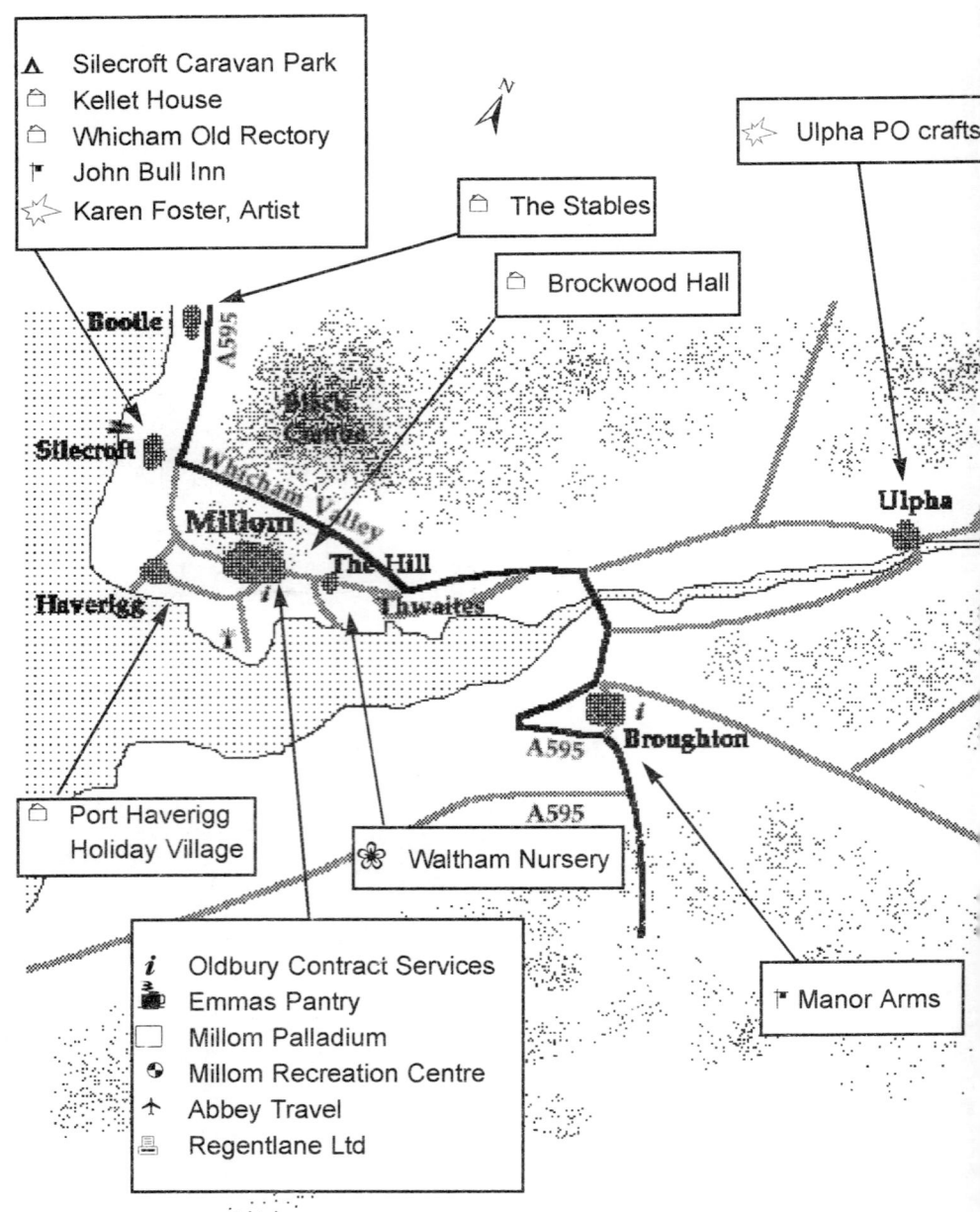

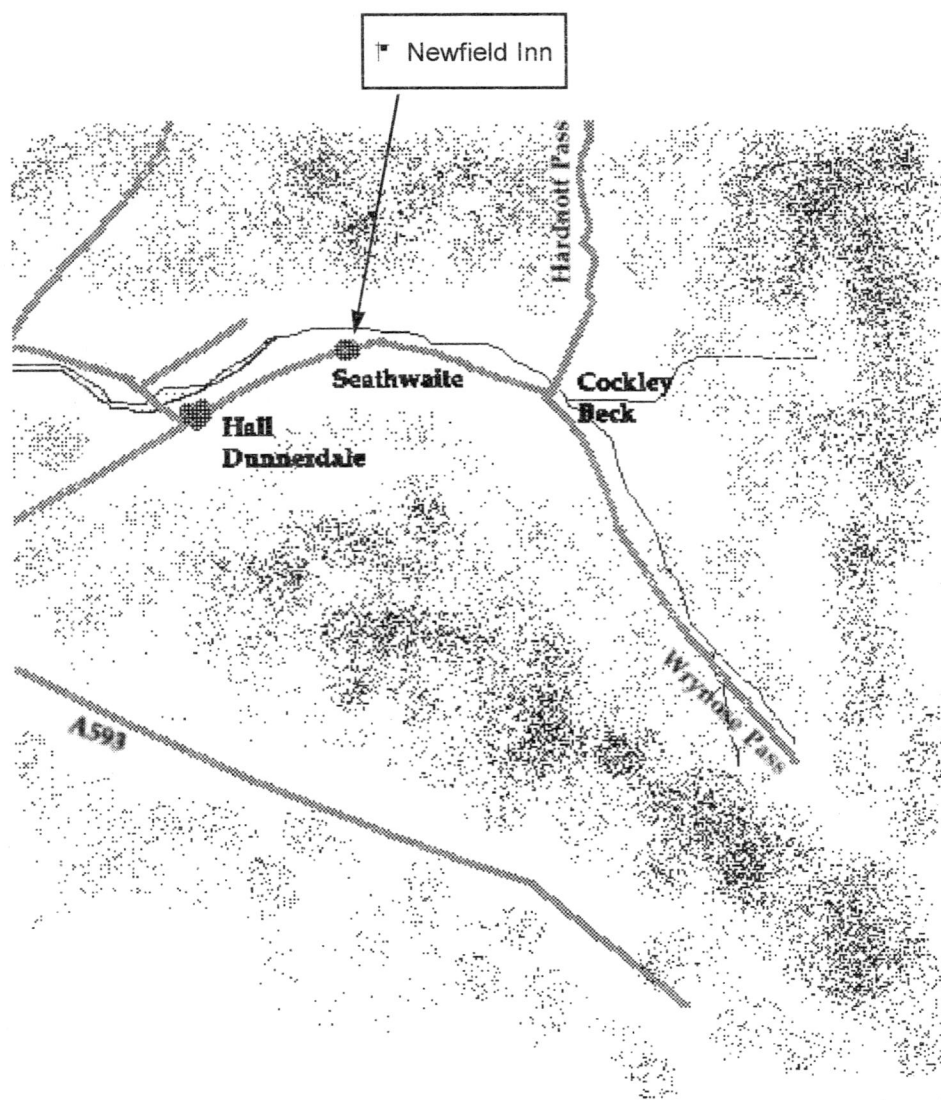

Travellers' Guide to Cumbria's Western Lakes & Coast

DUNNERDALE

THE DUDDON VALLEY

In common with many parts of the British Isles, particularly in Cumbria, the name of the river which flows through Dunnerdale, the Duddon, has Celtic origins. It is a compound of ddu (dark, as in Dublin) and denu (valley, as in Danube). For a period of several centuries, much of the west coast area was once part of the county of Cumberland, Westmorland being the more eastern part of Cumbria. Originally, of course, the two names were synonymous: Cumberland was the land the Cwmry (the brotherhood) whereas the Angles in the east of England referred to this same part of Britain as Westmorland (Westmaringasland–the land of the people who live by the western sea). Few of these Angles reached Cumbria, as is borne out by the relatively low number of English place names. However, they did out of ignorance of Gaelic, add endings of their own. Hence Denu (valley) became to them Dunnerdale (denudael–valley valley).

How the name Dark valley came to be applied to the area is unknown. A fault line which stretches from the Pink Graphite Igneous Intrusion at far-away Shap, across part of the High Street range and out under the sea close to Millom, goes right over the peak of Coniston Old Man, separating the Coniston Limestone from Brathay flags. For centuries, this could have belched volcanic ash and smoke, causing the area to appear dark. An alternative is that the name could have come from the massive basalt boulder which almost blocks the Dunnerdale Gorge above Seathwaite.

The River Duddon rises close to the Three Shire Stone (where Cumberland and Westmorland met the County of North Lonsdale–part of Lancashire). It then flows westward from Wrynose Pass through a barren landscape reminiscent of the surface of the moon, as far as Cockley Back where it is joined by its main tributary, Moasdale Beck. Here the fell road splits and one part continues west over Hardnott Pass to Boot and Eskdale. A Roman road once traversed the entire valley, culminating in Hardnott Fort (Mediobogdum).

After Cockley Beck, the river turns South-West through a gradually narrowing valley to tumble through the Froth Pot and under the narrow Birks Bridge. It is then joined by Grassguards Gill to fall through the Duddon Gorge below Wallabarrow Crag. Below the pretty village of Seathwaite is the confluence with Tarn Beck, bringing the overflow of Seathwaite Tarn, now a reservoir.

At Hall Dunnerdale (literally Upper Dunnerdale from the Norse word Hallr meaning high), the roads fork. One goes up and over Kiln bank through the oddly-named Hoses Farm. The other follows the Duddon past the new water works towards Ulpha (wolf-hill). Ulpha has little more than a post-office, church and school. It once had a pub which appeared in the film "The One That Got Away".

Below Ulpha, the river races southward to Duddon Bridge and almost erupts into the wide estuary, once dominated Millom Castle but, more recently, the iron mines on Hodbarrow Point (closed in 1968).

The lower valley is wide and the river sluggish and has always been difficult to cross because of the shifting soft sands which have claimed many a foolhardy victim. Many proposals have been put forward for a bridge crossing from Askam-in-Furness to Millom, saving many agonising miles of road (cart track) from Barrow, and even a suggestion to make a tidal barrage with which to generate electricity. This, however has been criticised by nature lovers who would seemingly prefer power from Sellafield.

THE COAST AND BEACHES

Millom is a small industrial town on the sandy estuary of an unpolluted river, ...it has the splendour of the hill of Black Combe along with the Eskdale fells around, and with views of the hills of Furness just across the water...which one day may be reached by bridge rather than the current fifteen mile drive around the Duddon estuary.

At one time Millom was a busy port with boats arriving almost on a daily basis to be loaded with hematite from the busy blast furnaces close by. These day Millom is a quiet town with few visitors arriving to 'enjoy' its coast. Little remains of the old port other than the odd post seen to be sticking out of the dunes...but nevertheless the area has a quiet charm suited to those who just enjoy sitting by the water.

Close by though lies Hodbarrow nature reserve, a man-made lagoon which has been successfully colonised by a variety of wildlife....as have the lighthouse and the other abandoned buildings to be seen hereabouts. In summer great crested grebe, tufted duck and shelduck can be seen on the open water with ringed plovers, oystercatchers and little terns on the sea bank, whilst the scrubby areas provide shelter for summer migrants such as warblers, kestrel, sparrowhawk and barn owl also occur frequently over the reserve. This reserve is open to the public at all times.

Haverigg Dunes, almost 70 feet high in part sweep around Haverigg Point where the sands are more than a mile wide at low tide. Haverigg is a small but today quite attractive village, with a sandy beach crossed by a stream. There is a broad expanse of shingle to the east. Bathing is safe close inshore when the tide is rising, but be warned as there are deep steep-sided channels and fast currents about half a mile out.

Silecroft has a long sandy beach some seven miles in length, and reported as being the cleanest beach in the North West having had a 'clean bill of health' continuously since 1987. This safe beach (popular with many for beach combing, for many Roman flints have been discovered) is approached over a broad strip of shingle dappled with pools at low tide. More visitors are to be found enjoying its charm year after year. (see editorial feature)

Gutterby Spa has got to be the least frequented beach in the north-west of England, and can often be found deserted on sunny days even in the height of summer. It is approached down a narrow, rutted track from the A595. The shore north of the access point has scattered patches of sand at low tide among its boulder strewn acres of shingle. The beach, which becomes sandy to the south, is backed by shingle and overlooked by high cliffs of grass covered clay.

Annaside has a sandy beach, located some two miles from the nearest tarmac road, and is strewn with boulders. There are literally hundreds of shallow pools at low tide. The beach is approached by a narrow rough lane which starts from the unclassified road between Bootle railway station and Bootle village. Cars would need to be parked at the approach to a private bridge over the River Annas, some ten minutes walk away from the sea.

Selker Bay has low but sheer cliffs of grass-topped clay, undercut and liable to sudden collapse, overlook a beach of shingle and boulders. The falling tide reveals patches of sand and many pools. Access is by a narrow, unmade lane from Bootle railway station.

Bootle

Bootle, the name means 'the dwelling'..is a former market town with its charter issued by Edward III in 1347, and later renewed by Queen Elizabeth I in 1567. Once said to be the smallest market town in England.

Bootle, in fact, consists of two small villages, the old on the roadside, the new by the railway station. The town(s) are situated just one mile south-east of Bootle railway station and boasts of being more than a 1000 years old. The earliest record in fact is a mesolithic site at Eskmeals where numerous Stone Age tools have been found, together with the remains of a Bronze Age settlement many cairns hereabouts testify to that fact.

These day the town is little more than a quiet country village with narrow lanes connecting the village with the attractive pebble and sandy beaches, together with its market cross.

St Michael's church is Norman in origin. the tall 15th century font here has shields around the bowl carved with initials and old lettering signifying the Trinity. A fine little brass portrait is shining on the chancel wall. It shows Sir Hugh Askew who was knighted by Edward VI at the battle of pinkie, when Protector Somerset marched against the Scots, slew thousands of them, and gained nothing by his victory. But Sir Hugh gained his knighthood, and here he stands in his armour with his hands in prayer.

About a mile to the north is the remains of Seaton Nunnery....a Benedictine foundation dating back to before 1227, and dedicated to St Leonard.

Dominating the skyline is the mass of Black Combe at a height of 1970 feet. From here travellers will have the most extensive view from any point in Britain......14 counties in England and Scotland can be seen, together with Snowdon, Isle of Man, and the Mountains of Mourne..Such a view may well explain why William Wordsworth visited here on occasions.

'The Stables'
Bootle Village, Nr. Millom,
Cumbria, LA19 5TJ
Tel: (01229) 718644

Bed & Breakfast Accommodation
You are sure of a warm and friendly welcome from Rodney and Jennifer Light when you stay at 'The Stables'. We offer Bed & Breakfast with an optional Evening Dinner. One room has full en-suite bathroom facilities, the other an adjoining bathroom. Quiet surroundings with lovely views of fell and river. Open all year. Prices from £15.00 per person per night (B&B). Please phone or write for more information.

Broughton-in-Furness

Until Ulverston stole its thunder by linking itself by canal to the sea in 1847, Broughton in Furness was an important market town serving a wide area of Furness. It still has a cattle market but now it's just like a friendly unspoilt vil-

DUNNERDALE

lage. Broughton nestles in a hollow between wooded hills midway between Barrow in Furness and Millom. Many of the houses are Georgian including those in the elegant square, set out by the Lord of the Manor to resemble a London square. In the middle stands an obelisk erected in 1810 to commemorate the Jubilee of George III, together with the ancient fish-slabs once used for the sale of fish caught in the nearby River Duddon. Also adjacent is the town stocks, no doubt well used in times gone by, but nowadays very much a sense of amusement to the town's many visitors. Opposite is the 'Town Hall' dating from 1766, at one time a market hall with lock-up shops, now housing the Tourist Information Centre. Broughton was at one time the centre of the wool trade, together with the manufacture of oak baskets (swills). Visitors will find several yards which lead to many old buildings often with unusual restrictions placed upon them, still in force today - because of the 'rights of way' necessary to reach the wells.

The town is ancient in origin having been mentioned in the Domesday Book, and the two important buildings - the church and the castle - are Norman. The church of St Mary Magdalene was consecrated in 1547 and was rebuilt during Victorian times. It has a ring of ten bells - most unusual for such a small place. Broughton Tower, an 18th to 19th century mansion built around a 14th century defensive tower, is set in parkland a little to the north of the village. The ruins are complete with dungeons. Broughton Tower unfortunately is not open to the public

Just three miles from Broughton in Furness is Broughton Mills, so called because of the woollen mill that was at one time located here. There are remains of old kilns where lime was made for the land and buildings.

In the eighteenth century, a busy forge stood by the River Duddon one-and-a-half miles to the west. The ruins of Duddon Forge are open to the public on application to the National Park Authority.

THE Manor Arms

A FREE HOUSE — FOUNDED IN 1768

The Square, Broughton in Furness,
Cumbria LA20 6HY
Telephone: 01229 716286

"I have known the southern Lake District for Thirty years and for me Broughton in Furness is a kind of personal gateway to that wonderful country of hills, sheep, honest beer and honest people.......we'd start the holiday with breakfast at the 'Manor'. The 'Manor' used to be one of the three best pubs I have ever known....."
from " A Personal Portrait of Broughton in Furness" by Richard Adams, Author of 'Watership Down'.

**Wide selection of beers, wines & spirits.
(range of bitters available at all times)
Bed & Breakfast available all year.**

Travellers' Guide to Cumbria's Western Lakes & Coast

DUNNERDALE

Haverigg

'Haverigg'...meaning 'ridge where oats are grown'.

Just one mile north of Millom, it is close to the R.S.P B nature reserve, and has attractive views out to the Irish Sea. Its a good place for families to visit with a children's playground and safe beaches. Haverigg is ideal for walking, pony-trekking, water sports and sea-fishing. Dunes almost 70 ft high in places sweep round Haverigg Point where the sands are more than a mile wide at low tide. Seals can sometimes be seen basking on the sandbanks. There is a water ski school on the lagoon which is surrounded by a mile and a quarter long outer barrier. On the remains of the original wall which collapsed in 1897 is a 7¼" gauge miniature railway open to the public.

Haverigg's front and old fishing harbour have recently been renovated tastefully and it has a sandy beach crossed by the stream which descends from Whicham Valley. There is a broad expanse of shingle to the east. Bathing is safe close inshore when the tide is rising, but there are deep, steep-sided channels and fast currents about half a mile out.

During World War II, Haverigg and the surrounding area was a vital centre for training aircrew, and even today its memories are kept alive by a group of enthusiasts who founded the RAF Museum here in 1992. The museum has limited seasonal opening and is located in some of the original airfield buildings. Here through a collection of memorabilia and items rescued from various crash sites, visitors can learn some of the unique stories of the airmen who trained at Haverigg.

Port Haverigg Holiday Village
In Association with Butterflowers Holiday Homes
Haverigg, Millom, Cumbria LA18 4HB

We are situated on the beautiful Duddon Estuary, with magnificent beaches and sand dunes, yet ideally suited for exploring the Lake District's many delights.

We can offer you a choice of 2 caravan parks with excellent facilities for touring and camping, luxury caravans for hire and indoor heated swimming pool. One of our parks has its very own private 200 acre lake which it share with the RSPB, a small part which is protected for the benefit of the birds and wildlife, but sailing, windsurfing and water ski-ing can be enjoyed on the rest, as well as trout and sea fishing.

- INDOOR HEATED SWIMMING POOL
- BAR SERVING MEALS
- RESTAURANT • PRIVATE LAKE
- MINIATURE RAILWAY
- WATERSKI SCHOOL • WINDSURFING
- TROUT FISHING • SEA FISHING
- R.S.P.B. NATURE RESERVE
- LAUNDERETTE

OPEN 11 MONTHS OF THE YEAR
Telephone : 01229 772880

Travellers' Guide to Cumbria's Western Lakes & Coast

DUNNERDALE

Oldbury Contract Services

Devonshire Rd Ind Estate
Millom, Cumbria LA18 4JS
Tel: 01 229 770 465
Fax: 01 229 770 339

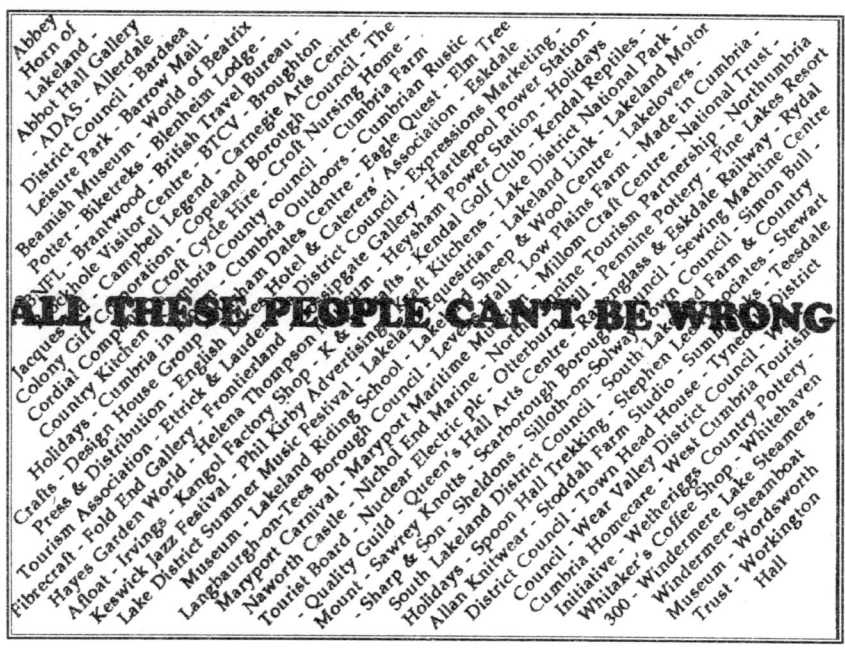

Any kind of business can benefit from effective promotion

WHY NOT YOURS?

Speak to the experts today!

Find out how little it costs to

advertise in the right way

MEMBER OF

ADVERTISING–PROMOTIONS–LEAFLET DISTRIBUTION

Travellers' Guide to Cumbria's Western Lakes & Coast

Millom

Millom was once a small village complete with its Norman castle. To many visitors the town seems out of character with its setting, set as it is in a sparkling landscape of sea, sand and mountains. The estuary of the River Duddon bites deeply into the Millom coastline, and to the north the land rises sharply to the summit of Black Combe Fell.

In the 19th century, it became a boom town. Rich iron ore deposits were discovered south of the town at Hodbarrow in 1843. By 1880 the mine was producing over 300,000 tons of ore annually. The decline (to many regretfully) came in the 1920s

There is a rather pleasant folk museum here which effectively tells the Millom story...its history of the mines...the development of the iron trade.

Millom was the birthplace of Norman Nicholson, the Lake Poet, and the town figures prominently in his poetry and books.

ABBEY TRAVEL
34, LAPSTONE RD, MILLOM
TEL. 01229 773622

THE WEST COASTS SPECIALISTS IN WORLD

AIR, COACH & CRUISE HOLIDAYS

• PACKAGE HOLIDAYS • FLIGHTS • FERRIES • CRUISES •
• HOTELS • THEATRE RESERVATIONS • CAR HIRE •
• DISCOUNT AIR TICKETS • INSURANCE •

BUS·NESS AND LEISURE TRAVEL

ABBEY TRAVEL - YOUR FIRST CHOICE

ALL MAJOR CREDIT CARDS ACCEPTED

DUNNERDALE

Emma's Pantry

at Millom Craft Centre
Tel: 01229 771590
OPEN 9-5 Mon-Sat
Wholesome Homemade
Food to Suit Everyone

**FUNCTIONS, PARTIES
& OUTSIDE CATERING
BY ARRANGEMENT**

MILLOM PALLADIUM

for details of forthcoming events and shows
Telephone: 01229 772779 or 716733

The Mouse That Roared

WALTHAM NURSERY
THE GREEN
MILLOM
CUMBRIA
01229 773494

Large selection of summer bedding plants, perennials, and herbs.
Hanging baskets, Window boxes & Patio pots ready filled
or
Have your own baskets, pots & boxes filled with the plants of your choice
also
Garden furniture and ornaments for sale

OPEN HOURS: TUES 10am - 3pm
WED 10am - 3pm
THUR 10am - 3pm
SAT 10am - 5pm
SUN 10am - 5pm
Closed: Monday & Friday
(except Bank Holiday Mondays)

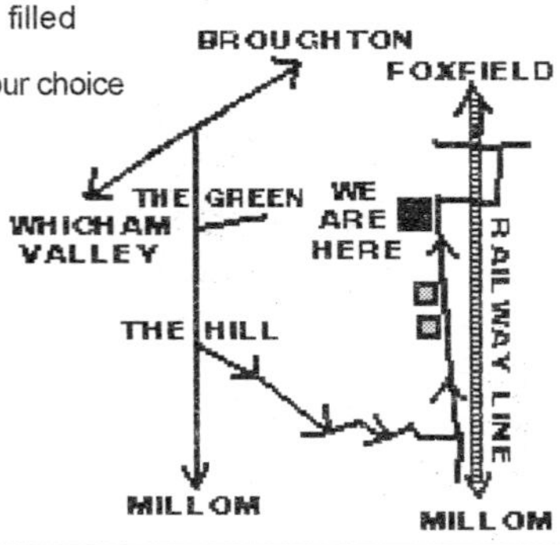

Travellers' Guide to Cumbria's Western Lakes & Coast

DUNNERDALE

Nearby at Haverigg is an extensive RSPB reserve on the old iron mine site at Hodbarrow, and which shares an artificial lake with a water ski centre. Very many species of sea birds can be seen here.

The parish church of Holy Trinity dates back to the Norman period...in fact during a recent restoration, fragments of a cross shaft and head were found in the north wall of the chancel...the workmanship clearly dating it as late 11th century.

The 14th century Millom Castle stands in a position where lines of approach were limited, and observation easily maintained, and was originally the Hudleston family home. (John Hudleston was the man who administered the last sacrament to Charles II at his bedside).

In its great days the castle stood in a fine park, and though never very big it was very strong, some of the walls still left are seven feet thick. The Lords of Millom wielded power of life and death over a very wide area, and we are vividly reminded of this in what is known as the Gallows Field not far away.

MILLOM RECREATION CENTRE

Aerobic Classes, Step Classes, Bums n'Tums, Multi Gym, Circuit Training.

We have something to suit everyone's level of fitness

Over 50's Tuesday afternoon
Children's Activities include:
Junior Badminton, Football, Roller Skating
every Friday 7-8pm
For more details ring Linda, Pauline or Rachel on 01229 774985

The castle was largely destroyed around 1460 during the War of the Roses, but in the 16th century the pele tower was built and today is the only part of the castle which is inhabited...as a farmhouse!

RegentLane Publishers & Printers

are a refreshing new concept in quick-printing.

- *Business starter packs from £25*
- *A5 promotional flyers from £15 per 1000*
- *A4 posters from £20 per 1000*
- *Brochures and leaflets (flat or folded)*
- *Books and booklets*
- *Tourist guides*
- *Business Forms*
- *Wedding and personal stationery*
- *Full advertising and design facilities*
- *Invitations and tickets*
- *Laminating & Binding*
- *Nationwide Distribution also available*

Unit 13B Devonshire Rd Ind Est, Millom

01229 770465

Seathwaite

Not to be confused with Seathwaite in Borrowdale, this village was the home for 67 years of the remarkable Reverend Robert Walker (1709-1802) known as 'Wonderful Walker' because, as Wordsworth put it " good works formed an endless retinue".

Born at Undercrag in 1709 the 12th son of Nicholas Walker, one of the valley farmers... the runt of the litter...he was undoubtedly destined for the church. He went to village schools at Ulpha and Eskdale, and even 'taught school' at Gosforth, where the building in which he taught still stands at the road-junction at the northern end of the village, now a private house. From there he went to Loweswater, still as a teacher, then on to Buttermere. He would sit up until the 'small hours' by candlelight studying Divinity, even after he had been given the curacy of the knoll-top Buttermere Church...in those days the smallest church in England. However within a year he was asking for an even lonelier ministry and in answer to his wishes was moved to Seathwaite at a stipend of £17 per year where he was to stay until his death at the grand age of 93.

His wife apparently had a dowry of £40 but he refused to touch a penny of it. Instead, proudly independent, he worked ceaselessly ; as a farm labourer, as a practical Christian weaving and spinning (even as he was teaching the village children beside the Communion Table); as a scrivener and lawyer. bringing up his three sons and seven daughters with a sound education.... even as an innkeeper when the Parsonage was turned into a hostelry in his brothers name. Yet he always had time to visit the sick and needy.

His pleasures were simple, an occasional game of whist.....and meat on Sundays. When he died he had saved in excess of £2,000. He is commemorated by a plaque in Seathwaite's church of the Holy Trinity, itself built in 1874 to replace an earlier church. A chair made by 'Wonderful Walker' can still be seen in the church, while an inscription on a stone outside the porch records that he clipped sheep there. He and his wife died in the same year and are buried in Seathwaite churchyard.

Just upstream from Birks Bridge ...famous for its deep clear rocks pools below...is the romantic Wallowbarrow Gorge, where the River Duddon is

---

The NEWFIELD INN

Seathwaite, Duddon Valley, LA20 6ED Tel: (01229) 716208

VISIT THIS FAMOUS 16th c INN SITUATED IN WORDSWORTH'S FAVOURITE VALLEY.
TRADITIONAL ALES AND BAR MEALS.
SUPERB VIEWS. OPEN ALL YEAR.
ACCOMMODATION AVAILABLE

DUNNERDALE

squeezed between two craggy hills. The stepping stones a short way downstream are described by Wordsworth in one of his sequence of 34 sonnets on the River Duddon. Visitors should also look for the unusual rock which has been shaped by the river over the years and today has the nickname 'Giant's Leg'.

Silecroft

Silecroft village lies on a long road between the main coast road and the sea, just three miles from Millom.

Not one style of house here, but a variety of stone houses, farm buildings, bungalows, and terrace houses, most of which were built originally to house the railway workers together with the employees of the small local ironworks.

The oldest house here has a well in its kitchen. Cobble walls line the streets between the houses, and it still has its own railway station.

The beach here is safe and popular with visitors and local alike...beach combing is a popular sport, often turning up early Roman flints.

Silecroft has its own hill...Black Combe, lying to the north, and which besides being a perfect beacon hill, also acts as a shelter from the worst of the winter weather.

THE COVER OF THIS BOOK
WAS DESIGNED BY:

KAREN FOSTER

PAINTER

&

ILLUSTRATOR

COMMISSIONS WELCOME

4, Commerce Terrace, Silecroft, Millom, Cumbria LA18 4NR Tel: (01229) 773976

Whicham Old Rectory

Silecroft, Millom, Cumbria LA18 5LS. Tel: Millom (01229) 772954

WHICHAM OLD RECTORY stands at the foot of Black Combe in the Whicham Valley. It has central heating throughout, H & C and tea making facilities in all guest rooms. One room en-suite. Lounge and separate dining room, ample private parking together with a large garden. Home grown food, home-baked bread and homespun hospitality are our specialities. Here you can relax in Victorian surroundings in the tranquillity of Western Lakeland and explore the nature reserves, historic houses and ancient monuments.

Travellers' Guide to Cumbria's Western Lakes & Coast

DUNNERDALE

BROCKWOOD HALL
Quality Lodges
Self-Catering

Set in 26 acres of mature woodland within easy reach of fells, coast and lakes.

• Indoor Pool • Sauna • Spa bath •
• Solarium • Indoor and Outdoor childrens play areas • Kids Club in all school holidays • Pets welcome •
• Television, video and telephones •
• On-site restaurant and bar •
• Short breaks welcome •

Why not come for the day?

Daily and weekly memberships available for all the family

On the A595 between Broughton in Furness and Silecroft

FREE FULL COLOUR BROCHURES
☎ 01229 772329

and say I saw you in the Travellers Guide

DUNNERDALE

SILECROFT CARAVAN & CAMPING PARK

We offer luxury 2 & 3 bedroom holiday homes for hire and sale. Just 200 yards from the beach and golf course, yet only 1 mile from the fells this is the perfect holiday location.

☆ Heated Indoor Pool ☆ Spa ☆ Sauna ☆ Luxury touring ☆ Camping facilities.

Tel: 01229 772659 For Colour Brochure

The JOHN BULL Inn

A595 SILECROFT

01229 772394

Open Daily for Home-made Meals and a Selection of Ales.

Opening Hours:
Mon - Fri 9am - 11pm
Saturday 11am - 11pm
Sun 12 noon - 10.30pm

⌐ Our Kitchen Never Closes ¬
⌊ During Opening Hours ⌋

Thwaites

Thwaites is situated on the Duddon estuary roughly halfway between Millom and Broughton-in-Furness, and consists of three hamlets, namely, The Green, Hallthwaites and Ladyhall.

The village has been populated for years....many years! Evidence abounds that Neolithic man at one time lived here, and in fact is thought to have been responsible for the stone circle to be seen at Swinside. Visitors to Thwaite Fell can also see remains of their rounded dwellings.

On a hill above Hallthwaites is the parish church dedicated to St Anne. The first of the churches to stand here was built in 1725 originally as chapel of ease for Millom. In 1805 the "new" church was built complete with steeple and two bells.

From the Middle Ages until the early 20th century there were several industries in the parish and deriving the power they needed from the river Duddon or the Black beck. At one time there was a bloomery in the woods (near Duddon bridge) which was established in 1737. Fortunately a great deal of the earlier buildings are being preserved and are open to the public. There was also a thriving woollen mill dating back to the 16th century at Hallthwaites. Some of the carpets and blankets, woven and dyed, are still in use in the district even today.

Travellers' Guide to Cumbria's Western Lakes & Coast

DUNNERDALE

Ulpha

We must be grateful to it for ever, for Wordsworth loved it, and its beauty stirred his heart. It comes into his sonnets of the Duddon.

Between the fine Duddon Bridge and Ulpha village are three miles of an entrancing valley where the river divides Furness from what was at one time Cumberland. Three miles of thrilling delight it is as we come up the steep and tortuous road threading in and out of the rocks high up on the Furness side; we look down on a scene of exquisite beauty where hills clothed in trees and bracken rise from the clear stream. A glory of gold and green in autumn, it is in spring and summer too a scene of delight which Wordsworth himself could hardly paint.

It is an ancient stone bridge which brings us over the river, and the houses of Ulpha deck the valley. In a charming spot on the spur of a hill the little church stands as Wordsworth knew it.

The lychgate brings us to the lovely old church in which the light is pouring through windows which need no other pictures than the hills around. Its spick and span white walls have fragments of 18th century decoration, with the arms of Queen Anne, and there are old timbers in the black and white roof. The font bowl and the piscina are old, but Ulpha church is loved for its simplicity and there is little more. It was strange to find two pairs of handcuffs in the vestry, relics of the days when the sexton was the village policeman.

Wordsworth must have often sat and looked across at the romantic ruins of Frith Hall silhouetted against the sky, once a wayside inn where coaches changed horses on the way to Whitehaven. Within a mile of it are the ruins of the tower of Ulpha Old Hall, which has among its stories that of a lady who was drowned in the ravine below while fleeing from a wolf.

However much further back goes the story of the hills, for there are ancient British settlements, and on the top of the huge mass of solid stone known as the Wallowbarrow Crag, is a tiny stone circle. The crag belongs to us all, for the National Trust has it in its keeping, 75 acres by the river, lovely always, but a favourite place when spring flowers are blooming.

The sonnets Wordsworth wrote on the little River Duddon have an interesting place in the story of his genius. He knew and loved the river from early boyhood as a frequent visitor to Broughton-in-

---

Ulpha Post Office & Craft Shop
Duddon Valley, Nr. Broughton-in-Furness

A variety of wooden items from pine kitchen furniture & bookcases to letter racks are made on the premises along with decorative folk art, traditional chair caning restoration, black leading, specialist joinery and sale of antique furniture. Open all year seven days a week for groceries, ice cream & Craft Shop. Ring for daily opening times: 01229 716255. Looking forward to welcoming you in the Duddon Valley.

Travellers' Guide to Cumbria's Western Lakes & Coast

DUNNERDALE

Furness, near where the Duddon enters Duddon Sands. He traced it so far into the hills on one occasion with the help of local fishermen, that he had to be carried home pick-a-back, tired out. He was 36 years of age, a poet of ever-increasing renown, when he wrote his first sonnet on the stream, at a place where it cleaves a passage through the wilderness attended only by its own voice, the clouds and the birds.

Rising close by the summit of Wrynose Pass the Duddon river fed by many becks from two counties, reaches the sea on Duddon Sands, 14 miles away, without having on its banks a single village with grouped houses. There are only broad-spread towns with a scattering of houses here and there. It is a lonely river, and a lovely spot.

Whicham Valley

Upon crossing the ridge close to Thwaites, many an unwary traveller finds himself compelled to stop suddenly, and sometimes dangerously, at the sight of the sea at the bottom of what must be the shortest valley in the area. It is not the length of the valley which is spectacular (about 3 miles), nor the width (less than a mile). It is the amount of varying scenery in such a short space.

The valley, once flooded to a depth of over 70 metres, is flanked on the north by the massive hump of Black Combe and the south by the granite outcrops above Ghyll Scaur Quarry (off the Millom Road).

Black Combe (just a few metres short of being able to be called a mountain) is made up of one of the earliest Cambrian rocks, Skiddaw Slate. Although resembling a volcano from a certain angle, there is no trace of igneous activity. The sole evidence of heat being a white metamorphic scar crossing the tiny beck which drains the combe into Whicham Beck.

There has been, however, much igneous activity on the southern side where the craggy outcrops contrast the smooth bulk of Black Combe. The name of the hill has nothing to do with black (the colour) nor combe (the valley). Rather it is a corruption of Bleak Camber (the rounded hump upon which nothing would grow). There is not a single tree on Black Combe due to the acidity and shallow depth of the soil. There is, however, sufficient depth to produce a great variety of grasses and heathers. Perhaps this is the reason why the area has been noted for centuries as excellent grazing pasture for sheep.

The shape of the original lake can be clearly recognised by the perfectly flat area with its head just below Applehead Farm and its foot near Whicham Old Hall. It was likely a glaciated valley as the humps at the foot which acted as a dam resemble terminal moraines.

On a clear day, several mountains of the Snowdonia range in North Wales can be seen across the sea at a distance of over 70 miles.

The lane which runs parallel to the main road (to the south) offers beautiful views of the whole of the valley but beware of the narrow steep incline terminating in a tight bend around Po House at the foot. This is not a drive to be attempted by the uninitiated in winter conditions.

Half way down the valley is a set of cottages...once the Fox and Goose Inn.

Travellers' Guide to Cumbria's Western Lakes & Coast

ANTIQUES.
Corner Cupboard Antiques, Church Street. Broughton in Furness. Tel: 01229 716669.

ART & CRAFTS SHOPS.
Cumbria Crafts, 1 School Terrace. Millom Tel: 01229 773443.
Haverigg Gift Shop, 3 Main Street Haverigg. Tel: 01229 774470.
I-Spy 10, St Georges Terrace, Millom. Tel: 01229 774367.
J Kelly, 9 St Georges Terrace, Millom. Tel: 01229 772385.
Millom Craft Centre, The Station, Millom. Tel: 01229 770000
Stem Crafts, Ulpha Post Office. (see advert)

ATTRACTIONS.
Millom Folk Museum. Tel: 01229 772555.
Millom Folk Museum is home to vivid displays, including a reconstruction of a drift mine, recording this aspect of Millom's past. Poetry too has played a part in the cultural life of Millom in the 20th century, for it was in this town that the writer Norman Nicholson was born and lived. A permanent exhibition in the Folk Museum records his life and works.
Millom Craft Centre. Tel: 01229 770000.
Located in the former Millom Railway Station buildings, the Craft Centre provides workshop units offering a variety of crafts which visitors can see being made as well as for sale. There are also continually changing exhibitions and a bistro-style cafe/restaurant which, like the centre, is open throughout the year
RAF Museum, the Old Airfield, Haverigg.

AUCTIONEERS.
Harrison Coward. 24, Lapstone Road. Millom. Tel 01229 772314.

BAKERS & CONFECTIONERS.
Dansons, 18 St Georges Terrace, Millom Tel: 01229 772614.
J Green & Sons, 37-39 Wellington Street, Millom Tel: 01229 772466.
Harvest Bakery, 15 Holborn Hill, Millom Tel: 01229 774779.
Haskets the Bakery. Princes Street Broughton in Furness. Tel: 01229 716284.

BANKS.
Barclays, Market Square, Millom. Tel: 01229 824383.
Midland, Market Square, Millom. Tel: 01229 772251
National Westminster, 5 Market Square, Millom Tel: 01229 835488

BOARDING KENNELS.
Spunham Boarding Kennels. Whicham Valley. Millom. Tel: 01229 772609.

Travellers' Guide to Cumbria's Western Lakes & Coast

DUNNERDALE

BOWLING.
Bootle Bowling Club, Bootle. Crown Green.
Millom Park, Millom. Crown Green.

CAR & VAN HIRE.
Port Haverigg Car Centre. Haverigg Ind Estate, Haverigg. Tel 01229 774500.

CARAVAN & CAMPING SITES.
Butterflowers Holiday Homes, Haverigg. Tel 01229 772880.
Port Haverigg Holiday Village, Haverigg. Tel 01229 774228. (see advert)
Silecroft Caravan Park. Silecroft. Tel: 01229 772659. (see advert)

CHEMISTS.
Boots the Chemists, 30 Lapstone Road,
Kenneth Robson, 43 Wellington Street, Millom Tel: 01229 772262.
Wm Wilson, 1 Princes Street, Broughton in Furness. Tel: 01229 716303.

CHURCHES.
Holy Innocents Church of England, Broughton Mills. Tel: 01229 716305.
Holy Trinity Church of England, Millom Tel: 01229 772889.
Holy Trinity, Seathwaite. Tel: 01229 716305.
Kingdom Hall of Jehovah's Witnesses, Holborn Hill, Millom. Tel: 01229 773088
St Anne Church of England, Thwaites. Tel: 01229 772889.
St George the Martyr, Millom Tel: 01229 772889.
St John the Baptist Church of England, Corney. Tel: 01229 718223.
St John the Baptist Church of England, Ulpha. Tel: 01229 716305.
St John the Evangelist Church of England, Woodland Tel: 01229 716305.
St Luke Church of England, Haverigg Tel: 01229 772889.
St Mary Church of England, Whitbeck, Tel: 01229 718223.
St Mary Magdalene Church of England, Broughton Tel: 01229 716305.
St Marys Church of England, Whicham Tel: 01229 718223.
St Michaels Church of England Bootle. Tel: 01229 718223.
Salvation Army, Nelson Street, Millom. Tel: 01229 772775.

CITIZEN ADVICE BUREAUX
Entrance B St Georges Road, Millom Tel: 01229 772395.

CLUBS & ASSOCIATIONS.
Cumbria Club, 3 Market Street Millom Tel: 01229 772413.
Haverigg Working Mens Club, 41 Main Street Millom Tel: 01229 772352.
Millom Rugby Union Football Club, Wilson Park, Haverigg. Tel: 01229 770401.
Millom Working Mens Club, Market Square, Millom Tel: 01229 772444.
Rotary Club of Millom, (Meetings Tuesdays) 12.30pm. Bankside, Kirksanton. Tel:

01229 772276.
Royal British Legion Clubs, Wellington Street, Millom Tel: 01229 772396

COACH & COACH HIRE.
Hodgsons Coaches, Crown Street, Millom.
Woods Coaches, Unit 3 Haverigg Ind Estate. Haverigg. Tel: 01229 772390.

CRAFT WORKERS.
Ashdown Smokers. Skellerah Farm, Corney, Nr Millom Tel: 01229 718324. Traditionally cured foodstuff
Karen Foster. Silecroft. Artist. (see advert)
Broughton Craft Shop, Griffin Street,.Broughton Tel: 01229 716413. Slate jewellry.
Mountain Method, Unit 11c, Devonshire Road, Millom. Tel: 01229 771180. Waterproof clothing.
TWM's Tack. The Beck, The Knott, Millom Tel:01229 772753. Hand crafted saddlery.
Waberwood, Newbiggin House Farm, Waberthwaite. Nr Millom Tel: 01229 717689. Miniature and full size furniture.

CYCLE SHOPS & HIRE.
Charles McIntosh, 63 Queen Street, Millom. Tel: 01229 772294.

DENTISTS.
AB Smith, Lodge Terrace, Broughton in Furness. Tel: 01229 716746.
Joan Stevenson, 1 Horn Hill, Millom Tel: 01229 772319.

DOCTORS.
T H Bates. The Surgery, Park Stile. Broughton in Furness Tel: 01229 716337.
Millom Surgery, Waterloo House, 42 Wellington Street. Millom Tel: 01229 772123
Bootle Surgery, Chapel Lane, Bootle. Tel: 01229 718711.

ESTATE AGENTS.
Bairstow Eves North West, 32 Lapstone Road, Millom Tel: 01229 774809

GARDEN CENTRES.
Foxfield Garden Centre. The Laurels, Foxfield. Tel: 01229 716314.
Waltham Nursery, The Hill, Millom. (see advert)

GIFT SHOPS.
Cumbria Crafts, 1 School Terrace, Millom Tel: 01229 773443.
Haverigg Gift Shop, 3 Main Street Haverigg. Tel: 01229 774470.
I-Spy, 10 St Georges Terrace, Millom. Tel: 01229 774367.
Kelly, 9 St Georges Terrace, Millom Tel: 01229 772385.

DUNNERDALE

GOLF COURSES.
Silecroft Golf Club. Silecroft. Tel: 01229 774250.

GUEST HOUSES and B&B
Buckman Brow House, Thwaites. Tel: 01229 716541.
Cockley Beck Cottage, Cockley Beck.
Croft Cottage, Kirksanton. Tel: 01229 772582
Dunelm Cottage, 4 Main Street, Haverigg. Tel:01229 770097.
Fairview Guest House, 4 Salthouse Road, Millom Tel: 01229 772027
Foldgate Farm B&B. Corney. Tel: 01229 718660.
Gilgarth GH, Caton Street, Haverigg. Tel: 01229 772531
Havelock GH, Seathwaite.
Kellet Country Guest House, Silecroft. Tel:01229 770836. (see advert)
Oak Bank, Ulpha. Tel: 01229 716393
Old School, Whicham Valley.
Whicham Old Hall, Silecroft. Tel: 01229 772637
Whicham Old Rectory, Whicham Valley. (see advert)

HILL TARNS.
There are many hill tarns in the Lake District which offer free fishing for brown trout and perch. The trout tend to be small but the perch are often numerous and sometimes big. These hill tarns vary in size and depth, but they seldom exceed 15 acres in area. The fishing in these tarns is unlikely to be scintillating but anglers who appreciate solitude and wide open spaces will enjoy the challenge they offer. The hill tarns have one thing in common, and that is they all require fell walking to reach them.

HOSPITALS & CLINICS.
Millom Hospital, Lapstone Road, Millom. Tel: 01229 772631.

HOTELS.
Bankfield House Hotel, Kirksanton.Tel: 01229 772276.
Duddon Pilot Hotel, Devonshire Road, Millom.Tel: 01229 774116.
Eccle Riggs Manor Hotel, Foxfield Road, Broughton-in-Furness. Tel 01229
High Cross Inn, Broughton in Furness. Tel: 01229 716272.8.
Old Kings Head Hotel. Station Road, Broughton in Furness. Tel: 01229 716293.
Station Hotel, Bootle Station. Tel:01229 718207
West County Hotel, Market Square, Millom. Tel: 01229 772227.

INNS & PUBLIC HOUSES.
Black Cock Inn, Princes Street, Broughton in Furness. Tel: 01229 716529.

Brown Cow Inn, Waberthwaite. Tel: 01229 717243. (see advert)
Castle Inn, 47 Holborn Hill, Millom. Tel: 01229 772721
Devonshire Hotel, Devonshire Road, Millom. Tel: 01229 774912
Harbour Hotel, 2 Main Street, Haverigg. Tel: 01229 772764.
John Bull, Silecroft. Tel: 01229 772394. (see advert)
King William IV, Kirksanton Tel: 01229 772009.
Kings Head Hotel, Main Street, Bootle. Tel: 01229 718239.
Manor Arms, The Square, Broughton in Furness. (see advert)
Miners Arms, Silecroft. Tel: 01229 772325.
Newfield Inn, Seathwaite. Duddon Valley. Tel: 01229 716208. (see advert)
Peel Inn, Bedford Street, Millom. Tel: 01229 772245
Plough Inn, 41 Holborn Hill, Millom. Tel: 01229 772597.
Prince of Wales, Foxfield. Tel: 01229 716238.
Punch Bowl, The Green, Millom. Tel: 01229 772605.
Red Lion, 101 Holborn Hill, Millom Tel: 01229 773159.
Rising Sun Inn, Main Street, Haverigg. Tel: 01229 774752
Ship Inn, Holborn Hill, Millom Tel: 01229 773079.
Station Hotel, Salthouse Road, Millom Tel: 01229 772223.

LEISURE CENTRES.

Millom Recreation Centre. Lancashire Rd. Millom. Tel: 01229 774985. (see advert)

NATURE RESERVES.
Hodbarrow Bird Reserve, Millom. Tel: 01229 773281.

NURSING & RETIREMENT HOMES.
Croft Nursing Home Kirksanton. Tel: 01229 772868.
St.George's Residential Home. Millom. Tel: 01229 773959.

POLICE.
Millom. Tel: 01229 772213.

PONY TREKKING.
Bridle Mount, Haws Lane, Haverigg. Tel: 01229 770304.

POST OFFICES.
Bootle. 4, Main Street. Tel:01229 718233
Broughton in Furness. 11, Princes Street. Tel: 01229 716220
Haverigg. 96, Main Street. Tel: 01229. 772338.
Holborn Hill. 49, Holborn Hill. Millom. Tel: 01229 772570.
Millom. 9, St. Georges Road. Tel: 01229. 772574.
Silecroft. 1-3,Main Street. Tel: 01229 772595

DUNNERDALE
Ulpha. Tel: 01229 716255.
Waberthwaite, Lane End. Tel: 01229 717237.

PUBLIC LIBRARIES.
St Georges Road, Millom. Tel: 01229 772445.

PUBLIC PARKS.
Pleasure Ground, Millom.

RESTAURANTS & CAFES
Beach Cafe, Sea Front, Haverigg.
Bengal Balti Take-away, 50 Lapstone Road, Millom. Tel: 01229 771997
Beswicks Restaurant, The Square, Broughton in Furness Tel: 01229 716 285
Bridge Cafe, St George's Road, Millom. Tel: 01229 772416.
Brockwood Hall, Whicham Valley, Millom (see advert)
Commodore Country Club, Haverigg Holiday Village, Haverigg. Tel: 01229 774388.
Emma's Pantry, Millom Craft Centre, Millom. (see advert)
Nicholson House, 14 St Georges Terrace. Millom Tel: 01229 774534.
Square Cafe, Annan House, Broughton in Furness. Tel: 01229 716388.

RIDING SCHOOLS.
Bridle Mount Stables, Haws Lane, Haverigg. Tel: 01229 770304.

SAILING / SEA
Launching facilities are available at Haverigg and Silecroft.
Haverigg Water Sports Centre. Haverigg. Tel: 01229 774228.

SCHOOLS & COLLEGES.
Black Combe Junior School. Moor Road, Millom. Tel: 01229 772862.
Broughton in Furness Primary School, Kepplewray. Tel: 01229 716206.
Captain Shaw's School, Bootle. Tel: 01229 718279
Haverigg Primary School, Atkinson Street, Haverigg. Tel: 01229 772502.
Millom Infants School, Lapstone Road, Millom Tel: 01229 772679.
Millom Secondary School, Salthouse Road, Millom Tel: 01229 772300.
St James Roman Catholic Primary School, Lonsdale Road, Millom. Tel: 01229 772731.
Thwaites School, Hallthwaites, Millom. Tel: 01229 772554.
Ulpha School, Ulpha, Broughton in Furness. Tel: 01229 716267.
Waberthwaite Church of England Primary School, Waberthwaite. Tel: 01229 717664.

SELF CATERING ACCOMMODATION.
Brockwood Hall, Whicham Valley. Tel: 01229. 772329. (see advert)
The Dower House. High Duddon, Duddon Bridge. Tel: 01229 716279.
Harriet Trust. Borwick Rails, Millom Tel: 01229. 772345.
Kellet House, Silecroft. Tel: 01229 770836. (see advert)
Ring House, Woodland, Broughton in Furness. Tel: 01229 716578.
Seathwaite Lodge, Seathwaite.

TAXIS.
Millom Taxis, 27 Main St.Haverigg Tel: 01229 772256
Pete's Taxis 32 Festival Road, Millom. Tel: 01229 774995

THEATRES.
Millom Palladium, St Georges Road, Millom. Tel: 01229 772441, 772779 or 716733 (see advert)

TOURIST INFORMATION CENTRES.
Cumbria Tourist Board, Ashleigh, Holly Road, Windermere. Tel: 015394 44444.
Folk Museum, Millom. Tel: 01229 772555
The Square, Broughton-in-Furness. 01229 716115

TRAVEL AGENTS.
Abbey Travel, 34 Lapstone Road, Millom Tel: 01229 773622. (see advert)

ESKDALE

Regentlane Publishers & Printers

are a refreshing new concept in quick-printing.

RING NOW FOR A QUOTATION

01229 770444

FAX: **01229 770339**

CUMBRIA'S WESTERN LAKES & COAST.

ESKDALE.

ESKDALE

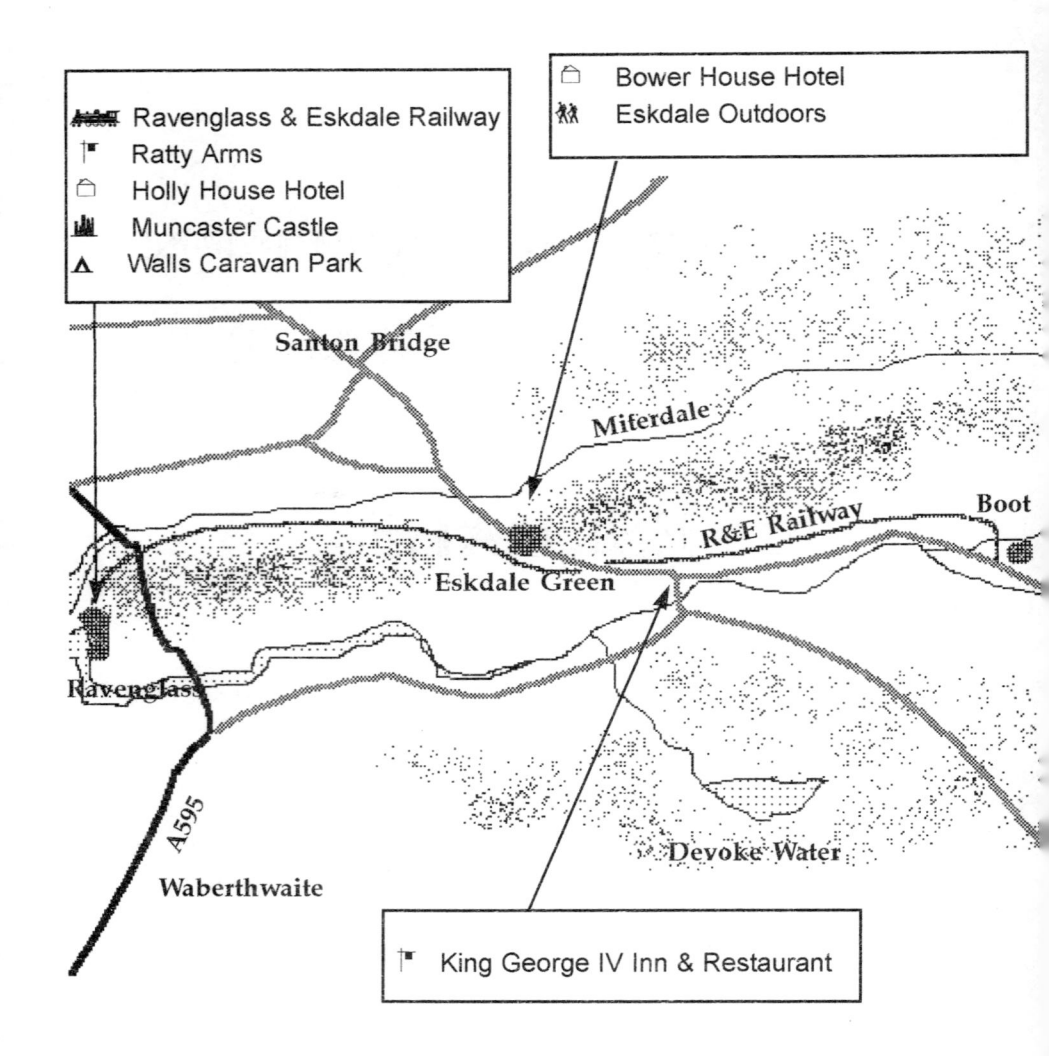

- 🚂 Ravenglass & Eskdale Railway
- 🍺 Ratty Arms
- ⌂ Holly House Hotel
- 🏰 Muncaster Castle
- ▲ Walls Caravan Park

- ⌂ Bower House Hotel
- 🚶 Eskdale Outdoors

Santon Bridge

Miterdale

R&E Railway

Boot

Eskdale Green

Ravenglass

A595

Waberthwaite

Devoke Water

- 🍺 King George IV Inn & Restaurant

40 *Travellers' Guide to Cumbria's Western Lakes & Coast*

ESKDALE

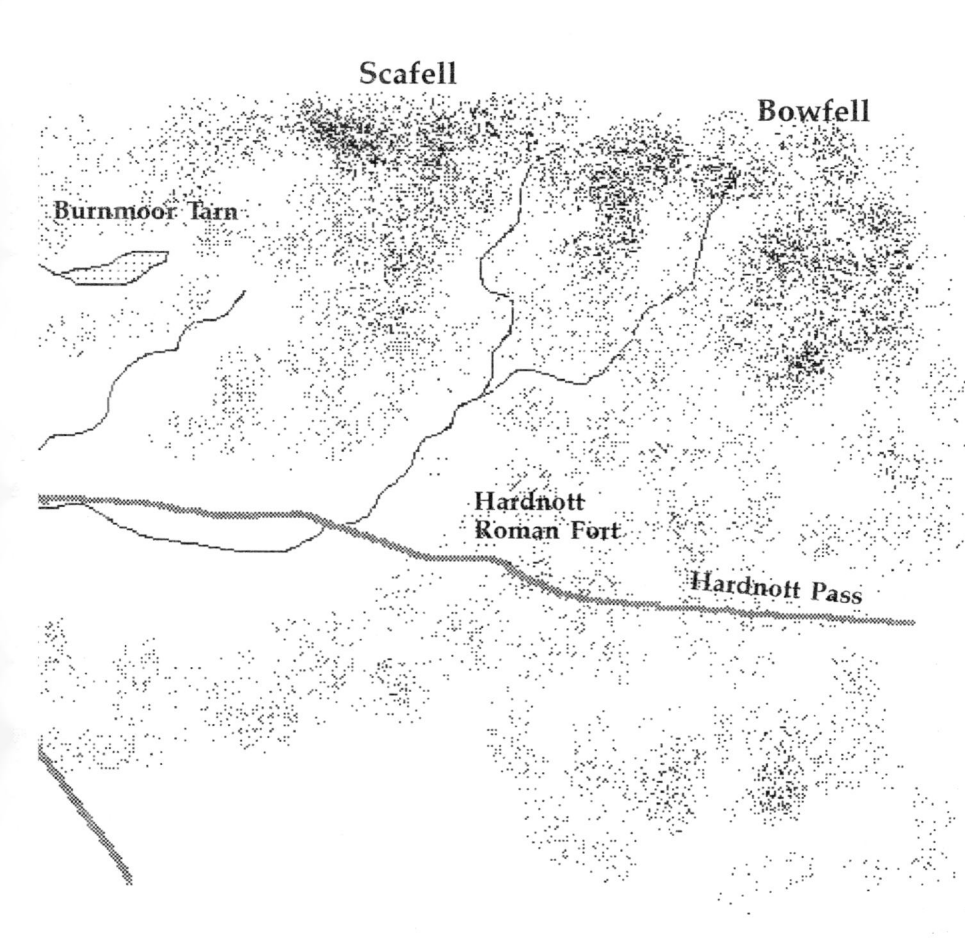

Scafell
Bowfell
Burnmoor Tarn
Hardnott Roman Fort
Hardnott Pass

THE ESK VALLEY

Most of the water which makes up the Esk River descend from the eastern slopes of England's highest mountain. The name (Aesc) is of Indo-European derivation and means "powerful". The Latin "Isca" which the Romans would have used has the same meaning.

It is an apt description as the growing torrent froths over numerous waterfalls, its size increased after the confluence with Lingcove Beck and Scale Gill. Below Hardnott Fort (the Roman Mediobogdum–literally, in the middle of waters), the valley widens into a rich alluvial area once farmed by monks allied to Furness Abbey, hence the name Brotherikeld. Hardnott Fort guards one end of the pass over to Ambleside from a commanding position on a crag some 800 feet high, and glorying in some of the finest mountain scenery in the country, with a magnificent view of Scafell Pass less than four miles away. It has been excavated and the remains show it to be roughly a square of 125 yards, enclosing just three acres, with the base of a tower at each corner, and a gateway at each side. The north tower on the highest point was perhaps a signal station, and the walls or rampart of the fort are five feet thick.

For two miles, the now-sluggish river meanders past the Woolpack Inn where Eskdale 'Tup' Show is held on the last Friday in September. 'Tup' Fair origins...when rams are hired out or sold for breeding purposes...later turning itself into a social gathering, and now currently, the Eskdale Show. A mile down the river is Penny Hill which is one of the farms which Beatrix Potter bought for the National Trust...and two miles further on is Stanley Ghyll with Dalegarth Force. The Stanleys of Austhwaite have farmed the valley for 600 years, and are still doing so to this day.

The valley narrows once more after passing Boot. Erosion has been so significant on this stretch that the rock is worn away in places right down to the Pre-Cambrian crust.

Elsewhere, the landscape is obviously volcanic. Early theories as to the origins of what is known generally as the Borrowdale Volcanic Series of rocks include the belief that there was once a huge volcano in the area between Borrowdale, Wasdale and Eskdale (these valley virtually meet in the central lakes) or that the original slate was covered in lava and then covered with limestone which has gradually been worn away.

More recent surveys suggest that Cumbria was originally fairly flat, covered in shale and slate, overlaid with limestone in some parts of the south and east, and coal seams in the west around Workington. Then, some time geologically recent, there was a tremendous upheaval which pushed up Black Combe, Skiddaw and other slate-based mountains, but which burst out in numerous igneous extrusions like mud bubbling through the joins in crazy paving. Hence, the crazy, mixed-up landscape with little regular form which constitutes much of the Lake District. Eskdale is a perfect example of how this may have happened.

Much of the valley below here can be seen best from the narrow-gauge "La'al Ratty", the local name for the Ravenglass and Eskdale Railway. Originally built to carry ore from drift mines above Boot, it now carries Tourists up and down the valley in relative comfort.

The terminus is at Dalegarth and everyone should travel the full length of the track to Ravenglass at least once in their lives.

Below Boot, the river begins to meander again as it swerves away from the village of Eskdale Green and the accompanying road meets the fell track from Broughton-in-Furness via Ulpha.

On the right (north) is the huge black basaltic extrusion of Muncaster Fell. The rock here is so hard that only one road crosses it and does so with difficulty. The railway doe not follow the river but loops around the far side of the fell to parallel the tiny River Mite to Ravenglass.

After passing under the A595 coast road, often liable to flooding in severe weather and high tide, Muncaster Castle can be clearly seen on a outcrop, seemingly perched right on the edge of the outcrop. There is a ford across the river at Hall Waberthwaite, negotiable only with extreme care, and the Newbiggin to Eskmeals road is often under water at Eskmeals Viaduct where the main railway crosses the estuary.

The river then does a dog-leg to the north to meet the Mite and the Irt in Ravenglass Harbour, first passing close to the Roman Bath House (Glannoventa) south of Ravenglass village.

The meagre population of the valley is swelled almost beyond belief by visitors during the holiday season. They come to camp at one of several locations along the valley, stay in self-catering cottages which are numerous, or in serviced accommodation at an Inn or guest house.

There is a great deal of choice for the walker, cyclist, bird-watcher or one of the many who come simply to admire the scenery. The lanes are few, narrow and cramped so do not expect to race through the area. Eskdale is a valley to be absorbed slowly.

THE COAST & BEACHES

Stub Place is a sandy, boulder-scattered beach looking deceptively similar to other quiet stretches along this Cumbrian coastline, is backed by a broad bank of shingle and is an ideal place to watch guns being fired from the Ministry of Defence's 'Proof and Experimental Establishment' at Eskmeals. The peace and quiet here however is often shattered by the shells screaming out to sea. Firing generally takes place between 8am and 5pm Monday to Friday. Warning flags fly when the shore in front of the range is closed during firing.

Eskmeals. At weekend this pleasant sandy beach is as quiet and pleasant as so many others along this coastline. But, like Stub Place, the weekdays are shattered by the sound of guns firing Between 8am and 5pm weekdays, the beach is closed and red flags can be seen flying. When the range is is used outside those times, black and yellow flags are flown. The firing area extends to 15 miles out to sea and is patrolled by a launch.

Ravenglass. Steep wooded slopes rise up behind this tranquil fishing village, where the only street ends on a shore of shingle and muddy sand. The beach is carved by deep channels and bathing is unsafe because of fast currents. Ravenglass has undoubtedly lost its old fame as the foremost port in north-west Britain, but its wide street still straggles along the estuary where the Irt and the Mite and the Esk all fall into the sea. Sheltered by fine hills and the glorious woodlands of Muncaster Castle close by, it is perhaps the oldest seaport in Cumbria and is said to have been built from Roman materials. One's imagination could quite easily picture a Roman fleet at anchor in its harbour, where great sandy stretches are left bare by every tide, feeding grounds for oystercatchers and ringed plovers. Across the water among nearly 600 acres of sand dunes is a controlled nature reserve with many interesting wild plants and the largest black-headed gullery in Britain. (see editorial feature)

Boot

Boot is a beautiful little village just north of the Eskdale valley road. Parking here being next to impossible, most motorised visitors park in the car park at Dalegarth station a short distance away.

The village of Boot, to all who visit, is a delightful spot, with its restored corn mill, a packhorse bridge, church, shop/post office, art/craft gallery and, of course, its traditional inns. (In fact there is a choice of five both in Boot and nearby Eskdale).

This is magnificent walking country visitors may take a leisurely stroll across the lane to the waterfalls of the tumbling Whillan beck and on level ground to the stepping stones of the River Esk. Eskdale descends from the highest and wildest mountains in the district to the sands of Ravenglass in a swift transition from grandeur to beauty. "The finest of all valleys for those whose special joy is to travel on foot and a paradise for artists" (Wainwright).

Within walking distance are Scafell Pike, Englands highest mountain, its steepest mountain road, Hardknott Pass, and its deepest lake, the dramatic Wastwater. There is also the well preserved Hardknott Roman Fort, and the 60 foot Stanley Force. High on the Birker Fell above is wild and lonely Devoke Water (the Lake District's largest tarn) surrounded by heather moors, with Bronze Age cairns around its shores.

Beyond a short range of cottages, and over a pack-horse bridge will be found Eskdale Mill, an ancient corn mill on the Whillan Beck which operated from the sixteenth century until the 1920's. Milling has been a feature of the Eskdale valley life since the 12th century. The first documented evidence of Eskdale Mill itself dates from 1578, when brothers Henry and Robert Vicars were the tenants paying an annual rent of 8 shillings! (40p in todays currency).

The mill continued to grind cereals until the early 1920's when a dynamo was installed for the last miller Edward Bibby who died in 1924. The upper wheel of the mill continued to make electricity until 1955 when mains power came to the valley.

Inside the mill today will be found a quite informative exhibition with display stands and old photographs, and the atmosphere is well re-created even to the point of cobwebs and a moth-eaten bowler hat on a chair.

A delightful wooded area to the rear of the mill is well worth a visit. Impressive waterfalls provide a powerful head of water to feed ponds and sluices, necessary to power two huge water wheels. A wonderful setting for a picnic.

Boot is in fact a railway terminus, The Ravenglass and Eskdale Railway winds its way from Ravenglass on the coast to Dalegarth Station, close by a seven mile journey completed in 40 minutes by miniature train.

Corney

Corney is a parish on the south coast, between Bootle and Waberthwaite.

Coming to its little church on a lonely hilltop we are rewarded with a splendid view of this fascinating countryside. Far in the valley below a mountain stream chatters under a tiny bridge, and here and there among the hills the farms are dotted. Over the lowlands we look to the sea, and inland rise Black Combe and Buck Barrow.

The church here is dedicated to St John the Baptist and at its height of 600 feet looks protectively over the parish. This church is a little over 100 years old, though there has been one here since the 12th century. In the churchyard is a sundial dated 1882, the gift of one Edward Troughton, Corney's most famous son. Despite being colour blind and deaf he became famous for his work on scientific instruments, and was awarded the Copley medal by the Royal Society.

The Brown Cow Inn built around 1800, and in its early days provided bed and board for huntsmen and hounds. It wasn't until the late 1950's that electricity first came to Corney...lighting until then had been by oil lamps and candles.

Corney people have a reputation for longevity. A gravestone here shows one John Noble lived here 1658-1772 (114 years)..his life stretching from the end of Cromwell's to the beginning of Napoleon's.

Eskdale Green

Eskdale is one of Cumbria's most delightful valleys, full of interest and beauty, with little hamlets dotting along it, and with great rocky crags crowning lovely wooded slopes. The valley has a network of old routed, some of which are tarmac, but most are unspoilt, together with pony tracks. One of these leads over the bridge at Boot, up and over Burnmoor, and down to Wasdale.

Bordering on Eskdale is Birker Force, a fine waterfall to see after heavy rains, along with Dalegarth Force, one of the country's gems, a waterfall leaping over

---

ESKDALE OUTDOOR SHOP & POST OFFICE
ESKDALE GREEN

Boots
Waterproofs & Outdoor Wear
Camping spares
Maps & books
Newsagent
Boots for hire

P & B Hyde
(019467) 23223

Travellers' Guide to Cumbria's Western Lakes & Coast

ESKDALE

sixty feet into a wooded ravine. Not far away is Devoke Water, the small lake a mile long and half as wide, high up in the fells nearly 800 feet above the sea. It is famous for its trout.

The churchyard here was not consecrated for burials until 1901. Over this (aptly named) Corpse road, the coffins from Wasdale were carried to St Catherine's... Locals here still talk of the day that a pack-horse took fright and disappeared into the mist with the body of one Thomas Porter strapped to its back. St Catherine's Church is down by the river in an idyllic setting. It is typical of a small dale church, built like a barn and largely 17th century. The monks from Furness Abbey, which owned much of Eskdale, built the original chapel here long before this church was built.

Note the Holy Well in a small plateau above the path, along with the tombstones of Tommy Dobson and Willy Porter,

King George IV Inn
COUNTRY INN & RESTAURANT
HARRY & JACQUI SHEPHERD

Bed & Breakfast offering en-suite facilities
We pride ourselves on having over 200 varieties of Single Malt Whisky
Open All Year
A La Carte & Bar Meals served lunchtime & evenings
Restaurant Available for Bookings

Eskdale Holmrook Cumbria CA19 1TS
(019467) 23262 • Fax: (019467) 23334

BOWER HOUSE INN

ESKDALE GREEN,
CUMBRIA CA19 1TD
Tel: 01946 723 244
Fax: 01946 723308

A COUNTRY INN AS IT SHOULD BE

AA★★

GARDEN MEALS
BAR MEALS - FIVE REAL ALES
SUPERB RESTAURANT
(AA ROSETTE)

COMFORTABLE ROOMS - ALL EN-SUITE
NO MUSIC, NO FRUIT MACHINES

huntsmen of the Eskdale and Ennerdale pack, and of great local renown.

The village of Eskdale Green was changed considerably around a hundred years ago, when the Rea family bought Gate House Farm, and developed the Gate House Estate. These days the centre of the village is the post office cum shop, the owner of which is a cousin to the maker of Woodall's Cumberland Sausage.

The pub here 'The King George'..was at one time named the 'King of Prussia', but had its name changed at the outbreak of World War I.

'La'al Ratty', the steam train from the Ravenglass and Eskdale Railway, makes a loop around the village, but has stations on either side.

Above Eskdale Green is 'Miterdale' where a ruined farmhouse is haunted by the ghost of a gypsy, known as 'Beckside Boggle' gurglings can still be heard on moonlight nights!

Ravenglass

Ravenglass is an ancient and delightful Cumbrian coastal village, situated at the junction of the rivers Esk, Irt and Mite, where they form an estuary flowing into the Irish Sea.

Throughout the 17th and 18th centuries, this little urban centre enjoyed a good coastal trade, for its ships could in those days dock right by the single main street for loading and unloading. The proximity of the Lakeland fells, the lower cost involved for shipping, and its handiness in avoiding expensive Whitehaven, encouraged growth of the village.

In Roman days, Ravenglass was the second largest port in Britain. In fact, it was the only natural harbour on the west coast between the Dee and the Solway.

Additionally, the Romans under their General Agricola, built an important fort here in AD79, known at Glannaventa, though little remains of the fort these days. "Walls Castle" was the bath house for the fort and this can be visited just outside the village.

WALLS CARAVAN & CAMPING PARK
RAVENGLASS CUMBRIA CA18 1SR
TEL: 01229 717250

Walls Caravan and Tent Park was constructed in the spring of 1978, to the specifications of the English Tourist Board. The facilities have been landscaped into an existing woodland so that the setting is amongst a variety of established and mature trees. The site extends to 5 acres and is limited to 51 caravans, tents and touring caravanettes. There are no static caravans. All pitches are hard standings, and there is a hard internal road. There are electric hook-ups.
The site is managed by Keith & Stephinie Bridges who provide a warm reception to all their visitors and are on hand to help during your stay. Site open 28th February until 15th November. Pets allowed under proper control and on leads.

Travellers' Guide to Cumbria's Western Lakes & Coast

ESKDALE

It is interesting to note that it has the highest standing walls of any Roman ruin in the North of England. They are over twelve feet high in parts. Roman cement can be seen clinging to the inside of the walls even today. It is thought by many that the fort had associations with King Eveling and King Arthur. Today, if you wish, you will still find Neolithic flints on the sand dunes.

The village received a market charter in the 13th century, drawing large numbers of people to its annual fairs and markets.

Today, the village is more famous for its railway...the Ravenglass and Eskdale Railway, better known as the "La'al Ratty". The R & ER operates a steam train service starting from this picturesque estuary and winding its way through the fells to the terminus at Dalegarth in the heart of Eskdale. Such is the prospect of riding in open carriages over this seven-mile route, from coast to the mountains, so to speak...that it attracts thousands of tourists almost daily during the season.

Muncaster Castle...the home of the Pennington family since 1208 is just a short distance away. The castle grounds in themselves have been one of Cumbria's principle attractions for many years, and thousands have flocked in spring and summer to see the massed rhododendrons and azaleas in the castle park. But as many visit to see the wonders of this beautifully kept castle too and be shown around on a hi-tech tour introduced personally by one of the family who still own and run the castle and grounds. There is also a display of owls.

The Penningtons have been one of the great families of "Cumberland" since the 11th century, and their forebears lived in Walls Castle before building, in the 13th

Muncaster Castle

The Castle is set in an idyllic corner of the Western Lake District. The breathtaking views over Eskdale were described by John Ruskin as "Heaven's Gate". Muncaster has something for everyone. The Castle has been the home of the Pennington family since 1208 and is still their family home. The Pele Tower, standing on Roman foundations, has been developed and extended over the centuries to form the Castle as it is seen today.

The Castle brings you seven centuries of glorious history. The 40 minute audio tour contains a wealth of interesting and humourous family anecdotes which add immensely to the enjoyment and create a unique atmosphere in which to view the superb antique furniture, portraits by famous artists, beautiful tapestries and many other articles of historical and artistic merit.

A walk through Muncaster's Gardens and woodland will be a joy to anyone who loves nature. The Gardens are spectacular and enjoy a world-wide reputation for the outstanding collection of rhododendrons and azaleas with many varieties first propagated here. There is also a wide variety of rare and beautiful trees and exotic plants.

Muncaster is also home to the World Owl Trust which strives to conserve owls world-wide. The Owl Centre has one of the finest collections of owls in the world. Visitors can view at close range some of the rarest owls on earth and thanks to video cameras installed in selected nesting boxes observe the private lives of these mystical creatures. There is an opportunity to "Meet the Birds" daily at 2.30pm (end March to end October). This is an informative talk and display when, weather permitting, the birds fly.

The Stables Buttery serves light refreshments and full meals and the Gift Shops offer that special memento of your visit.

Muncaster Castle is situated on the A595 one mile east of Ravenglass on the west coast of Cumbria.

Ravenglass, Cumbria, CA18 1RQ
Tel: 01229 717614   Fax: 01229 717010

ESKDALE

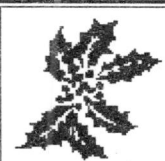

Holly House Hotel
Ravenglass, Cumbria, CA18 1SQ
Tel: 01229 717230

Mine Hosts: Ed & Anita extend to you the warmest of welcomes to their small country hotel overlooking the picturesque estuary and sand dunes. The 'Holly' gives you all the comforts, home cooking & en-suite accommodation.

~ PLUS ~
☆ Fully licensed bar and dining room (for both residents & non residents) ☆
☆ Extensive bar menu also a fish & chip cafe & take away ☆
☆ A haven for boating enthusiasts ☆

An ideal starting point for all Cumbrian pursuits & coast to coast travellers.

OPEN ALL YEAR
THE SUNSETS ARE SOMETHING ELSE!

Enjoy a complete and delightful day out
THE RAVENGLASS & ESKDALE RAILWAY

England's oldest narrow gauge steam railway transports you through some of the most glorious landscape in the world. From the coast at Ravenglass to the foot of Lakeland's highest mountains you will ride behind a small locomotive and traverse gradients as steep as 1 in 35. Almost the steepest possible for normal railways. You will also have the opportunity to visit Muncaster Water Mill, The Railway Museum and enjoy food and refreshment at The Ratty Arms.

For further information or for party details Telephone: 01229 717171

The Ravenglass & Eskdale Railway Co. Ltd., Ravenglass Cumbria CA18 1SW

Travellers' Guide to Cumbria's Western Lakes & Coast

century, the pele tower which was the corner stone of the present castle.

The castle in its present form is relatively modern, no later than the 18th century, but the pele tower with its walls ten feet thick, still stands on the right of the castle facade.

Probably the most magnificent room on view to the public is the library, a vast octagonal chamber which soars up through two floors of the castle with a fine brass railed balcony running all around to bring thousands of rare books within reach.

Several of the bedrooms are open to the public, including what is referred to as the "King's Room". Solid carved oak Elizabethan four-posters are the focal points in these rooms and two of them have carved stone Elizabethan fire places which were brought by the Pennington from dismantled homes many years ago. Among the treasures on show are some excellent old tapestries, the best by far being four small framed pieces hung in the bedroom corridor, depicting allegorical scenes, including the destruction of Sodom and Gomorrah, Lot's wife and all.

Muncaster Water Mill stands between the Ratty Railway and the River Mite and is open to visitors who can watch flour being ground as it has been for centuries.

Waberthwaite

Waberthwaite is a hamlet some one and a half miles north east of Eskmeals on the Esk.

The name Waberthwaite is of Norse origin and is believed to mean 'Wyburgh's Clearing'

Its a lonely little place near the coast. Here the River Esk flows around the finely wooded hill of Muncaster Castle, with its beacon tower 250 feet up, and here on the edge of a sandy creek, crouches one of the county's ancient white-walled churches.

Low and simple, it has only five windows to light it, some of them 16th century. The east window is enriched with a picture of the Good Shepherd. The 300 year old pulpit has carved panels and borders, and hidden in one of the old box-pews is a Norman font two feet high, looking rather like the base of a pillar. The bell turret was rebuilt in Queen Anne's reign. In the graveyard will be found a 9th century cross shaft which at one time stood on a well used route for travellers heading north from the village.

At the start of the century, quarrying was the name of the game for this village. It had started at Broad Oak with granite sets of different sizes being sent to many Lancashire towns. For years the quarry offered work to around 50 men until 1946 when it was closed. The quarry site is now a site of Special Scientific Interest.

The village shop here opened by a Mrs Hannah Woodall in 1828. Its still there today, incorporating the local Post Office, under the same family ownership, though today it now proudly displays a Royal Warrant for traditional Cumberland sausage...and is better known for its ham, bacon, and sausage nationwide labelled 'Woodalls of Waberthwaite'.

ESKDALE

ART & CRAFT SHOPS.
Fold End Gallery, Boot Tel: 019467 23213.

ATTRACTIONS.
Dalegarth Station.
Is the terminus of the Eskdale Railway, providing a cafe in the very centre of the valley. From here it's an easy walk to the lovely St Catherine's Church in its tranquil riverside setting or to Dalegarth Waterfall or charming Boot Village. For the more ambitious, there are scores of walks, from a pleasant meander by the River Esk to a hike up Englands highest peak...mighty Scafell Pike.

Dalegarth Fells.
Magnificent waterfalls in a lovely wooded gorge. Here you may catch a glimpse of Heron, Peregrine Falcons, or the Buzzards which are Wild Eskdale's trademark. Here too you may spot if you are lucky deer, fox and badgers.

Ravenglass & Eskdale Railway. Tel: 01229 717171. (see advert)
The Ravenglass & Eskdale Railway better known as "La'al Ratty", was open in 1875 to bring iron ore to the Furness Railway and started carrying passengers the following year. Since then the railway has had a very unsettled history. The iron ore traffic dwindled to nothing, the line was in financial difficulty and granite quarries were opened to provide traffic. The 3 foot (914mm) gauge track was closed but was unexpectedly reopened by the famous model-maker Mr Basset-Lowke, the next year on the even narrower gauge of 15 inches.

The tiny trains were soon again carrying goods and passengers into and out of the valley and the granite quarries were busy through until 1953 when they were closed. The railway could not survive on the tourist trade there then was and was finally bought by a group of enthusiasts. A new company now operates the railway, supported by members of the Preservation Society. The nearly derelict line has been improved greatly since then and is now one of the foremost tourist attractions in the North-West of England.

Ravenglass Village.
The Romans used it as a port and called it Glanoventa. Later it was renowned for the activities of the smugglers. Today the small attractive estuary village is the home of the 15" gauge Ravenglass and Eskdale Railway with its station, workshops and museum. On the estuary bird sanctuary you can see a variety of sea birds and, if you're lucky, the famous Natterjack Toads. Visit also the Roman Bath House (the second tallest Roman remains in Britain) and Muncaster Water Mill.

Muncaster Castle. Tel: 01229 717614.(see advert)
Medieval Muncaster Castle opens its Pele Tower and treasures for all visitors...or alternatively stroll around its renowned rhododendrons and azalea gardens and the Owl Centre. Henry VI hid in the castle in 1464 after the battle of Hexham and presented the lovely glass "Luck of Muncaster" bowl. A replica is on display.

Visitors here are offered a free audio tour which explains and enlivens the treasures collected by the Pennington family over seven centuries with many interesting and

ESKDALE

humourous family anecdotes.

Muncaster Mill. Tel: 01229 717232.

Since 1455 flour has been milled here by water-power. You can break your journey on the miniature railway by alighting here at its own station beside the mill and see how flour is ground in the traditional way.

Muncaster Watermill is one of the few working water-powered corn mills in the country to have survived from the days when the village mill was a common feature. Indeed, in pre-railway days few communities existed without at least one watermill or windmill. The mill site at Muncaster has a long association with milling as this was the manorial mill for the Manor of Muncaster, Although the present mill building dates from about 1700, it is known that a mill has occupied the same site since at least 1455, when it was recorded that Thomas Senhouse leased the mill for £3 a year from Sir John Pennington.

Muncaster Owl Centre.

Muncaster Owl Centre boasts one of the finest collections of owls in the world ranging from tiny Pygmy Owls to gigantic Eagle Owls. Visitors can view at close range some of the rarest owls on earth and thanks to video cameras installed in selected nest boxes observe the private lives of these mystical creatures.

Eskdale Corn Mill. Tel: 019467 23335.

Eskdale Mill dates back to the 16th century and is located in one of the finest and most picturesque Lake District valleys. One of the few remaining corn mills with two water wheels, the mill also features an exhibition of milling machinery and related items associated with Eskdale and its people. Around the mill can be enjoyed a woodland picnic area and the waterside habitat often contains frequent visitors from the Lake District's own wildlife.

Lakeland Experience Adventure Holidays. Tel: 019467 24366.

Richard Woodall Waberthwaite (traditionally cured hams, bacon and sausage) Tel: 01229 717237.

Seven Acres Caravan Park & Childrens Animal Park. Gosforth. Tel: 019467 25480.

Here you can see, goats, pigs, hens, bantams, geese, ducks, deer turkeys, rabbits, guinea pigs, aviary birds, fox, etc.

Upper Eskdale.

Upper Eskdale takes visitors back to their wilder roots. Broad vistas of majestic fells enfold Hardknott Roman Pass...the sternest test to drivers in the kingdom. and beside it Hardknott Roman Fort, wonderfully preserved from the 1st century and commanding magnificent views of this superb valley.

CARAVAN & CAMPING SITES.

Walls Caravan & Camping Park., Ravenglass. Tel: 01229 717250. (see advert)

Fisherground Campsite, Eskdale Green. Tel: 019467 23319.

Hollins Farm, Boot. Tel: 019467 23253.

CHURCHES.
Kingdom Hall of Jehovah's Witnesses, Holborn Hill, Millom. Tel: 01229 773088
St Catherine Church of England, Eskdale. Tel: 019467 23242.
St Paul Church of England, Irton. Tel: 019467 23242.
St Michael Church of England, Muncaster. Tel: 019467 23242.
St Bega's Church of England

COACH & COACH HIRE.
William Sim & Son Hunholme Garage, Boot. Tel: 019467 23227

CRAFT WORKERS.
Ravenglass Crafts, Main Street, Ravenglass. Tel 01229 717209. Furniture.

FISHING. Stocked Tarns.
Knott End Farm Nr Ravenglass. Tel: 01229 717255.

GARDENS.
(National Gardens Scheme. Properties open all year on request)
Rydal Mount, Eskdale Green. Tel: 019467 23267.
Muncaster Castle. Tel: 01229 717614 (see advert)

GUEST HOUSES and B&B
Countrywide Holidays, Stanley Ghyll House, Boot. Tel : 019467 23327.
The Ferns, Eskdale Green. Tel: 019467 23217.
Foldgate Farm, Corney Fell. Tel: 01229 718660
Forest How Guest House Eskdale Green. Tel: 019467 23201.
Muncaster Country Guest House, Muncaster, Tel: 01229 717693
Muncaster Water Mill. Ravenglass. Tel: 01229. 717232.
Rosegarth, Main Street, Ravenglass. Tel: 01229 717275.
Stanley Ghyll House. Boot. Tel: 019467 23327.
The Stables. Bootle (see advert)

HILL TARNS.
There are many hill tarns in the Lake District which offer free fishing for brown trout and perch. The trout tend to be small but the perch are often numerous and sometimes big. These hill tarns vary in size and depth, but they seldom exceed 15 acres in area. The fishing in these tarns is unlikely to be scintillating but anglers who appreciate solitude and wide open spaces will enjoy the challenge they offer. The hill tarns have one thing in common, and that is they all require fell walking to reach them.

ESKDALE

HOTELS.
Brook House Hotel, Boot. Tel: 019467 23288.
Holly House Hotel, Ravenglass. Tel: 01229 717230. (see advert)
Pennington Arms Hotel, Ravenglass. Tel: 01229 717222.

INNS & PUBLIC HOUSES
Brown Cow Inn, Waberthwaite. Tel: 01229 717243
Bower House Inn. Eskdale Green. (see advert)
Burnmoor Inn. Boot. Tel: 019467 23224.
King George IV Inn, Eskdale Green. Tel: 019467 23262. (see advert)
Ratty Arms Ravenglass. Tel: 01229 717676.
Woolpack Inn, Boot. Tel: 019467 23230.

NATURE RESERVES.
Ravenglass & Drigg Dunes Nature Reserve. Tel: 01539 724555.
Please Note: Additional nature reserves will be found at Crimpfield Marsh, Glasson Moss National Nature Reserve and Fingland Wood National Nature Reserve, Drumburgh.

POST OFFICES.
Boot Post Office. Tel: 019467 23236
Eskdale Post Office, Eskdale Green. (see advert)
Ravenglass Post Office, Main Street. Tel: 01229 717281.

RESTAURANTS.
Dalegarth Station Cafe, Eskdale. Tel: 019467 23221.
King George IV Restaurant, Eskdale Green. Tel: 019467 23262.
The Ratty Arms, Ravenglass Tel: 01229 717676. (see advert)

SAILING. SEA
Launching facilities are available along the West coast at Ravenglass
Ravenglass RYA. Tel: 019467 28597.

SCHOOLS & COLLEGES.
St Bega's Church of England Primary School.

SELF CATERING ACCOMMODATION.
Character Country Cottages, Bridge End Farm, Boot. Tel: 019467 23100.

ESKDALE

Dyke Croft, Ravenglass. Tel: 01229 717326
Esk View Cottage, Church Lane, Boot. Tel: 019467 23235.
Fisherground Farm Cottages & Pine Lodges, Eskdale Tel: 019467 23319.
Hollin Head Cottage, Eskdale. Tel: 019467 23235.
Longrigg Green, Eskdale Tel: 019467 23201.
Old Brantrake, Eskdale. Tel: 019467 23340.

TOURIST INFORMATION CENTRES.
Cumbria Tourist Board, Ashleigh, Holly Road, Windermere. Tel: 015394 44444.
Ravenglass & Eskdale Railway Ravenglass. Tel: 01229 717278

YOUTH HOSTELS.
Eskdale Youth Hostel, Boot. Tel : 019467 23219.

Travellers' Guide to Cumbria's Western Lakes & Coast

RegentLane Publishers & Printers

are a refreshing new concept in quick-printing.

RING NOW FOR A QUOTATION

01229 770444

FAX: **01229 770339**

CUMBRIA'S WESTERN LAKES & COAST.

WASDALE.

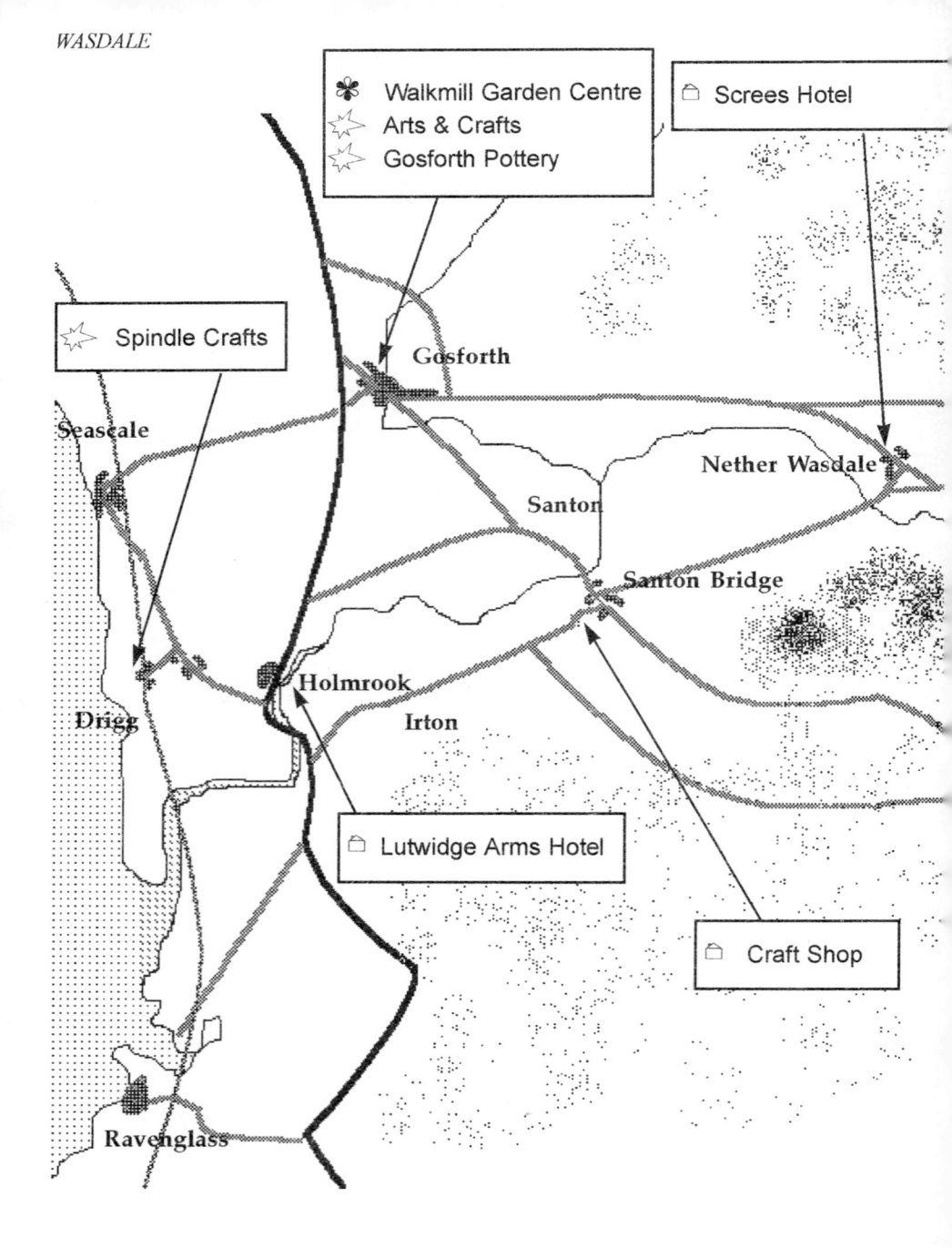

WASDALE

- Walkmill Garden Centre
- Arts & Crafts
- Gosforth Pottery
- Screes Hotel
- Spindle Crafts
- Lutwidge Arms Hotel
- Craft Shop

Seascale · Gosforth · Nether Wasdale · Santon · Santon Bridge · Holmrook · Irton · Drigg · Ravenglass

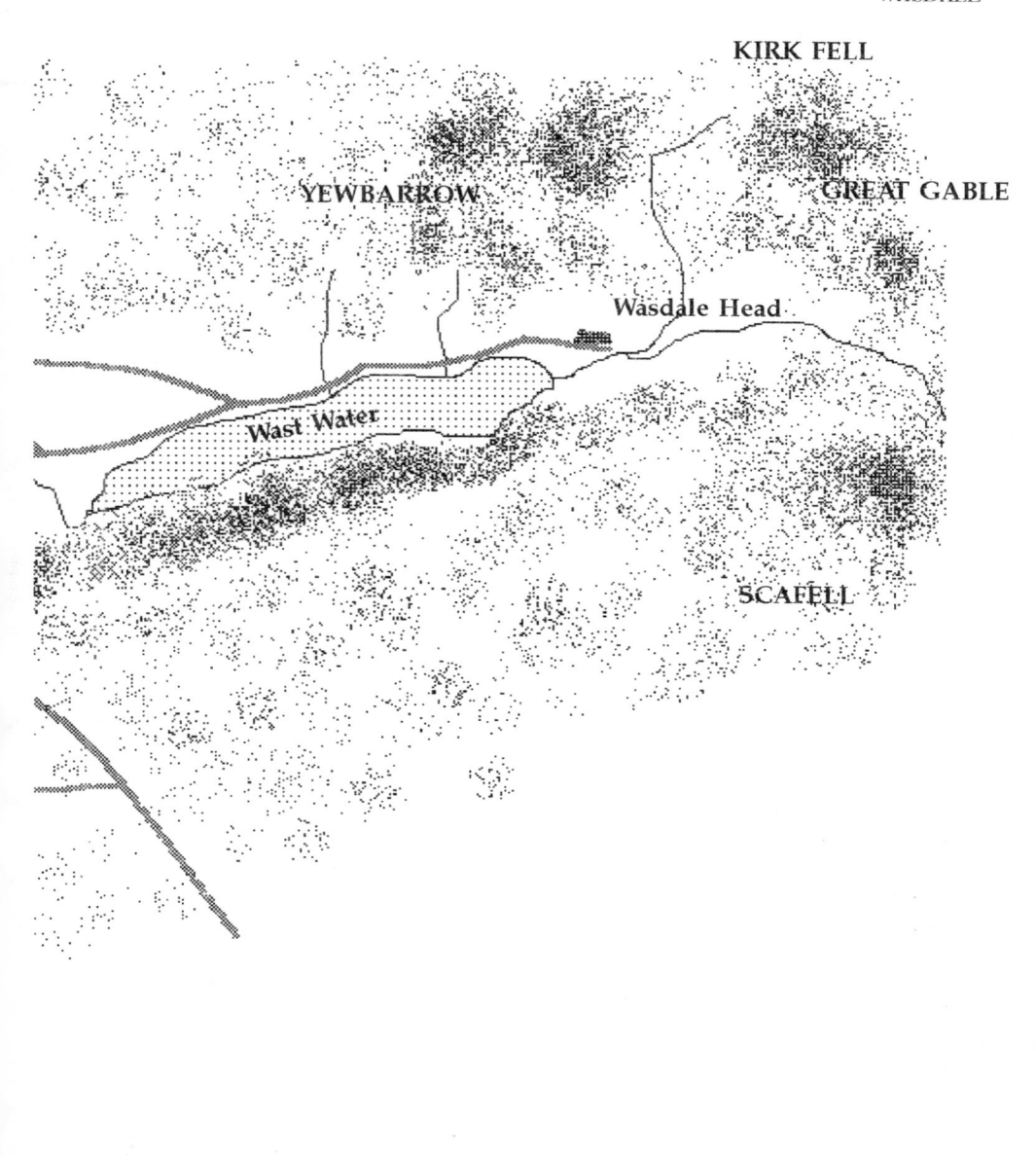

WASDALE

KIRK FELL

YEWBARROW

GREAT GABLE

Wasdale Head

Wast Water

SCAFELL

WASDALE

By rights, I suppose the valley which starts on the slopes of Scafell and Great Gable, running the short distance to join the Mite and Esk in Ravenglass Harbour should be named Irtdale. Instead, it retains the Old Germanic name for water. Hence Wasdale is "the valley full of water."

The silly part came later when someone who was obviously completely ignorant as to the meaning decided to call the lake Wast Water–literally "water water". Another etymological anomaly is the Copeland Forest (which gives its name to the local authority). Copeland means "the land of forests." Hence "forest forest".

Instantly recognisable by the unique screes on the southern bank, the lake fills most of the upper valley.

Above the lake, close to Wasdale Head, Mosedale Beck, Lingmell Beck and Lingmell Gill join together to keep the lake at a constant depth far in excess of any other Cumbrian lake.

Wasdale Head has that "hemmed in" feeling with the twin peaks of Scafell towering to the east, almost a thousand metres high. There are many theories concerning the name but the most plausible is the simplest–it is the fell (*Norse* fjall–open land) of the Esk (*Gaelic* Aesc–powerful) - hence Aescfjall, Scafell. On the opposite side of Lingmell Beck is Great Gable, resembling the end gable of a house, and Kirk Fell. To the west is Yewbarrow, the hill of Yew Trees.

The Becks (*Norse* Bekkr) rise and fall rapidly due to the sudden precipitation which can result from being high in the Lake District. Just over Sty Head Pass at the top of the valley are Langdale and Borrowdale. This region is by far the wettest in England.

At Wasdale Head, there is a Hotel, mountaineering shop (with mountain rescue post), a couple of farms, a campsite for none but the extremely hardy (and waterproof), and a famous church. It is a dead-end valley with a reasonable road along one side of the lake and a precarious footpath along the other, traversing the entire length of the screes.

The Lake itself is administered by the National Trust as is much of the land in the Lake District.

At the foot of the lake is a youth hostel beside which the Irt begins its short tumble down to the sea. Below the lake is Nether Wasdale with two Hotels, and an Inn. There is also a campsite run by the farmer's wife, Mrs Knight.

Below the village, the Irt meets the Bleng which has just left Gosforth, a village full of craft shops and pubs. At Hollins Bridge, there is the remnant of an ox-bow and, shortly after this, the river passes under Santon Bridge with its popular Bridge Inn. There is also a campsite here run by the Thwaite family who, for years, kept the village post office in their house.

Close by is a craft shop (on the road to Holmrook) and Irton Hall which now has self-catering accommodation for families.

The Irt then meanders across the flat valley bottom and over two weirs before passing behind Irton with its ancient cross.

After Holmrook, it is but a short run to the sea, passing Drigg where great controversy has arisen lately over the proposal to bury nuclear waste on the land between the village and the sea.

WASDALE'S BEACHES.

Drigg. From this tiny village a small road leads to high dunes that sweep down to a long, sandy beach, and a pool-dappled area of rocks and shingle known as Barn Scar. Unexploded shells are occasionally washed ashore and any unidentified objects should be left alone, but reported to the police. The dunes form part of the 400 acre nature reserve must in the previous feature and permits to enter must be obtained in advance. The entrance to the reserve is a quarter of a mile from the sea on the Drigg road. The largest breeding colony of the aforementioned black-headed gulls in Europe...and probably in the world....is the main feature, in fact at the last count over 11,000 nests were counted. The birds converge on the reserve in March, mate, rear their young and depart in July and August. The area is closed from late May to early July when the eggs are hatching. Many other birds can be seen too amongst them being terns, oyster-catchers, and ringed plovers. Adders, foxes, and natterjack toads also inhabit the dunes. (see editorial feature)

Seascale. A small, completely uncommercialised town with a sandy boulder-strewn beach approached over shingle. To the south the beach is backed by dunes and can be reached by a rough track from the B5344, one mile south-east of Seascale. The last 200 yards of the track are deeply rutted and it is unwise to try to take cars on to the sands. (see editorial feature)

Calder Hall. A rough track south of the station leads to a beach of shingle and low-tide sand near the confluence of the Rivers Ehen and Calder. The area is overlooked by the world's first nuclear powered station generating electricity. (see editorial feature Calderbridge)

Travellers' Guide to Cumbria's Western Lakes & Coast

Drigg & Holmrook

Drigg is a long village of scattered houses near the coast, it has fine views of the mountains towering up to the east. A long straight beach terminates in an extensive area of sand dunes and salt marsh between the River Irt and the sea, it is a bird sanctuary which may be visited, with a permit, during nesting time.

Here on a little hilltop the Normans built a church which was added to by 13th century builders, but what we see is a plain little structure refashioned in the last century, in which ancient masonry was used again. It has an arcade in 13th century style, and attractive woodwork in the door and reredos.

At one time Drigg had an annual fair which would have been held on Drigg Sands. A contemporary writer of the time described it as a fine sight that lasted for three days, and included such activities as horse racing. The description explains how officials from Egremont, the Sergeant and bailiffs would all meet the tenants of 'His Lordship' on the outskirts of Ravenglass and went in procession to open the fair. This eventually started a 'great trade' in cattle and produce, between the local people and those who came from as far afield as Ireland and Scotland, with the majority of them coming by sea.

Visitors to Cumbria are shore to hear the story of how Herdwick sheep first came to the County.

Legend has it that there was a shipwreck

DRIGG STATION
Holmrook • Cumbria • CA19 1XQ
Tel. (019467) 24335

CRAFTS & COFFEE

While in West Cumbria do not miss the opportunity to visit Spindle Craft situated in the old Victorian Station buildings.

Here you can browse around at your leisure an seek inspiration for that special gift.

Knitwear, Original Paintings, Leather Bags, Pottery, Toys, Novelties.

Coffee in the old Lamp Room.

Spindle Craft

Open 7 days 9.30am to 5.30pm.

Ample Parking.

Disabled Entrance - with care.

Winter Opening: open every day until Christmas.

January to Easter: open 6 days (closed Thursdays only).

BR Mainline Station.

on the coast at Drigg many centuries ago and about forty sheep which were being carried in the Spanish vessel managed to make their way to land, upon which they were subsequently taken possession of by the Lord of the Manor. The animals evinced a propensity for high ground and noting that they were capable of taking care of themselves the practice was started of letting them out in small herds to farms...and this apparently is the origin of the name Herdwick.

Lutwidge Arms Hotel

Holmrook, Cumbria, CA19 1UH
Resident Partners: IAN KELLY
019467 24230

Comfortable, informal ☆☆ Inn close to beautiful Eskdale, Wasdale and the Coast.
Great home cooked food and fine beer served lunchtime and evening

WALKING PARTIES WELCOME

✻ Special Weekend Breaks: £32 pppn DB&B ✻

All our 19 bedrooms are fully central heated and have bath or shower en-suite
☆ Colour TV and tea-making facilities in all bedrooms ☆ Direct Dial telephones ☆
☆ Full English breakfast included ☆ Packed lunches available on request ☆
☆ Full a la carte, or bar meals, available lunch and evening ☆ Fully licensed
(with approx. 100 different whiskies!) ☆ Ample car parking ☆

Gosforth

Gosforth is a village three miles southeast of Seascale. Once a Viking settlement as one can see from the famous Gosforth crosses, and hogback tombstone. Worn, but very fine, it is a remarkable sandstone monolith nearly 15 feet high..the tallest ancient cross in the country..it is thought to be a relic from the Scandinavian settlement here in the generations just before the Norman Conquest. The slender tapering shaft is partly round and partly square, and is crowned by a fine four-holed head carved on the arms with the triquetra, the emblem of the Trinity. The cross head is said to be unique in the north of England for being carved with a crucifix.

The Viking influence is also to be seen in the name of the river ...the Bleng, together with the names of the surrounding fells and farms.

As to be expected in a country parish, many events centre around the church.

Travellers' Guide to Cumbria's Western Lakes & Coast

WASDALE

Gosforth has the largest church in the united benefice with Nether Wasdale and Wasdale Head. The Norman church dating from the 12th century also contains the Viking 'fishing stone'..representing the Edda story of Thor, together with many monolith's of Norse mythology. The church's other claim to fame is reputed to be the country's most northerly cork tree.

The church itself has two old chairs, and a new oak lectern. There is a neat modern font with traceried panels, and there are some curious old collecting boxes in the vestry. A most unusual relic on one of the window sills is a Chinese iron bell, perhaps the only one of its kind ever to ring in an English church. Though cracked, it is finely ornamented in Eastern fashion. It was given to Gosforth by Lady Senhouse after her husband Sir Humphrey Senhouse brought it from a fort he captured on the Canton River in 1841, and a tablet tells of his death on board HMS Blenheim after Canton was taken. By the bell are two old stone cannon balls from forts in the Dardanelles.

Part of the village hall incorporates one of the oldest buildings in Gosforth. This was built by John and Margaret Shearwen in 1628 and now houses the library and the Supper Room. In 1658 Gosforth Hall was built using local sandstone. Here still are some fine stone pillars of the gate, along with an old fireplace, a newel stair, and some splendid old beams in the roof. In a corner of the field above the Hall is the site of an ancient chapel built over the Holy Well.

The Hall was the seat originally of the Copley's, and is in fact the house where Bishop Nicholson used to go courting Barbara Copley when he was a young archdeacon.

Visit
GOSFORTH POTTERY AND SHOP
For an exceptional range of pottery

Gosforth pottery is a small working pottery run by Dick and Barbara Wright in converted barn.

The ground floor is the pottery workshop, where many of the pots for sale in the shop are made. Upstairs we sell pots by over twenty potters with different materials, designs and techniques.

Regular stocks include a good range of garden pots for use in the home: bread crocks, dinner plates, casseroles, mugs and jugs. Also decorative pots: slipware, raku pots, smoked pots and other unusual pots.

Summer: Open each day 10.00 - 5.30
Winter: Open 10.00 - 5.00,
Sunday 12.00 - 5.00, closed Mondays (Restricted opening hours January and February for maintenance - phone for information)

Gosforth Pottery, Gosforth, Nr. Seascale, Cumbria CA20 1AH
Telephone and fax 019467 25296

Just outside the village in a long narrow field are the remains of an early Viking homestead known locally as Danes Camp.

ARTS & CRAFTS
Gift Shop & Cafe
Gosforth, Nr. Seascale

Shop open daily 9.30 - 5.30
(Cafe Closed Mondays)
TEL: Gosforth (019467) 25258
Cafe: (019467) 25287

We have an excellent and ever changing range of Craft lines and gifts as well as Basketware, Home Furnishings, Cane & Pine Furniture at reasonable prices. Enjoy shopping in a pleasant atmosphere. Then you can relax in the Cafe and enjoy good food.

Irton with Santon

Irton with Santon is a scattered parish, along with the hamlets of Santon, Hall Santon, and Santon Bridge, nestled between the hills and the sea. About two miles long and one and a half miles wide it is bounded by the river Irt and Mite...the Irt at one time being famous for its pearl producing mussels...regretfully no more.

Evidence exists of an Anglo-Saxon settlement here dating the village more than a 1000 years old. In fact there has certainly been a church on the site of St Pauls Irton since the 13th century, being built on an elevated position with spectacular views of the Wasdale Valley. In the churchyard will be found an ancient Celtic 8th century 10 feet high sandstone cross, ranking only second to that wonderful cross at Gosforth.

This solid little church was re-fashioned last century and has a fine tower with an imposing turret above the battlements. Its eight bells must echo far and wide among these hills and vales. The tower archway is screened by attractive wrought iron gates, and the attractive chancel arch has black marble shafts.

Amongst its many memorials there is a marble tablet with cannon and anchor in memory of one Skeffington Lutwidge who commanded a ship in an expedition of polar discovery in 1773, and it is interesting to learn that serving under him on HMS Carcass was a certain 14 year old midshipman by the name of Horatio Nelson.

Approximately one mile away is the Manor House of Irton Hall...a mansion built around a pele tower. In the grounds is a huge oak tree where it is said Henry VI hid in 1464 when seeking refuge dur-

Travellers' Guide to Cumbria's Western Lakes & Coast

ing the War of the Roses.. The Hall still has its embattled tower and some other remains of the 14th and 16th centuries.

Santon Bridge, located on the banks of the Irt at Bridge Inn is where the well known 'Biggest Liar Competition' is held annually. Santon Bridge is where the crystal waters of the River Irt come rushing over a rocky bed from Wastwater, the deepest of all the lakes.

The Craft Shop
SANTON BRIDGE • NR HOLMROOK
CUMBRIA CA19 1UY
Tel. Wasdale (019467) 26281

Set in beautiful countryside, this General Gift Shop has been established for almost 40 years now. It is often described as Aladdin's Cave, this is because it is so well stocked with a wide variety of goods to suit all pockets.

These are just a few: Border Fine Arts; Lilliput Lane Cottages; Arden Sculpture; Tutbury Crystal; China & Pottery; Jewelery including Hematite and Amber; a wide range of Leather Handbags, Wallets and Purses including Jane Shilton bags; Stainless Steel; Horn items; Walking Sticks, Walking Socks, Hats and Caps; Wool Rugs; Sheepskin Rugs; Slippers; Baskets; Books; Indian Clothes; Aromatherapy products and much more.

Well worth a visit!
Open Daily 9.30am to 5.30pm

Seascale

South along the coast from Whitehaven and Workington Seascale still has a popular following, partly due to its rail link and fine sandy beach, and a backdrop of splendid accessible mountains.

It is still a lovable little seaside place for many things...for its fine open stretches of sand and for the beauty of the hills and mountains which rise magnificently in the east. Monarch of all the fine array is the wild twin-peaked mountain mass which climbs 12 miles away to the highest point in England, Scafell Pike, 3,210 feet above the sea.

There's been two distinct stages in the town's development over the years. The first would have been the coming of the railway in the 1850's, when it could be said Victorian Seascale really began, complete with bathing machines, ice-creams, deck chairs...even donkey rides.

It was the outbreak of war in 1939 which brought to an end the holiday trade, and from the mid 40's an atomic station was set up at Sellafield close by...(though then it was known as Windscale)

Following the war the holiday trade started up all over again though this time it was the Sellafield workers and their families who were enjoying all that Seascale could offer.

The spacious church stands proudly at a high corner of the village, near a war memorial cross carved with vines and knotwork. Hardly older than the 20th century, the nave has five round bays built in Norman fashion.

An old farmhouse a little way off was built as the manor house in the 17th century, and there is also in the neighbourhood about a mile away, one great stone standing near the golf links, the only stone remaining of a prehistoric Circle of the Stone Age, the others sunk into the ground. Quite near is yet another circle of standing stones, their purpose still remains a mystery however.

Over the years as we all know, Sellafield has expanded enormously, and the visitors these days are the thousands who visit for an exciting tour of the site.

Wasdale

"Wasdale"....meaning "valley of the water". Wasdale, reputed to be the home of the highest mountain, the deepest lake, the smallest church...and the greatest liar in England...

It has to be the Lake of Wastwater that attracts so many people to this delightful part of the Lakes.

Wastwater is perhaps the most awe-inspiring of all the English lakes. It is hemmed in by the great mountains of Red Pike, Kirk Fell, Great Gable and ,of course, Scafell Pike. Its waters can look decidedly ominous, for this is also the deepest of the English lakes. It takes the form of a fissure which plunges beneath the surface of the water for more than 250 feet...in fact the bottom of the lake is below sea level.

Adding an extra element of grandeur are the famous screes on the south-east side of Wastwater. These extend the whole length of the lake and have been formed by gradual erosion.

Wastwater and Wasdale have been described as "as grand a combination as can be found in the British Isles". In the little churchyard at Wasdale Head one may find the graves of those who have died scaling the dangerous heights of the Gable and Scafell. In the early days Wasdale Head was united with Eskdale for burials, and the coffins were carried on horse-back across the moor.

Every year many people come to Wasdale for their annual "Biggest Liar in the world" competition, originated by Will Ritson, one time landlord of the Wasdale Head Inn. He was famous for his stories...one of them being the story of the eagle with a broken wing which was put in a chicken run and mated with a foxhound bitch in order to breed winged hounds that hunted along the screes.

It is said of him that he entered a competition at the dale sports for the man who could tell the biggest lie, but when it came to his turn he asked to withdraw.

"Why?" he was asked. "Because I cannot tell a lie," he replied. He won!.

Locked in the heart of the mountains at the end of the lake is the remote little village of Wasdale Head, with narrow walled lanes, grey stone houses, and streams cascading down the hills. It is famous as the centre for the highest climbs in Lakeland. Here amid Nature's pageantry is one of the smallest churches in the land, just 40 feet long and 17 feet wide, with only three windows and a roof which on one side is less than six feet high.

**Nether Wasdale
Cumbria
CA20 1ET**

THE SCREES HOTEL
**(019467) 26262
Your Host Edward Simpson**

This delightful 300 year old Inn, one time Temperance Hotel (though not any more) offers home from home comforts, as well as a selection of mouth watering menus, which includes vegetarian specialities.

Meet (?) 'Lucy' our resident ghost.
5 bedrooms (2 en-suite)
OPEN ALL YEAR

Good selection of ales including:
Yates Bitter -Jennings- Theakstons Best & Theakstons Old Peculiar.
We even have two beer festivals every year. Details on request.

WALKMILL GARDEN CENTRE
& COFFEE SHOP

10% off for OAPs on Tuesdays

Situated on the Wasdale Road, Walkmill provides a peaceful setting in which to enjoy a stroll and a snack in the coffee shop.

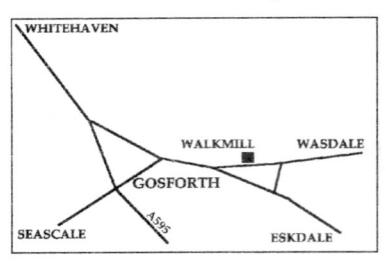

We have a large selection of shrubs, trees, plants, flowers, giftware and garden sundries.

Open Monday to Saturday 9 am–5pm and Sunday 11am–5pm

WASDALE ROAD, GOSFORTH. TEL: 01946 725293

ANTIQUES.

Orchard Antiques. Orchard Cottage. Gosforth. Tel:019467. 25460.

ART & CRAFT SHOPS.

Acorn Studio. Ghylwood House. Gosforth. Tel: 019467 25516.
Arts & Crafts Gosforth Tel: 019467.25258 see advert.
The Craft Shop, Santon Bridge. Tel: 019467 26281. (see advert)
Gosforth Pottery. Gosforth Tel: 019467 25296. (see advert)
The Hobby Shop, Gosforth. Tel: 019467 25702
Spindle Crafts, Drigg Station. Tel: 019467 24335. (see advert)

ATTRACTIONS.

Gosforth Pottery. Gosforth. Tel: 019467. 25296.see advert.
A busy country pottery selling earthenware and stoneware pots made in the pottery. Also pots by other potters. Pottery course and raku evenings. Demonstration and 'have-a-go evenings.
Seven Acres Falcon Centre & Childrens Animal Park. Gosforth. Tel: 019467 25480.
Sellafield Visitor Centre, Seascale. see advert.
Enter the Sellafield Visitor Centre and computerised technology takes excitement all the way into the 2st Century. Its a totally different experience that explores and explains the fascinating world of BNFL. Designed to inform and entertain the whole family, it features 'hands-on' interactive scientific experiments, intriguing shows and fascinating displays of technology. There is a total of ten amazing zones to investigate. Discover all the facts and have your questions answered. Guided tours around the Sellafield site. ...and the beauty of it all is...it's free!

BAKERS & CONFECTIONERS.

Sylvia's Bakery, 5 South Parade, Seascale. Tel: 019467 27242.
B & G Unsworth, Meadow View, Gosforth Tel: 019467 25525.

BANKS.

Midland Bank. Denton Hill. Gosforth. Tel: 019467 25224.
National Westminster Bank.11, Gosforth Road, Seascale. Tel: 019467 28346.

BOOKSELLERS.

Archie Miles Bookshop. Beck Place.Gosforth. Tel: 019467 25792.

BOWLING.

Gosforth Road, Seascale. Flat Green.

WASDALE

CAFES & CAFETERIAS
Craftshop Cafe, Croft Foot, Gosforth. Tel: 019467 25287.
The Lakeland Habit, Main Street, Gosforth. Tel: 019467 25751.

CARAVAN & CAMPING SITES.
Santon Bridge Camping, The Old Post Office, Santon Bridge.
Seven Acres Caravan Park. Gosforth. Tel: 019467 25480.
Church Stile Camp Site, Nether Wasdale. Tel: 019467 26388.

CHEMISTS
Seascale Pharmacy, 6 The Crescent, Seascale. Tel: 019467 28223..

CHURCHES.
Nether Wasdale Church of England. Tel: 019467 25251.
St Cuthbert Church of England, Seascale. Tel: 019467 28217.
St Josephs Roman Catholic, Seascale. Tel: 019467 28731.
St Mary Church of England, Gosforth. Tel: 019467 25251.
St Peter Church of England, Drigg Tel: 019467. 28217.
Wasdale Head Church of England. Tel: 019467 25251

CLUBS & ASSOCIATIONS.
Rotary Club, St Bees. Meetings Thursday.6.30pm. Seacote Hotel. Tel: 01946 822777.
Beckermet. Egremont. Tuesdays 7.30pm. Blackbeck Hotel. Tel: 01946 841661.
Windscale Club, Gosforth Road, Seascale. Tel: 019467 28468.

CRAFT WORKERS.
Ann Galloway. The Rectory, Gosforth Tel 019467. 25251.Batik on cotton.
Ann Southward Designs. The Rectory, Gosforth Tel: 019466 91737.Greetings cards.
Cumbria Art & Design. 2, South Parade. Seascale. Tel: 019267 27217.Art Gallery. Debbie Oram 2
Gosforth Garden replicas. The Barn, Gosforth Hall. Gosforth. Tel: 019467 25753. Garden ornaments

CYCLE SHOPS & HIRE.
Doctor Foster Cycle Practitioner. 1a, South Parade. Seascale Tel: 019467 21161.

DENTISTS.
M J Davison. The Glen, The Crescent, Seascale. Tel: 019467 27667.

DOCTORS.
Walker, O'Neill, Stevenson, Illsley, & Jay, Seascale Health Centre, Gosforth Road, Seascale. Tel: 019467 28101.

ESTATE AGENTS.
Huntley Property Services, Copeland House, Gosforth. Tel: 019467 25217.

GARDEN CENTRES.
Boonwood Garden Centre. Gosforth. Tel: 019467 25330.
Walk Mill Garden Centre. Gosforth. Tel: 019467 25293. see advert.

GOLF COURSES.
Seascale Golf Club. The Banks. Seascale. Tel: 019467 28202.

GUEST HOUSES.
M.Holmes, The Banks, Calderthwaite, Seascale. Tel: 019467 29000.
Bridge End Farm, Santon Bridge.
Burnt House Farm, Nether Wasdale. Tel: 019467 26224
Burnthwaite Farm, Wasdale Head. Tel: 019467 26242.
Cookson Place Farm, Irton. Tel: 019467 24286.
Ghylwood House, Gosforth. Tel: 019467 25516.
Hill Farm, Holmrook. Tel: 019467 24217.
Longacre Country Guest House. Santon Bridge Road. Gosforth. Tel: 019467 25328.
Low Holme, Drigg Road, Holmrook. Tel: 019467 24219.
Windsor Farm, Nether Wasdale. Tel: 019467 26249.

HOTELS.
Calder House Hotel, The Banks, Seascale. Tel: 0119467 28538.
Globe Hotel, The Square, Gosforth. Tel: 019467 25235.
Gosforth Hall Hotel, Gosforth. Tel: 019467 25322
Lowood Hall Hotel, Nether Wasdale. Tel: 019467 26289
Lutwidge Arms Hotel, Holmrook. Tel: 019467 24230
Scawfell Hotel, The Banks, Seascale. Tel: 019467 28400.
Screes Hotel, Nether Wasdale Seascale. Tel: 019467 26262. (see advert)
Seafield Hotel, Drigg Road, Seascale. Tel: 019467 28298.
Stanley Arms Hotel, Calderbridge. Tel: 01946 841235.
Strands Hotel, Nether Wasdale. Tel: 019467 26237.
Victoria Hotel, Drigg. Tel:019467 24231.

WASDALE
Wasdale Head Inn, Wasdale Head. Tel: 019467 26229.
Westlakes Hotel, Gosforth. Tel: 019467 25221.

INNS & PUBLIC HOUSES
The Bridge Inn, Santon Bridge. Tel: 019467 26221.
Golden Fleece Inn, The Square, Calderbridge. Tel 01946 841250.
Horse & Groom, Santon Bridge Road, Gosforth. Tel: 019467 25254
Red Admiral, Gosforth. Tel: 019467 25222.
Wasdale Head Inn, Wasdale Head. Tel: 019467 26229.
Wheatsheaf Inn, The Square, Gosforth. Tel: 019467 25821.

POST OFFICES.
Calderbridge Post Office. Tel: 01946 841220.
Gosforth Post Office. Tel: 01946 725234.
Holmrook Post Office, Drigg Road. Tel: 019467 724277
Seascale Post Office, Rose Bank, Gosforth Road. Tel:01946 728218.

PUBLIC LIBRARIES.
Public Hall, Gosforth. Tel: 019467 25425.
Seascale Library. Tel: 019467 28487,

SAILING, SEA
Launching facilities are available at Drigg,, Ravenglass and Seascale.
Winscale Boat Club. Seascale. Tel: 019467 28624.

SCHOOLS & COLLEGES.
Gosforth Church of England School, Wasdale Road, Gosforth. Tel: 019467 25244.
Harecroft Hall School, Gosforth Tel: 019467 25220
Seascale Primary School, Seascale. Tel: 019467 28403.

TAXIS.
Unicorn Cabs 12, Coniston Avenue, Seascale. Tel: 019467 27634.

TOURIST INFORMATION CENTRES.
Sellafield Visitor Centre, Seascale. Tel: 019467 76510.

YOUTH HOSTELS
Wasdale Foot YHA, Nether Wasdale. Tel: 019467 26222

CUMBRIA'S WESTERN LAKES & COAST.

ENNERDALE.

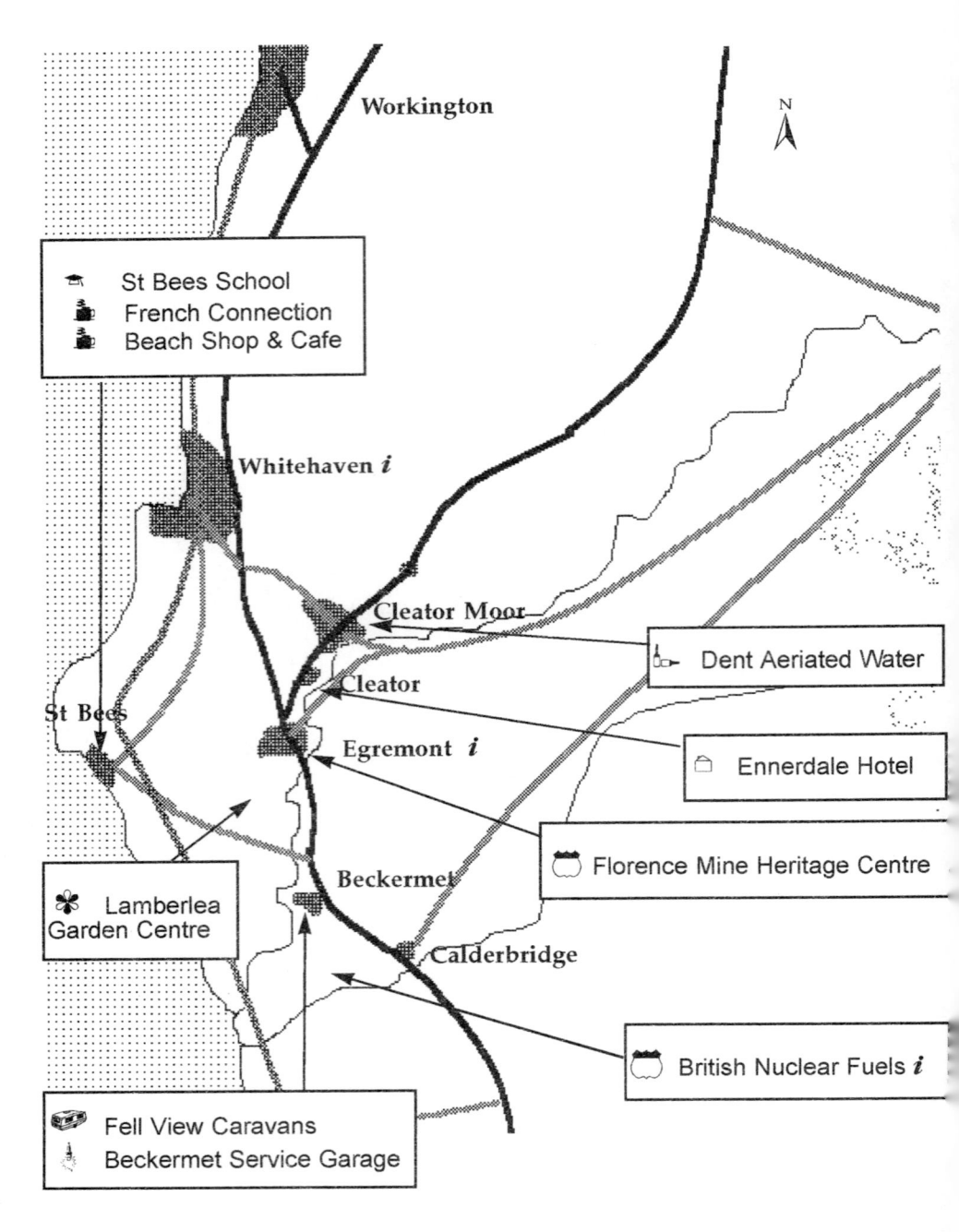

ENNERDALE

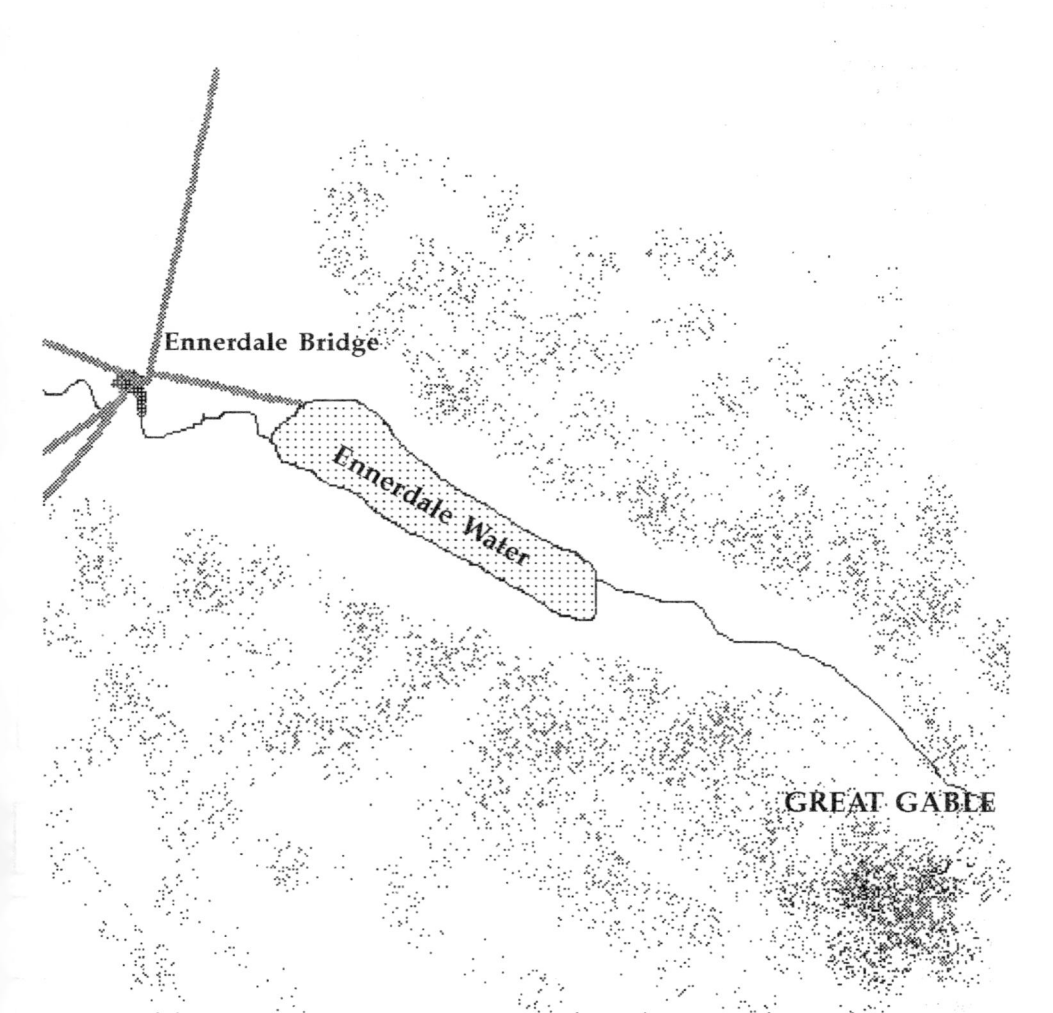

ENNERDALE

ENNERDALE

If you are expecting another Wasdale, you will be disappointed with Ennerdale. Although surrounded by the same king of mountains and, in a couple of cases, the identical mountains, its appearance and topography is quite different.

For one thing, the upper valley is densely forested with numerous plantations on either side of the tiny River Liza (it only becomes the Ehen below the lake). Rising on the north side of Great Gable, the river tumbles through the trees which are crisscrossed by numerous forest trails (there is no public vehicular access above the car park at the mid point of the lakes northern shore).

It is the least frequented of all the Cumberland lakes. Its beautiful setting however is all the village has to offer, for it lies where the Ehen and the Crossdale Beck meet near their bridges, as they come from lake and fell. The mountains and peaks which tower at its head...Great Gable, Kirk Fell, Pillar, Steeple, and Haycock, are typical of the Borrowdale Volcanic series.

Below the lake, the valley widens out suddenly and dramatically onto the coastal flood plain. The river then meanders lazily across it to the sea.

Many books on place names explain that the name "Ehen" derives from the Old English word for Swan and try to convince us that the river was, perhaps, once alive with these birds. However, the root meaning of Ehen goes further back than English history. The Celtic equivalent, used widely in France, for example, is Sqan which is where we get our English word Swan (the Latin equivalent brought by the Romans was similar–Sequana). In Gaul, the river which wound its way from Lutetia (Paris) to the English Channel was the Sequana (Seine) as was the one which flowed from the Alps to join the Rhône at Lyon (Saône).

Now what on earth have any of those rivers to do with swans, I hear you ask? The answer is–absolutely nothing at all. The connection is that sequana was also the old word for snake or serpent and was used, in a geographical sense, to describe a winding river (the swan got its name from the fact that its S-shaped neck resembled a snake). The Seine and middle Saône both meander considerably as does the Ehen between Ennerdale Bridge and the place where it dribbles out into the sea just south of Beckermet.

En route, it passes close to Cleator Moor at a place called Wath where there is an old bridge. The word wath comes from the Germanic word for water from which also derives our English verb to wash. Just north of London is a place where the people went forth (spelled fordd) across the water (wath), hence Watford.

Below the relatively modern community of Cleator Moor is the older Cleator and then the ancient town of Egremont.

Included in this area is the much shorter (and insignificant) Calderdale, famous only for the Abbey at Calder Bridge and the nuclear power station beside the River Calder at Calder Hall.

ENNERDALE'S COASTAL RESORTS.

St Bees. This is a village that grew up around a 7th century priory and a 16th century school in the valley of Pow Beck. The sandy beach is backed by a broad bank of shingle and a promenade that acts as a sea-defence. Lanes and footpaths climb north to St Bees Head and follow the top of the red-sandstone cliffs which rise to 310 feet and are topped by a further 100 feet of grassy slopes. On a clear day, the Isle of Man, 30 miles to the southwest can be seen.

The lighthouse on the North Head is open Monday to Saturday except during fog. Between the lighthouse and the village, a footpath leads down to Fleswick Bay, a secluded shingle cove with low-tide sand crossed by a small stream...there are strong currents. The shores to the south of St.Bees can be reached by lanes and footpaths from Coulderton, Nethertown Halt, Nethertown and Braystones. (see editorial feature)

CRUMMOCK WATER.

Crummock Water lies between Buttermere and Loweswater, near Keswick. This lake has depths in excess of 100 feet. The lake contains brown trout and some salmon and sea trout enter the lake when they come upriver to spawn. The perch are plentiful, and there are also a few pike. In the deeper water there are also char. Season. 1st April to 31st October (salmon), 3rd April to 31st October (sea trout), 20th March to 14th September (brown trout) and 16th June to 14th March (coarse fish)

ENNERDALE

Beckermet

The parish of Beckermet occupied for 5,000 years according to pre-historic finds...is situated just two miles south of Egremont and is actually two villages. St John's Beckermet, and St Bridget Beckermet, named somewhat naturally after its respective churches.

The church of St John has many interesting pre-Norman stones in the churchyard, which include the old font, a collection of corbels, coffin lids, together with fragments of eleven crosses.

The 13th century St Bridgets church stands between the sea and the village...has four services a year, though the churchyard is still occasionally used for burials.

These two churches are reputed to have been a nunnery (St Bridget) and a monastery (St John) in pre-Norman times, though unfortunately there is nothing to confirm this. Both however were served by secular monks from the Cistercian Abbey at Calder until the suppression of that Abbey in the 16th century.

In the churchyard of St Bridget's stand two interesting cross shafts; the heads vanished long ago. They are of a form not found anywhere else in the locality. One carries an inscription that has long baffled antiquarians..so far five translations have been produced.

The natural mounds located hereabouts actually mark the motte of Caernarvon Castle, the Roman area itself offering views towards Scafell Pike and the Roman fort of Hard Knott.

Lamberlea Garden Centre

Aquatic centre

Large selection of Ponds, Pondpumps, Filters, U.V.C.s, Fishfoods, Treatments, Plants and Fish.

A member of the Horticultural Trades Association.

Gift and Coffee Shop

On site Plant Nursery

At Lamberlea we propagate and grow nearly all our own shrubs, conifers, heathers, alpines and herbaceous.

We also have large selections of roses, trees (both fruit and ornamental), soft fruit bushes and climbing plants.

Being situated so close to the sea, we know that if they grow in our garden they will thrive in yours!

How to find us!

From Egremont follow signs for Nethertown. We are on the left approximately 50 yards AFTER SEAVIEW NURSERY.

Telephone
01946 820536

ENNERDALE

Visitors should note, on common land opposite the river, the old open truck, a relic of Beckermet's iron ore mining days. A railway engine is reputed to be buried in the bogland close by.

Village events here include fete, sports days, and Christmas fair and party.

J.W. JACQUES & CO.
BECKERMET SERVICE GARAGE
M.O.T. TESTING STATION
BECKERMET

Telephone 01946 841200

FELLVIEW CARAVANS
ABI CARAVANS, CALOR GAS
ACCESSORIES - SERVICE REPAIRS
BECKERMET

Telephone 01946 841274

Calderbridge

Calderbridge is an inland village situated on the A.595, close to Seascale and Sellafield, the river Calder runs through the village, from whence it gets its name.

Calderbridge's most famous building is undoubtedly the Abbey. Calder Abbey is a small picturesque ruin about one mile east of the village. Founded in 1134 by Ranulf Meschines, Lord of Copeland, for a colony of monks from Furness Abbey, originally as a Benedictine monastery, which some fourteen years later adopted the reformed order of Cistercians...The Abbey has been described as being one of the most enchanting of any of the monastic ruins in the British Isles.

During its long life the Abbey made great contributions to the lives of the community...alms to the poor, animal husbandry, crop production, and bee-keeping...Even 'Abbey Mead'. Not too surprisingly, for a property of this great age, the Abbey is reputed to be haunted.

Calder Abbey lies just within the National Park and may be visited by prior arrangement with the owner. The ruins stand in the grounds of a private residence and can only be glimpsed from a public footpath which passes a few hundred yards away. This path, known as the Monk's Road, begins close to the church at Calder Bridge and goes through an area of pasture-land adjoining the river. Behind a group of converted buildings it meets the drive of the private house and from here the Abbey ruins are just visible, a few graceful arches in the Early English style in a sylvan setting.

Calder incidentally, was amongst the first of the monastic foundations to be dissolved and in 1538 its lands were acquired by the chief agent of the dissolution Dr Thomas Legh. It has remained in private hands ever since. The highest detail of the Abbey is the remaining portion of the church tower, supported by four aches. Other parts of the church, including the north arcade of the nave, and the chapter house, remain. A late

Travellers' Guide to Cumbria's Western Lakes & Coast

ENNERDALE

Georgian private house occupies part of the site on what was the monks frater and dormitory.

Nearby is Pelham House on the site of the manor house of the Stanley's, who settled in Ponsonby in 1388. Along by the stream is Sella Park with interesting old houses with pele-like walls and an old oak recalling the country life of 300 years ago.

The church of St. Bridget's, built in 1842 by Thomas Irwin of Calder Abbey, is located in the centre of the town. Ponsonby parish has been a united benefice with Calderbridge since 1957, and today is served by the vicar of Beckermet. Ponsonby church stands in the park of Pelham House which at one time was Ponsonby Hall. The tower and spire were built by the Stanley family in 1840.

Ponsonby Old Hall is today farmed by the Stanley family.

Cleator & Cleator Moor

Cleator and Cleator Moor are situated some four miles from Whitehaven, and three miles from Ennerdale, lying in beautiful countryside. The villages lies on the edge of the great hills of Lakeland in a countryside once rich in iron but now dotted with the desolation of red waste heaps of the haematite mines. Great industrial depression has passed this way and many left, but new industries in the area are bringing people back again.

Just outside the town, close to St Mary's Roman Catholic Church is a small grotto similar to the one at Lourdes in France.

Under the capable supervision of Father Clayton...in 1926 utilising local people during the height of the depression years, he built a grotto which he wanted as near as possible to be an exact replica of the one at Lourdes. It took the workers a little over a year to build. It was opened and blessed on the 30th October 1927 by the Abbot of Douai. Dom. Edmund Kelly O.S.B. President of the English Congregation of the Benedictine Order.

Each year many thousands of pilgrims and visitors come to the grotto...though in September there is a pilgrimage which attracts many thousands from all over the country. There have been many stories of pilgrims being restored to full health after visiting the grotto. The most famous visitor here was his Eminence Cardinal Basil Hume, who came on the 27th July 1980 and re-dedicated the Grotto.

DENT AERATED WATER Co.
FRIZINGTON ROAD, CLEATOR MOOR, CUMBRIA, CA25 5EW
Tel: Cleator Moor 01946 810251 Fax: 01946 810456

So, what has Lakeland Spring Water got that some other spring waters haven't?...

"Nothing!" ..that's right, *nothing*...no additives, no processing, no brackish aftertaste - just natural spring water that doesn't taint other flavours. Which is why it is the perfect accompaniment to serve with both alcoholic and soft drinks.

This refreshing Lakeland Spring Water is collected above beautiful Ennerdale, at Standing Stones. The spring is situated 860 feet high in the fells, close to the North Western Lakes, and has probably effused ice-cold, crystal clear water since the last ice age.

WINNERS 1992 & 1995

Lakeland Spring Water...
naturally pure.

ENNERDALE

Besides Cleator's most popular attraction, other interesting features are in the market square. One is the memorial to the iron ore and coal miners, produced by the well known local artist Conrad Atkinson, and the Victorian awning around the Co-op store.

A popular beauty spot on the River Ehen is Wath Bridge, known locally as 'Hen beck' This is an ideal picnic spot where children can normally swim safely.

The Ennerdale

A Traditional Country House Hotel
in the Western Lakes
Cleator, Cumbria, CA23 3DT
Tel: 01946 813907 Fax: 01946 815260

Situated at the top of the lakes between Whitehaven and Keswick, The Ennerdale is surrounded by fine countryside, whilst being close enough for visitors to explore the coast. A delightful country house hotel with an enviable reputation for food and hospitality. Relax by log fires in sumptuous leather sofas and partake in afternoon tea in The Garden Room. Peace and tranquillity abound with fine hospitality and quality standards being the order of the day.

Weekend Special Rates, per person, per night.
Bed and full English breakfast, complimentary newspaper - single £40.00
Bed and full English breakfast, complimentary newspaper - double £80.00
Dinner, bed and full English breakfast, complimentary newspaper - £34.95
Rates based on a minimum two nights stay, per person, per night.

Egremont

Egremont is a small market town (charter from 1267) inland from St Bees.

Here William de Meschines built his castle in 1135.The gatehouse and the surviving curtain wall survive today from the original building, and the herring bone pattern of the stone-work is very typical of the Norman period. It was one time home of the deLucy family.Between the inner and outer courts is the stern ruined front of the great hall which has stood since about 1270 and has still a row of open windows and a doorway, the most effective part of the castle seen from the town, silhouetted against the sky.From this meagre fragment of a great stronghold is a fine view of the town and the distant mountains.By one of the paths bringing us down from it is a piece of a cross believed to be some 700 years old.

The legend here of the horn which could be blown only by the true Lord of

Travellers' Guide to Cumbria's Western Lakes & Coast

ENNERDALE

Egremont was told by Wordsworth. Hubert de Lucy, brother of the true Lord Sir Eustace, villainously assumed possession of the castle when he thought that he had successfully organised the murder of his brother who was away on the Crusades. Sir Eustace returned when his brother was feasting, and blew the horn. Exit Hubert in haste by a side door!

A bugle horn, stringed, is carved on the tomb of Sir John Hudleston who died in 1493 at Millom, representing his deBoyvill ancestry. The de Boyvills were kinsfolk of the powerful William de Meschine and were lords of Millom. The town has typically wide Cumbrian streets built apparently originally to accommodate market stalls.

Egremont was once a busy haematite iron mining area, and this would have supplied the industries around Workington and Whitehaven. Records here show that mining was popular here in Norman days. The only ore mine still working is Florence Mine nearby. Specimens of ore are on sale here and underground visits can be made by prior arrangement.

The church dating from about 1220 has been restored and contains early sculptures. Wordsworth enthusiasts will remember his ode 'The Boy of Egremont'... meaning in effect...young William de Romilly, nearest in succession to the throne of Scotland.

The 16th century Lowes Court is now a gallery on the main street combining an interesting gallery, with regularly changing exhibitions, a local crafts shop, and the town's Tourist Information Centre.

In late autumn the town celebrates the very popular 'Crab Fair' which goes back seven centuries, when the Lord of Egremont started a tradition of giving away crab apples. The apple-carts still

---

Florence Mine is all that remains of a once great industry, but it still mines some of the best quality Haematite Iron Ore in the world.

Haematite has been mined in this area since Roman days, with production hitting its' peak during the Industrial Revolution of the last century. Similarly further north towards Whitehaven, coal was mined. West Cumbrian towns were developed and grew, as a result of the mining industry, and in the early part of the 20th Century, there were almost 6000 employed in the iron mines, with a similar number for the coal mines.

FLORENCE MINE
HERITAGE CENTRE

At the Florence Mine Heritage Centre, the story of the miners is told. Underground tours take the visitor into the actual workings of the mine, where the visitor can try to appreciate what life was like for the "Red Men". For those unable to make the underground trip, there are simulated workings on surface, together with a mining and geological museum, coffee, and souvenir shop, where unusual gifts, and haematite jewellry can be bought. There are facilities for the disabled.

The Centre is open 1st April - 31st October 10.00am - 4.00pm.

Underground tours run every Saturday, Sunday and Bank Holiday 10.30 am & 1.30 pm. Tours also run daily through July and August. Winter tours on request.

Telephone: 01946-820683

"Enjoy an Underground Experience"

make this 'generous' gesture, these days showering the spectators with crab apples from lorries and trailers. Another famous amusement held at the same time, for which Egremont is renowned is the celebrated 'gurning' competition, where contestants try to pull the ugliest face framed in a horse collar. There is also a pipe smoking event, a greasy pole competition when youngsters try to scale a 30 feet high vertical slippery pole, along with the singing of hunting songs.

St Bees

St. Bees is a small village on the west coast of Cumbria, and lies five miles south of Whitehaven.

Tradition has it that it got its name from St. Bega, an Irish lady who fled in the 7th century from Ireland to avoid an unsuitable marriage, and landed on the beach by chance, and founded a nunnery. It is thought that the Nunnery was destroyed by Viking raiders, but in the 12th century a Norman Priory was built on the same site. The Dissolution by Henry VIII just left the church of St Mary. There are Norman details to be seen, the most striking ones being in the doorway with three orders of columns and zig zag patterned arches. Most of the chancel has been walled off and used by St Bee's School.

The most interesting possession of St Bees is an ancient relic of the nunnery itself, a remarkable stone believed to date from the 8th century. It is to be seen

The French Connection

The Old Station House, Main Street, St. Bees, Cumbria, CA27 0DG

Wonderful food, a warm welcome from our can-can girls and the chance to dine in a pullman dining carriage.

What more could you want?

Well, if you arrive early you can enjoy a 3 course meal for £10.95 !!

For more information or to reserve a table (essential at weekends) phone 01946 822600

ENNERDALE

between the churchyard and the vicarage where it forms the lintel of an alcove. It is carved with an ugly dragon turning to snarl at a tiny armed figure attacking it from behind. One end of the stone is decorated with plaitwork, and with the knotwork at the other end is a very curious carving which looks like a boar's head. Standing in the alcove is another relic, a stout stone cross on which the bearers of a coffin would rest their load.

Among other stones here are a stoup, a piscina, and a mortar all of the 12th century. Others are probably part of still older cross shafts with primitive carving and one is the upper part of a 10th century shaft decorated on each side with chain and scroll. There are coffin stones 800 years old, carved with crosses and swords and shears.

The church has one of the most perfect old registers in the County, the entries beginning in fine writing in 1538.

In company with the church is the school attractively built round three sides of a quadrangle. One wing is the original 16th century building, and over the doorway is a stone with the arms of its founder Archbishop Grindal, who gave the church one of its three Elizabethan chalices. Archbishop Grindal was born in a house on Cross Hill, just off Finkel Street.

The village main street has many ancient houses of much interest to visit and there is an extensive sandy beach.

In the 1980's when excavations were taking place near to the Priory, a lead coffin was found. It contained the mummified remains of what is believed to be a knight of the 13th century. The body has since been re-interred and the shroud, which covered the body is now on display in Whitehaven Museum.

A bird sanctuary is situated at the top of St Bees, and here will be found guillemots, puffins, terns, razorbill, kittiwake and herring gull.

A mile or two away is St Bees Head with lighthouse and field patterned crown, thrusts a blunt nose out into the Irish Sea. Its red sandstone cliffs honeycombed by weathering offer convenient nesting ledges during the summer months to noisy throngs of birds. St Bees Head is an ideal stroll, providing very fine views of coastal scenery. Beneath it incidentally there is a cove at Fleswick where interesting pebbles and crystals can be found.

The Coast to Coast walk, devised by A.W. Wainwright in 1973, starts from the Irish Sea at St Bees and stretches 190 miles across the north of England to the North Sea at Robin Hood's Bay. This is an enjoyable and challenging walk with

---

Beach Shop & Cafe

Beach Road,
St. Bees, Egremont,
Cumbria CA27 0ES

Tel: 01946 820175

The ideal spot to start your coast to coast walk rested and refreshed

Open daily: March to October

OPEN WEEKENDS ALL YEAR

Bed & Breakfast accommodation available
Details upon request.

the route passing through three National Parks, the Lake District, The Yorkshire Dales and the North Yorkshire Moors. The walk has been divided into 14 daily stages to suit walkers of average ability.

COMMUNITY

St. Bees School

An Independent HMC Boarding / Day School for boys and girls aged 11 - 18

Founded 1583

Excellent record of success in public examinations and entry to Higher Education

Superb cultural, sporting and recreational opportunities

and much more besides......

Entrance Awards and Government Assisted Places available

For further details please contact:

**Mrs. Helen Miller, The Registrar,
St. Bees School, St. Bees,
Cumbria, CA27 0DS
Tel: 01946 822263**

St. Bees School is a registered charity for the education of boys and girls. Charity No: 526858

COMMITMENT — *ACHIEVEMENT* — *TRADITION*

Woodend

Woodend is a quiet dormitory hamlet literally tucked away between the A595 Whitehaven to Egremont road, and the A5086 Cleator to Egremont road, close to the banks of the River Ehen.

At one time it was a busy iron-ore mining area, and the village was, no doubt, an important junction between the mines and the railway shunting yard at close by Moor Row. A row of railway cottages is built here, with Woodend railway station being a popular freight link. The railway as such, doesn't unfortunately stop here anymore, but the old station master's house is still here and still occupied (though not by the station-master), and the adjoining waiting rooms are now converted into an attractive bungalow.

Hidden behind the trees is Clintz Quarry, a protected conservation site, where rare species of wild flowers may be seen. Close by too is Woodend Mill, one time corn mill, and the Longlands Lake and Country Park...once an iron ore pit and flooded over in 1938.

Travellers' Guide to Cumbria's Western Lakes & Coast

RegentLane Publishers & Printers

are a refreshing new concept in quick-printing.

RING NOW FOR A QUOTATION

01229 770444

FAX: **01229 770339**

ANTIQUES.
Orchard Antiques, Orchard Cottage, Gosforth. Tel: 019467 25460.

ART & CRAFT SHOPS.
Lowes Court Gallery, 12 Main Street, Egremont. Tel: 01946 820693.

ATTRACTIONS.
Coast to Coast Walk. (190 miles)
Having dipped your toe in the Irish Sea at St Bees on the West Coast of Cumbria, walkers are now ready to set off on England's Coast to Coast Walk. You will pass through three National Parks before finally reaching the picturesque village of Robin Hoods Bay on the North Sea...190 miles distant.

For example, having left St Bees you travel through the Lake District passing through rocky and rugged country via Rosthwaite and Patterdale. From here you encounter the ancient Roman Road system over High Street and on through Shap to the old market town of Kirkby Stephen . The Yorkshire Dales are entered via Nine Standards Rigg, these are nine tall stone cairns atop of the watershed of Britain. The splendid Swaledale Valley takes you to the historic town of Richmond and on through the vale of Mowbray. After the Cleveland hills you pass into the heart of the heather covered North Yorkshire moors. Moorland walking makes a fitting conclusion to your Coast to Coast Walk Time to saviour the last cliff top views before making your way down to Robin Hoods Bay...and once you have dipped your toe in the North Sea, you can safely say that you have completed the exhilarating Coast to Coast walk.

Coast to Coast Pack Horse Service. West View Farmhouse, Hartley, Kirkby Stephen. Tel: 017683 71680
This is a walk which enables walkers of all ages to undertake the Coast to Coast walk.

In the Travel Advisory section of the New York Times, the newspaper reported " Travellers who are intrigued by Britain's Coast to Coast walk, but not by the prospect of carrying everything they need on their backs, can get a helping hand from the Pack Horse backpack shuttle service, a company started by Elizabeth and John Bowman who live in Hartley, which is a village about mid-point of the trail.

The horsepower is automotive, Each morning from March to October, Elizabeth drives west and John goes east, stopping at 17 pre-arranged pick up points in hotels and bed and breakfasts to transport walker's luggage to their next stop. This leaves walkers free to carry only a day pack.

Hikers can also get a ride along with their luggage if they are not able to walk for some reason. Transportation is also available , from the end of the trail back to the midpoint or beginning.

Egremont Castle.

ENNERDALE

Florence Mine, Egremont.Tel: 01946 820683. (see advert)
This unique museum includes the opportunity to go underground into a real iron ore mine, the last such working mine in Europe. The distinctive red ore lends colour to the story of the 'Red Men of Cumbria', the miners who gave everything including their lives to the mining of this valuable mineral resource. There is a surface museum, shop and refreshment room as well as the unique underground tours. (Old clothes recommended)

Kangol Factory Shop, Cleator. Tel: 01946 810312.
The Kangol Factory Shop has grown in popularity over the years and is now a major attraction in the area. The shop is always well stocked with a huge selection of the world famous range of Kangol headwear for formal and casual wear...for Men and Ladies. Also in stock is a large range of other products including belts, scarves and bags. Whilst there are a few items at full price, the vast majority of the merchandise in the shop is genuine factory seconds and ends of lines which are excellent value for money with many bargains.

Lowes Court Gallery, 12 Main Street Egremont. Tel: 01946 820693.
Fascinating gallery showing a wide range of paintings, print and craft work. Monthly exhibitions by emerging and established artists and craftspeople. Changing displays of work for sale by Cumbrian makers.

Cleator Grotto, Roman Catholic Church, Cleator

BAKERS & CONFECTIONERS.
J R Birkett & Sons, 2 High Street, Cleator Moor. Tel: 01946 811456.
J R Birkett & Sons, Leconfield Road, Cleator Moor. Tel: 01946 814040
J R Birkett & Sons, 42 Main Street, Egremont. Tel: 01946 820701.
Eldons, 31/32 Main Street, Cleator Moor. Tel: 01946 810347.
Kays Bakery, 237 Frizington Road, Cleator Moor. Tel: 01946 815344.
W Murphy, 27 Market Place, Egremont. Tel: 01946 820202.
Steads, 95 Main Street, Egremont. Tel: 01946 820346.
Pat a Cake, 81 High Street, Cleator Moor. Tel: 01946 810880.
Pat a Cake, 2b Main Street, Egremont. Tel: 01946 823156.
J Westworth, 17 High Road, Cleator Moor. Tel: 01946 814184

BANKS.
Barclays Bank, 26 Market Place, Egremont. Tel: 01946 820360.
Midland Bank, 58 Main Street, Egremont. Tel: 01946 820230.
National Westminster Bank, 59 High Street, Cleator Moor. Tel: 01946 810258.
National Westminster Bank, 39 Main Street, Frizington. Tel:01946 810219.
National Westminster Bank, 132 Main Street, St Bees. Tel: 01946 822282.
National Westminster Bank, 29 Market Place, Egremont. Tel: 01946 820217.

BOARDING KENNELS.
Bankend Boarding Kennels & Cattery, 2 Quarry Cottages, Bankend, Bigrig, Tel: 01946 813161.
Marlborough Boarding Kennels, Nindethana, Egremont. Tel: 01946 822745.

BOATING & SAILING
Buttermere Rowing Boats. Tel: 017687 70233.
Crummock Water Rowing Boat hire. Tel: 017687 70232.
Sea launching facilities are available at St Bees.

BOWLING.
Crossfield Road, Cleator Moor. Flat Green Indoor.
Egremont Bowling Club. Flat Green.

BOWLING CENTRES.
Copeland Bowls Centre. off Wyndham Street. Cleator Moor. Tel: 01946 815419.

CAR HIRE.
East Road Garage Ltd. Egremont. Tel: 01946 820266.
Kenning Car & Van Rental, Bridge End Ind Estate, Egremont. Tel: 01946 823459.
Lakeland Self Drive Ltd, 24 Main Street, Egremont. Tel: 01946 820226.

CARAVAN & CAMPING SITES.
Home Farm Caravan Park, Rothersyke, Egremont. Tel: 01946 824023.
Smithfield Caravan Park, Smithfield, Egremont. Tel: 01946 821245.
Tarnside Caravan Park & Club, Braystones. Tel: 01946 841308.
Lantern Moss, Braystones, Beckermet. Tel: 01946 84242.
Seacote Park, St Bees. Tel: 01946 822777.
St Bees Caravans, St Bees.
The Village Inn, Nethertown, Egremont. Tel: 01946 820476.

CHEMISTS.
J N Murray, 22 High Street, Cleator Moor. Tel: 01946 810373.
J N Murray, 31 Market Place, Egremont. Tel: 01946 820237.
L E Postgate, 67 Main Street, Egremont. Tel: 01946 820288.
PM Roberts, 6 Main Street, Cleator Moor. Tel: 01946 810352.

CHURCHES.
Haile Church of England, Egremont. Tel: 01946 820268.
St Bees Church of England. Tel: 01946 822279.
St Bridget with Ponsonby Church of England, Beckermet. Tel: 01946 841327.
St John Church of England, Beckermet. Tel: 01946 841327.
St Johns Church of England, Bigrigg. Tel: 01946 820268.

ENNERDALE
St John Church of England, Cleator Moor. Tel: 01946 810510.
St Josephs Roman Catholic, Frizington. Tel: 01946 810284.
St Leonard Church of England, Cleator. Tel: 01946 810510.
St Marys Roman Catholic, Cleator. Tel: 01946 810324.
St Marys Roman Catholic, Egremont. Tel: 01946 820251.
St Mary & St Michael Church of England, Egremont. Tel: 01946 820268.

CLUBS & ASSOCIATIONS.
Cleator Moor Working Men's Club, Birks Road, Cleator Moor. Tel: 01946 810414.
Egremont Catholic mens Club, St Bridgets Lane, Egremont. Tel: 01946 824671.
Egremont & District Conservative Club, Ehen Court Road, Egremont. Tel: 01946 820318.
Knights of St Columba, Market Square, Cragg Road, Cleator Moor. Tel: 01946 810476.
Knights of St Columba, St Bridgets Lane, Egremont. Tel: 01946 820401.
Moor Row Working mens Club, Scalegill Road, Moor Row. Tel: 01946 810286.
Royal British Legion Club, King Street, Cleator Moor. Tel: 01946 810489.
Royal British Legion Club, 64a Main Street, Egremont. Tel: 01946 820006
Royal British Legion Club, Stirling Lodge Masonic Hall, Market Square. Cleator Moor. Tel: 01946 810784.

COACHES & COACH HIRE.
J.Adams, Fairbourne, Ennerdale Road, Cleator Moor. Tel: 01946 810241.
S.H.Brownrigg, 53 Main Street, Egremont. Tel: 01946 820205.
Central Coaches & Limousine Hire, Central Garage, Market Square, Cleator Moor.

CRAFT WORKERS.
Debbie Oram, 2 Coronation Terrace, High Walton, St Bees. Tel: 01946 823010. Sculptured and hand painted wildlife and animal figurines.
Excellence & Elegance, 127 & 128 Main Street, St Bees. Tel: 01946 822705. Dried & Silk flowers
Haywood Enterprises, 14 Abbots Way, St Bees. Tel: 01946 822433. Haematite jewellry.
Keepsakes, 22 Towerson Street, Wath Brow, Cleator. Tel: 01946 813390. Pressed flowers.
Lyn Purnell Prints, High Rigg, Coulderton. Tel: 01946 822413. Pen drawings.

CUMBRIAN PRODUCTS.
Dent Aerated Water. Cleator. (see advert)

CYCLE SHOPS & HIRE.
Ainfield Cycle Centre, Jacktrees Road, Cleator Moor. Tel: 01946 812427.

ENNERDALE

DENTISTS.
R C & S E Broad, 74 High Street, Cleator Moor. Tel: 01946 812383.
N Forker, 36 North Road, Egremont. Tel: 01946 821275.

DOCTORS.
Beech House Group Practice, Beech House, 54 Main Street, Egremont. Tel: 01946 820203.
Beech House Group Practice, Ennerdale Road, Cleator Moor Tel: 01946 810427.
Beech House Group Practice, 44 Main Street, St Bees. Tel: 01946 822689.
Sydney, Godden, Sullivan, Rogers, Lewis & Boyle. Wyndham Street, Cleator Moor. Tel: 01946 810304.
Gallacher, Creed & Margerison, West Croft House, 66 Main Street, Egremont. Tel: 01946 820348.

ESTATE AGENTS.
Donald A Brownrigg, Wyndham Way, 73 Main Street, Egremont. Tel: 01946 820212.
Cumbria Estate Agency Ltd, 16 High Street, Cleator Moor Tel: 01946 812988.

FISHING
Longlands Lake, Cleator Moor. Tel: 01946 810377.
Meadley Tarn, Ennerdale Bridge. Permits from Tarn Bank.

GARDEN CENTRES.
Lamberlea Nursery & Garden Centre, Nethertown. 01946 820536 (see advert).
The Rustic Garden, Castlewent, Bookwell. Tel: 01946 820081.
Sea View Nurseries, Nethertown. Tel: 01946 820412.
Syke House Nurseries, St Bees. Tel: 01946 820489.

GOLF COURSES.
St Bees Golf Club. Tel: 01946 824300.

GUEST HOUSES and B&B
Alpha House, St Bees. Tel : 01946 822424
B.Durber, Crescent Guest House, St Bees. Tel: 01946 822748
Fairladies Barn Guest House, Main Street, St Bees. Tel: 01946 822718.
Far Head of Haile, Haile. Tel: 01946 841205.
How Hall Farm, Ennerdale, Tel: 01946 861266.
Khandalla. High House Road. St Bees. Tel: 01946. 822661.
Old Vicarage, Thornhill, Egremont. Tel: 01946 841577
Outrigg House, St Bees. Tel: 01946 822348
Stone House Farm, 133 Main Street, St Bees. Tel: 01946 822224.
Tarn Flatt Hall, Sandwith. Tel: 01946 692162
Tomlin Guest House, Beach Road. St Bees. Tel: 01946 822284.

Travellers' Guide to Cumbria's Western Lakes & Coast

ENNERDALE
Old Vicarage, Ennerdale Bridge.
Welcome Nook, St Bees.
White House, Main Street, St Bees.

HOSPITALS & CLINICS.
Egremont Clinic, St Bridgets Lane, Egremont. Tel: 01946 820310.
New Clinic, Ennerdale Road, Cleator Moor. Tel: 01946 810438.

INNS & PUBLIC HOUSES
Albert Hotel, North Street, Cleator Moor. Tel: 01946 810392.
Black Bull, 28 Market Place, Egremont. Tel: 01946 821491.
Blue Bell Inn, 6 Market Place, Egremont. Tel: 01946 820581.
Central Hotel, 70 Main Street, Egremont Tel: 01946 820241.
Commercial, 5 High Street, Cleator Moor. Tel: 01946 812712.
Derby Arms, 158 Ennerdale Road, Cleator Moor. Tel: 01946 810779.
Fox & Hounds, Ennerdale Bridge. Tel: 01946 861373.
Globe Hotel. Aldby Street, Cleator Moor. Tel: 01946 813123
Griffin Hotel, Mill Street, Cleator Moor. Tel: 01946 810298.
Horn of Egremont, 12 Market Place, Egremont. Tel: 01946 823034.
Keekle Inn, Keekle Terrace, Cleator Moor. Tel: 01946 815451.
Moffats, Birks Road, Cleator Moor. Tel: 01946 810372.
New Crown, Bowthorn Road, Cleator Moor. Tel: 01946 810136.
New Victoria, 12 Ennerdale Road, Cleator Moor. Tel: 01946 815918.
Oddfellows Arms Inn, Main Street, St Bees. Tel: 01946 822317.
Old Captains House, Bigrigg. Tel: 01946 814392
Park head Inn, Egremont.
Robin Hood, Bowthorn Road, Cleator. Tel: 01946 810477.
Ship Launch Inn, 68 North Road, Egremont. Tel: 01946 820928.
Stork Hotel, Rowrah. Tel: 01946 861232
Three Tuns, Main Street, Cleator. Tel: 01946 811166.
Tourists Hotel, Nethertown, Egremont. Tel: 01946 820477.
Wheatsheaf Inn, 24 Market Place, Egremont. Tel: 01946 824377.
White Mare, Beckermet. Tel: 01946 841246

HOTELS.
Albert Hotel, 1 Finkle Street, St Bees. Tel: 01946 822345.
Blackbeck Bridge Inn, Blackbeck, Egremont. Tel: 01946 841661.
Ennerdale Country House Hotel, Cleator. Tel: 01946 813907. (see advert)
Grove Court Hotel, Cleator. Tel: 01946 810503
Manor Arms Hotel, Main St, St Bees. Tel: 01946 822425.
Parkside Hotel, Parkside, Cleator Moor. Tel: 01946 811001.
Queens Hotel, Main St, St Bees. Tel: 01946 822287.
Royal Oak Inn, Beckermet. Tel: 01946. 841551.

ENNERDALE

Seacote Hotel, Beach Road, St Bees. Tel 01946 822777.
Summergrove Hall, Hensingham. Tel: 01946 811872.

KARTING.
Rally Round Off Road Buggy Hire, 52 John Street, Cleator Moor. Tel: 01946 811114

LEISURE CENTRES.
Copeland Bowls Centre, Off Wyndham Street, Cleator Moor Tel: 01946 815419.
Wyndham Sports Centre, Main Street, Egremont. Tel: 01946 821038

NATURE RESERVES.
St Bees Head Bird Reserve. Tel: 01229 773281.
Please Note: Additional nature reserves will be found at:
Crimpfield Marsh, Glasson Moss National Nature Reserve and Fingland Wood National Nature Reserve, Drumburgh.

NIGHT CLUBS & DISCO'S.
Beano's, Market Place, Egremont. Tel: 01946 822907.
Old Hall Night Club, 59 Main Street, Egremont. Tel: 01946 824394.

POST OFFICES.
Beckermet Post Office. Tel:01946 841372.
Cleator Moor Post Office, 15 Jacktrees Road, The Square. Tel: 01946 810201
Cleator Post Office, 31 Main Street. Tel: 01946 814205.
St. Bees Post Office. 122 Main Street. Tel: 01946 822343.
Wath Brow Post Office, Cleator Moor. Tel: 01946 810377.

PUBLIC LIBRARIES.
Market Square, Cleator Moor. Tel: 019946 810593.
The Charles Edmonds Library, Egremont Tel: 01946 820464.
Main Street, Frizington, Cleator Moor. Tel: 01946 810775.
St Bees Public Library, Main St, St Bees. Tel: 01946 822219.

PUBLIC PARKS.
Castle Park, Egremont.

RESTAURANTS & CAFES
Appletree Restaurant.47, Main Street Egremont. Tel: 01946 8200715.
Asha Tandoori 43, High Street.Cleator Moor .Tel: 01946 810090.
Beach Shop & Cafe, St Bees. (see advert)
Egremont Steak House. 59,Main Street.Egremont. Tel: 01946 824394.
French Connection, St Bees. (see advert)
Grove Court Hotel, Cleator Gate, Cleator, Tel: 01946 810503.

Travellers' Guide to Cumbria's Western Lakes & Coast

ENNERDALE
Raj of India. 8, Main Street. Egremont. Tel: 01946. 823186.
Wyndhams Country House Restaurant,Bigrigg. Cleator Moor. Tel: 01946 815447.

RIDING SCHOOLS.
Bradley Riding Centre, Low Cockhow, Kinniside Cleator. Tel: 01946 861354.
Yew Tree Trekking, Yew Tree Farm, Wilton. Tel: 01946 820105.
Wath Brow Post Office, Cleator Moor. Tel: 01946 810377.

SERVICE STATIONS.
Beckermet Service Garage, Beckermet. (see advert)
Forge Garage, Cleator Moor.

SCHOOLS & COLLEGES.
Beckermet Church of England School, Beckermet. Tel: 01946 841221.
Bookwell School, Bookwell. Tel: 01946 820408.
Ehenside School, Towerson Street, Cleator Moor. Tel: 01946 810306.
Ennerdale & Kinniside Primary School, Ennerdale. Tel: 01946 861402.
Montreal Church of England Infants School, Ennerdale Road, Cleator. Tel: 01946 810609.
Montreal Church of England Junior School, Ennerdale Road, Cleator. Tel: 01946 810346.
Moor Row School, Moor Row. Tel: 01946 810620.
Orgill Infant School, Croadilia Avenue, Egremont. Tel: 01946 820460.
Orgill Junior School, Southey Avenue, Egremont. Tel: 01946 820234.
St Bees School., Barony House, St Bees. Tel: 01946 822263. (see advert)
St Bees Village School, Main Street, St Bees. Tel: 01946 822392.
St Joseph's Roman Catholic School, Yeathouse Road, Cleator Moor. Tel: 01946 810702.
St Patrick's Roman Catholic Infant School, Birks Road, Cleator Moor. Tel: 01946 810643.
St Patrick's Roman Catholic Junior School, Todholes Road, Cleator Moor. Tel: 01946 810515.
Wyndham School Centre, Main Street, Egremont. Tel: 01946 820356.

SNOOKER.
Egremont Snooker Club, Old Castle Cinema, Bookwell. Tel: 01946 820495.

SPORTS CLUB & ASSOCIATIONS.
Cleator Cricket Club, Cleator. Tel: 01946 813222.
Egremont & District Sunday Football League. Tel: 01946 691707.
Egremont Rangers R L F C. Tel: 01946 820798.
Egremont Rugby Union Football Club. Tel: 01946 820645.

SPORTS GROUNDS.
Egremont Cricket Club, Gilfoot Park, Egremont. Tel: 01946 820955

SQUASH COURTS.
Winscale Squash Club, Falcon Club Field, Egremont. Tel: 01946 823130.

SWIMMING POOLS.
Wyndham School Swimming Pool, Egremont. Tel: 01946 824842.

TAXIS.
1A Castle Cabs, 2 Sunnyside, Egremont. Tel: 01946 820032.
R Basso. 9, Melbreak Avenue, Cleator Moor Tel: 01946 811924.
Bigrigg Cabs. 15, Croftlands Bigrigg. Tel: 01946 810024.
Castle Cabs, 2 Sunnyside, Egremont. Tel: 01946 820032.
Checkers Taxis, 14 Kinniside Place, Cleator Moor. Tel: 01946 812424.
Christine's Cabs, 39 Springfield Road, Bigrigg, Cleator Moor. Tel: 01946 812718.
Cleator Moor Cabs, 1, King Street, Cleator Moor. Tel: 01946 814635.
Egremont Cabs, 8a The Crescent, Thornhill, Egremont Tel: 01946 820913.
Martini Cabs, St Bees Trailer Park, St Bees. Tel: 01946 823555
Neils Cabs, Fawn Cross, Jacktrees Road, Cleator Moor. Tel: 01946 811806.
Sterling Cabs, 63 Main St, Egremont. Tel: 01946 823000.

TOURIST INFORMATION CENTRES.
Lowes Court Gallery, Main Street, Egremont. Tel: 01946 820693.

RegentLane Publishers & Printers

are a refreshing new concept in quick-printing.

RING NOW FOR A QUOTATION

01229 770444

FAX: **01229 770339**

CUMBRIA'S WESTERN LAKES & COAST.

WHITEHAVEN & DISTRICT

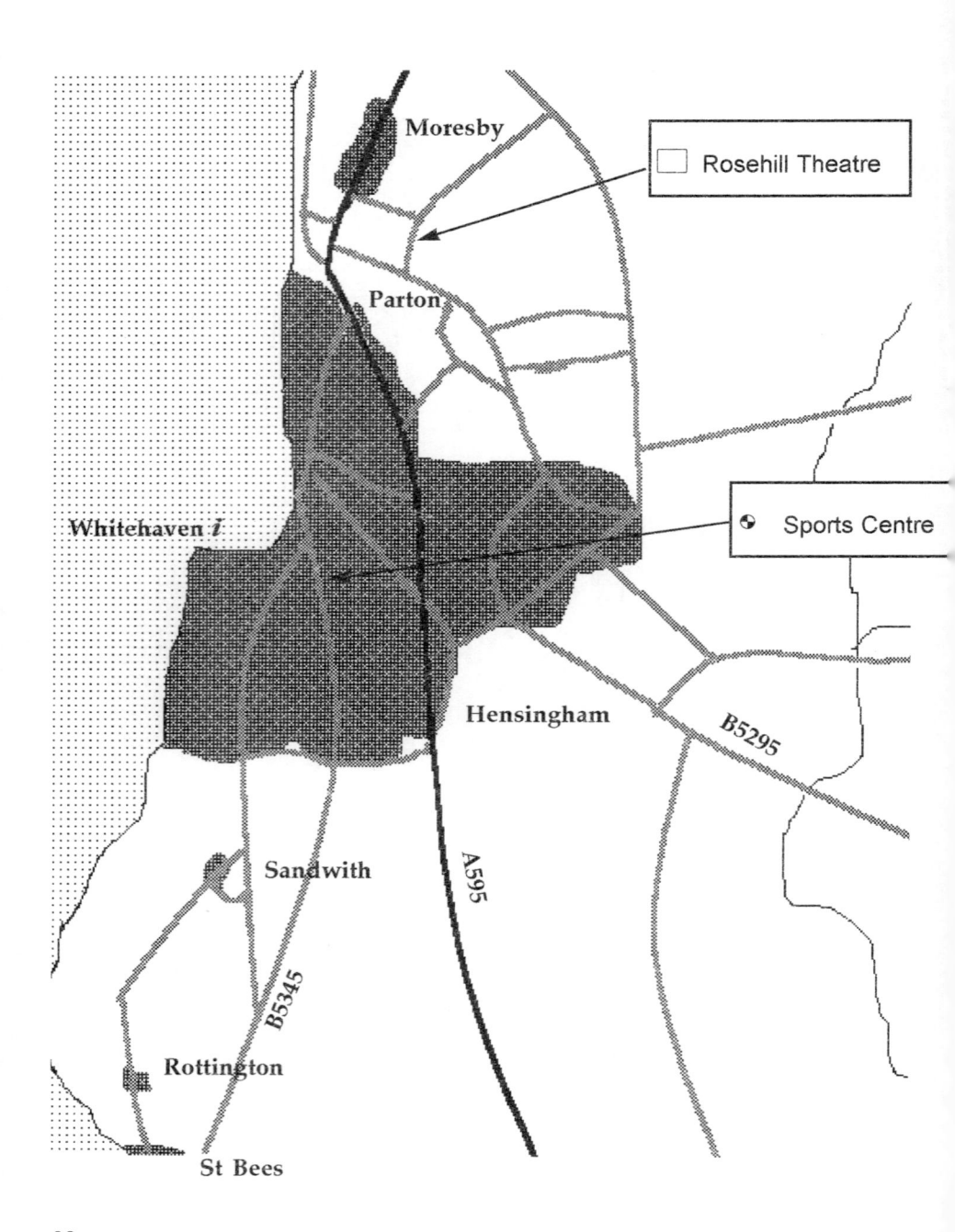

WHITEHAVEN

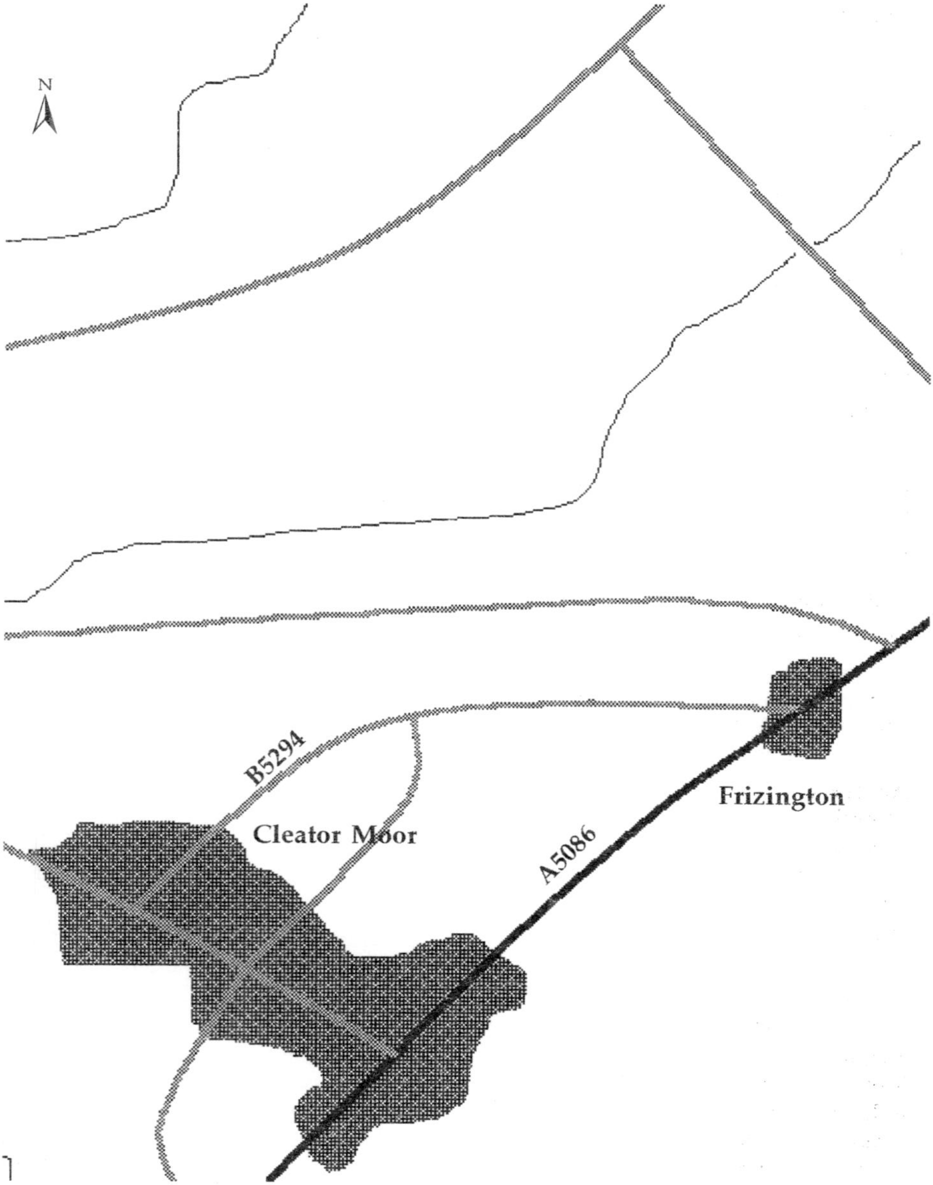
N
B5294
Cleator Moor
Frizington
A5086

Moresby

One and a half miles from Whitehaven stands Moresby Hall...though today it is a private guest house

Anyone well versed in the mysterious Druid Lore would be advised to pay a visit, for says legend, a vast fortune lies buried here somewhere...guarded so it is said by fairies...and the information only being released to someone who has that special Druid knowledge.

However there are two other pre-requisites necessary before that special person can lay claim to the fortune.

Firstly he must be there at the right time, that is on the one night of the year when an enchanted lake forms in the vaults beneath the house, from the fairy fountain, and secondly he must hear the dirge-like song wailed by the swan who glides across the lake, lamenting the extinction of the Moresbys.

The person fortunate enough to fulfil all three conditions will then have the power to enter the vaults, stop the flow of water, and retrieve the treasure.... Now, that doesn't sound too difficult does it?

Apparently there has been a settlement at Moresby since these days of the Roman occupation...possibly long before. The Romans built a fort here but were so strongly influenced by the Celtic culture that they built altars not only to their Roman Gods but to the Celtic Gods Rosmerta and Sylvanue too.

With the departure of the Romans and the arrival of the Christian missionaries Moresby again found itself in a sphere of influence for one of the nunneries dedicated to St Bridget was founded here in the sixth century.

The present day church of St Bridget lies within the ruins of the Roman fort and at one time an underground secret passage connected the church and Moresby Hall. The church is a formal little place with many pictures in its windows, and paintings on the pulpit of Christ teaching and Matthew and Paul with their books. On each side of the chancel arch is a bishop's head. A holy-water stoup, a stone coffin lid marked with shears and a cross, and a stone-head, all came from the old church, whose 13th century chancel arch stands in the churchyard.

The Moresby family (the name incidentally means 'Maurices Place') came into prominence after the Norman Conquest. The Moresby of the day found it expedient to offer his loyalty to the new ruling House in exchange for the privilege of retaining his land and property. From that point on the Moresby's never looked back. Advantageous marriages and loyal service to king and countries didn't do them any harm either...and increased their holdings. Several of them made their mark in other ways too, such as the Moresby youth who ganged up with other wild individuals and raided Fountains Abbey, making off with a haul of gold plate and jewels. He was apparently hastily packed off to the wars where he distinguished himself at Agincourt.

A few generations later a daughter lived to inherit Moresby...a pattern that was to be repeated in Tudor times. The heiress was unfortunate in her choice of husband, for he became romantically involved with Anne Boleyn, and Henry VIII certainly had no compunction in sending him to a similar fate that had befallen others who had upset him. it was this lady's son who sold Moresby Hall to the Fletchers of Cockermouth.

The Fletchers must have had a soft spot for the Royal Stuarts of Scotland... One earned fame in 1568 when Mary Queen of Scots sought refuge in England after the Battle of Langside. Because Cockermouth was unfit at that time to offer accommodation to the illustrious refugee, Henry Fletcher was asked to provide lodgings for her. He went the extra distance, he also gave her a rich velvet gown in which to receive all the wealthy folk from the district who called to pay their respects, a kindness which paid off in the next generation for Mary's son James knighted Henry's son when he became James I of England.

Whitehaven

Whitehaven is to many ideally situated on the West Cumbrian coast...just a few short miles from the Lake District National Park.

'Georgian' Whitehaven was in fact one of the first post-renaissance planned towns in the country, and is one of the forty-two 'Gem Towns' of England.

Almost unbelievable today, Whitehaven in the mid 18th century was a larger port than Liverpool. Indeed in business terms it was second only to London and Bristol. Its prosperity was built on coal and the enterprise of the Lowther family who owned the mines, and built the first quay here in 1634. It was actually Sir John Lowther who built the present town on a grid system...even specifying the type of buildings. His new town of Whitehaven he had laid out to plans inspired by Christopher Wren's designs for rebuilding London after the Great Fire of 166. He even went to the extent of having factory chimneys designed in the shape of his favourite silver candlesticks.

Only one coal mine in the area is still working today, but several pit structures have been preserved in the south beach recreation area as monuments of industrial archaelogy.

Here too in 1718 Carlisle Spedding invented one of the earliest steam engines...designed to pump water from the pits, as well as experimenting with coal gas...going so far as to lighting his own office with it.

Besides coal, much of Whitehaven's early prosperity was built on the import of tobacco from America and rum from the West Indies. Cumberland Rum Butter today is still very much a local delicacy.

The towns connection with the 'New World' goes much beyond trade. George Washington's grandmother... Mildred Warner Gale, lived in Whitehaven, and is buried in St Nicholas Gardens.

Travellers' Guide to Cumbria's Western Lakes & Coast

WHITEHAVEN

Additionally John Paul Jones, said to be the father of the American Navy (and later Admiral in the Russian Navy) made a raid on the town in 1778 during the American War of Independence. Historians of this era will note that two cannon used during the attack can still be seen near the old fort. Interestingly enough this sortie was the last occasion upon which the English mainland was invaded from the sea. Patriotic Scots regarded John Paul Jones as a traitor. He had physical courage, true..but he was considered despicable, particularly as he was in the slave trade for many years.

There was another, different attack in 1915 when Whitehaven sustained some damage as the result of shelling by a German U Boat.

The port today, though still busy is more geared to the activity of its fishing fleet, and as always, its many small pleasure boats...rather than the large ships of old. An indication of its famous past is shown in the following figures....In 1676 the town had 32 ships, in 1682- 40 ships, and in 1706...77.

Because of its unspoilt state, the entire harbour has been declared a conservation area. Here can be seen monuments to mining history...the candlestick chimney...the mine bogeys, and the winding wheel.

Many of Whitehaven's elegant Georgian buildings have been preserved, particularly in the Lowther Street area. The magnificent Georgian interior of St James Church is reputed to be the finest in the country.

Travellers' Guide to Cumbria's Western Lakes & Coast

Rosehill Theatre
Cinema & Bistro

Rosehill Theatre is splendidly located overlooking the Cumbrian coast near the Lake District. The charming and intimate silk-lined interior was the only one that Glyndebourne set designer Oliver Messel was ever to create and the theatre has attracted many world famous performers since it was opened by Peggy Ashcroft in 1959. Rosehill now provides the most comprehensive programme of high quality arts and entertainment in Cumbria.

- Drama • Classical Music •
- Jazz • Rock • Films • Lectures •
- Folk • Children's Shows •

Rosehill Theatre, Moresby, Whitehaven, Cumbria CA28 6SE
Box Office Tel: (01946) 692422 (24 hours)

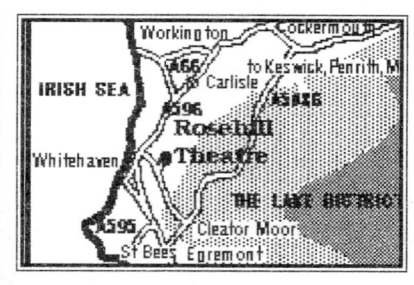

How to find us

Rosehill Theatre is approximately one mile north of **Whitehaven**. From the main A595, take the turning signposted **"Moresby Parks & Rosehill"**. The theatre is approximately half a mile on the left hand side and is clearly signposted. Ample parking is available in front of the theatre.

THE BEACON
WHITEHAVEN

What is The Beacon...?

Opened in July 1996, The Beacon tells the story of Whitehaven's social, maritime and industrial history.

The past, present and future of this, West Cumbria's Georgian port, are told using characters, sounds, graphics and audio visual presentations in exciting sets. Plus a Met. Office Weather Gallery with panoramic views of the town and harbour.

THE LORD INGLEWOOD CONSERVATION AWARD
1996

West Strand, Whitehaven, Cumbria CA28 7LY
Telephone: 01946 592302 Fax: 01946 599025

ACTIVITY/HOLIDAY CENTRES.
West Cumbria Field Centre. Tel: 01946 861029.

ANTIQUES.
Harbour Antiques. the old YWCA, Lowther Street. Whitehaven. Tel: 01946 590526.
Whitehaven Antiques. 5 Strand Street. Whitehaven.

ART & CRAFT SHOPS.
Holts Art Shop. 45 Roper Street. Whitehaven. Tel: 01946 62940.
Kittiwakes. Whitehaven. Tel: 01946 691273.
Pot in 3. Market Place. Whitehaven. Tel: 01946 695097.

ATTRACTIONS.
Michael Moon's Bookshop. 41-43, Roper Street, Whitehaven Tel: 01946 62936.
'The largest antiquarian bookshop in Cumbria'....This large old bookshop, as much a part of the townscape as the four old lighthouses and the beacon Heritage Centre on the Harbour, is built on the combined sites of the old Theatre Royal where tragedian Edmund Kean played to thunderous acclaim and where Donald Wolfit first got 'the bird'...recalled in his memoirs, and the Whitehaven News printing works.

The Beacon. Whitehaven Tel: 01946 592302.
The Beacon tells the story of Whitehaven's social, industrial and maritime heritage. The past, present, and future of this West Cumbria's Georgian port, are told using characters, sounds graphics and audio visual presentations.
What have Whitehaven, America, and the Meteorological Office got in common? The Beacon (which only opened in Summer of '96) Here you can discover the interesting and varied past of this Georgian port...the American Connection, slavery and smuggling, mining and shipbuilding. With interactive Met Office Weather Gallery where you can broadcast, forecast and monitor the weather. Enjoy spectacular panoramic views of the town and harbour. Full programme of events and exhibitions throughout the year.

Haig Pit Industrial Heritage. Whitehaven. Tel: 01946 695678.

Flagship of Fun Whitehaven. Tel: 01946 691986.

BAKERS & CONFECTIONERS.
Bells of Lazonby. Co-op Superstore. Church Street. Whitehaven. Tel: 01946 64297.
Bells of Lazonby. 52 Market Place. Whitehaven. Tel: 01946 61063.
Finkles Coffee Shop. 61 King Street. Whitehaven. Tel: 01946 694209
Grants. 97 Main Street. Distington. Tel: 01946 833958.

Travellers' Guide to Cumbria's Western Lakes & Coast

WHITEHAVEN

Pat a Cake. 1, Hicks Lane. Whitehaven. Tel: 01946 695618
16, Market Place. Whitehaven. Tel: 01946 590450
Rea's Bakers. 78, King Street. Whitehaven. Tel: 01946 61743
Confectionery. Sweet Treats. 105a, Duke Street.Whitehaven.

BANKS.
Abbey National. 43, King Street. Whitehaven. Tel: 01946 61241
Barclays Bank. Strand Street, Whitehaven. Tel: 01946 64444
Midland Bank. 69, Lowther Street. Whitehaven. Tel: 01946 692146
National Westminster. 71, Lowther Street, Whitehaven. Tel: 01946 67361
TSB. 59, Lowther Street. Whitehaven. Tel: 01946 66442

BOARDING KENNELS.
Benthow Kennels. Lowca, Whitehaven. Tel: 01946 832804
Fairview Holiday Kennels. Byersteads Road, Sandwith, Whitehaven. Tel: 01946 591064
Tutehill Farm Kennels. Tutehill Farm. Pia, Harrington. Tel: 01946 833502
Whinmill Farm Kennels & Cattery. Main Road, High Harrington. Tel: 01946 832002

BOOKSELLERS.
Cornerstone Christian Bookshop. 5, Church Street. Whitehaven. Tel: 01946 695460
Cribbs Bookshop. Church Street, Whitehaven. Tel: 01946 695111
Michael Moon. 41/42 Roper Street. Whitehaven. Tel: 01946 62936
W H Smith. 10-11, King Street. Whitehaven. Tel: 01946 61698

BOWLING.
Coach Road. Whitehaven. Flat Green.

CAR HIRE.
High Street Motors. Whitehaven. Tel: 01946 691291
Smith Self Drive Ltd. Preston Street ,Whitehaven. Tel: 01946 65281
N & M Walkingshaw. Monkrway Car Centre. 35, Central Road. Kells, Whitehaven. Tel: 01946 695078

CHEMISTS.
Boots the Chemists. 26, King Street Whitehaven. Tel: 01946 692042.
PW Davey (Chemist) Ltd. 1-2 King Street, Whitehaven. Tel: 01946 693084
W Fare. 11, Market Place. Whitehaven. Tel: 01946 692978

CHURCHES.

Assemblies of God Irish Street. Tel: 01946 66556
Kingdom Hall of Jehovah's Witnesses, Whitehaven. Tel: 01946 62907
St Andrew Church of England. Mirehouse. Tel: 01946 693565
St Beghs Roman Catholic. Tel: 01946 692342
St Benedicts Roman Catholic Nirehouse. Tel: 01946 692983
St Bridget Church of England. Moresby. Tel: 01946 693970
St James with the Tower Chapel. Church of England Tel: 01946 692630
St Johns Church of England. Hensingham. Tel: 01946 692822
St Marys Roman Catholic. Harrington. Tel: 01946 830234
St Marys Roman Catholic. Kells. Tel: 01946 692757
St Nicholas Church of England. Tel: 01946 692630
St Peter Church of England. Kells. Tel: 01946 692496
Salvation Army. 12, New Road. Tel: 01946 692883
United Reform Church. Harrington. Tel: 01900 871004

CINEMAS.

Gaiety Cinema. Tangier Street. Whitehaven. Tel: 01946 693012

CITIZEN ADVICE BUREAU'S

3, Duke Street. Whitehaven Tel: 01946 693321

CLIMBING & MOUNTAINEERING.

Jim Loxham Mountain Guide. Tel: 01946 861235

CLUBS & ASSOCIATIONS.

Calder Club. Meadow Road. Mirehouse. Whitehaven. Tel: 01946 692481
Distington Amateur RLFC Hinnings Road. Distington. Tel: 01946 830124
Gaiety Bingo Club. Tangier Street. Whitehaven. Tel: 01946 692336
Greenbank Pensioners Club. Greenbank Avenue. Whitehaven. Tel: 01946 693631
Harrington Social & Working Mens Club. 4, Sibson Place. Whitehaven. Tel: 01946 831937
Knights of St Columba. Cater Lane, Whitehaven. Tel: 01946 692872
Lowca Social Club. 1, Solway Road. Lowca, Whitehaven. Tel: 01946 695735
Marchon Sports & Social Club. Coach Road, Whitehaven. Tel: 01946 61496
Mirehouse Labour Social Club. Honister Road, Mirehouse, Whitehaven. Tel: 01946 693964
Moresby Sports & Social Club. School Brow, Moresby Parks. Tel: 01946 693939

WHITEHAVEN

Rotary Club. Whitehaven. Meetings Tuesdays 12.30.p.m. Chase Hotel. Inkerman Terrace.Tel: 01946 693656

Royal British Legion Club. Church Road. Distington. Tel: 01946 830292.

Royal British Legion Club. Salterbeck Road, Harrington. Tel: 01946 832670.

Royal British Legion Club. Hill Top Road. Whitehaven. Tel: 01946 692941.

St Beghs Social Centre. Coach Road. Whitehaven. Tel: 01946 694341.

St Benedicts Catholic Social Club. Whinlatter Road. Mirehouse. Tel: 01946 61753.

St Marys Catholic Young Mens Society. High Road. Kells. Tel: 01946 694273.

Thornhill Social Club. The Community Centre. Thornhill. Tel: 01946 820216.

Whitehaven Catholic Mens Assn. Queen Street.Whitehaven. Tel: 01946 69396.

Whitehaven Conservative & Constitutional Club. 82 Lowther Street.Whitehaven. Tel: 01946 692396.

Whitehaven Social Welfare Centre. Coach Road. Whitehaven. Tel: 01946 65421

COACH & COACH HIRE.

AA Travel. Bank Edge. Stocks Hill. High Harrington. Tel: 01946 832828

Apex Coach Travel. 41, Foundry Road, Parton, Whitehaven. Tel: 01946 693999.

Coachline.. Tangier Street.Whitehaven. Tel: 01946 693521.

CYCLE SHOPS & HIRE.

Coastline Cycles. Unit A10. Haig Enterprise Park, Kells. Freephone. 0500 221587.

Kershaw Cycles. 125, Queen Street. Whitehaven. Tel: 01946 590700.

Mark Taylor Cycles. 5-6 New Street. Whitehaven. Tel: 01946 692252.

DENTISTS

JEBird. 7, Church Street. Whitehaven. Tel: 01946 64144.

Bird & Sanderson. 6, Scotch Street. Whitehaven.Tel: 01946 692847.

AE Mercer. 22, Lowther Street. Whitehaven. Tel: 01946 66155.

Ray, Morrison Smith Watson & Robinson. 3 Scotch Street Whitehaven. Tel: 01946 692938.

DOCTORS.

Bagshaw, Campbell, Tranter & English. 27, Church Street. Whitehaven. Tel: 01946 693660.

Bates, Burgess, & Rudman. Hinnings Road. Distington. Tel: 01946 830207.

Moss, Proudfoot. 3, Catherine Street.Whitehaven. Tel: 01946 693094.

Sydney, Godden, Sullivan, Rogers, Lewis & Boyle..Flatts Walk Health Centre. Whitehaven. Tel: 01946 692173.

Griffin Close. Frizington. Tel: 01946 810777.

Rowrah House. Rowrah Road. Rowrah.Tel: 01946 861428.
Higgins, Pearson, Sullivan, Clarkson, Wignall, Stevenson & Watkinson. 1, Lowther Street Whitehaven Tel: 01946 692241.
Moss,Cassidy & Anderson. 3, Catherine Street. Whitehaven. Tel: 01946 693094.
Sumner & Ironside. 22, Irish Street. Whitehaven. Tel: 01946 694457.
Timney,Westhead, & Franklin. 17, Irish Street. Whitehaven. Tel: 01946 69341

ESTATE AGENTS.
Bairstow Eves North West. 18, Lowther Street. Whitehaven. Tel: 01946 61691.
Dixon Webb, Ingwell Hall, West Lakes Science & Technical Park. Moor Row.Whitehaven Tel: 01946 65835.
General Accident Property Services. 20, Church Street. Whitehaven. Tel: 01946 66311.
Mitchells Lakeland Properties. 20, Lowther Street. Whitehaven. Tel: 01946 693931.

FISHING.
Tackle Shack. Unit A, 17a, Haig Enterprise Park. Kells, Whitehaven.Tel: 01946 693233

GARDEN CENTRES.
The Garden Shop. Senhouse Street. Whitehaven. Tel: 01946 65200.

GIFT SHOPS.
Home Flair. Ltd. 5, Tangier Street. Whitehaven Tel: 01946 6921.
Pot in. 3, Market Place. Whitehaven. Tel: 01946 695097.

GOLF COURSES.
Distington Golf Driving Range. High Harrington. Tel: 01946 833688.

GUEST HOUSES AND B&B
Bell House Farm. St Bees Road. Whitehaven. Tel: 01946 692584.
Bonny Farm. Moresby. Whitehaven. Tel: 01946 692471.
Chapel House. Hensingham. Whitehaven. Tel: 01946 693434.
Corkickle Guest House, 1 Corkickle, Whitehaven. Tel: 01946 692073.
Cross Georgian Guest House, Sneckyeat Road, Hensingham. Tel: 01946 63716.
Glen Ard, Inkerman Terrace, Whitehaven. Tel: 01946 692249.
Glenlea Guest House, Stamford Hill, Lowca. Tel: 01946 693873.
Homecroft. 1a, Hensingham Road. Whitehaven. Tel: 01946 692185.
Lismore Guest House, 28 Wellington Row, Whitehaven. Tel: 01946 66028.
Read Guest House, 5 Cross Street, Whitehaven. Tel: 01946 61515.

WHITEHAVEN
Spout House, 4 Sandwith. Tel: 01946 62097.
Tarn Flatt Hall. Sandwith. Whitehaven. Tel: 01946 692162.
Tivoli Guest House, 156 Queen Street, Whitehaven. Tel: 01946 67400.

HOSPITALS & CLINICS.
Community Mental Health Centre. 21, Lowther Street, Whitehaven. Tel: 01946 592122.
Flatt Walks Health Centre. Flatt Walks. Whitehaven. Tel: 01946 695551.
West Cumberland Hospital. Hensingham. Whitehaven. Tel: 01946 693181.

HOTELS.
Chase Hotel, Corkickle, Whitehaven. Tel: 01946 693656.
Howgate Hotel, Howgate. Tel: 01946 66286.
Waverley Hotel, 13-14 Tangier Street, Whitehaven. Tel: 01946 692359.

INNS & PUBLIC HOUSES
Anchor Vaults. 25 Market Place. Whitehaven. Tel: 01946 692963.
Barrajacks. 37 James Street. Whitehaven. Tel: 01946 692119.
Beach Comber Club. 91, Foundry Road. Parton. Whitehaven. Tel: 01946 694884.
Beachcomber Club. The Shore. Main Street, Parton, Whitehaven. Tel: 01946 65694.
Brewers Arms. Old Arrowthwaite., Kells. Whitehaven. Tel: 01946 693442.
Captain Senny's 2, Senhouse Street, Whitehaven. Tel: 01946 62222.
Castle Hotel. Flatt Walks. Whitehaven. Tel: 01946 692190.
Central. 104 Duke Street. Whitehaven Tel: 01946 692796.
Crown & Anchor. Whinlatter Road, Whitehaven. Tel: 01946 692737.
Distressed Sailors Inn, Egremont Road, Hensingham.
Dog & Partridge Inn. Sandwith. Tel: 01946 692671.
Dolphin Hotel. Duke Street. Whitehaven. Tel: 01946 693681.
Dusty Miller, Albion Street. Whitehaven Tel: 01946 65031.
Ewe & Lamb.Inn. Padstow. Tel: 01946 813895.
Galloping Horse Inn. 95, Main Road. High Harrington Tel: 01946 830083.
Globe, Main Street, Hensingham.
Globe. Main Street Distington. Tel: 01946 833433.
Golden Fleece Inn. Chapel Street. Whitehaven. Tel: 01946 63194.
Heapo's Cellar Bar. 20/21 Tangier Street. Whitehaven Tel: 01946 66266.
Jubilee Inn. Low Road. Whitehaven. Tel: 01946 692848.
Kings Arms. Main Street, Hensingham. Tel: 01946 694899.
Lion, Woodhouse Road. Whitehaven. Tel: 01946 692267.

Lowther Arms. Main Street. Parton. Whitehaven. Tel: 01946 694427.
Lowther Arms. 18 Ribton Moorside. Whitehaven. Tel: 01946 695852.
Lowther Arms. Sandwith. Whitehaven. Tel: 01946 694378.
Lowther Arms, Hensingham.
Old Bank & Bistro. 132 Queen Street. Whitehaven. Tel: 01946 691554.
Pack Horse. Lowther Street. Whitehaven. Tel: 01946 693481.
Parkhead Inn Thornhill. Tel: 01946 820239.
Paul Jones Tavern. Duke Street. Whitehaven. Tel: 01946 63345.
Punchbowl, The Ginns, Preston Street. Whitehaven. Tel: 01946 692763.
Puncheon Inn. Chapel Street, Whitehaven. Tel: 01946 691140.
Queens Arms Inn. 19 Market Place. Whitehaven Tel: 01946 692640.
Richmond, Main Road. Hensingham. Tel: 01946 694152.
Royal Standard. West Strand. Whitehaven. Tel: 01946 691130.
Ship Inn. Lowca. Whitehaven. Tel: 01946 61217.
Ship, Duke Street, Whitehaven. Tel: 01946 692574.
Shipwright Arms. Tangier Street. Whitehaven. Tel: 01946 692327.
Silhouettes. 28, New Street. Whitehaven. Tel: 01946 592177.
Smugglers, Bransty Road. Whitehaven. Tel: 01946 69491.
Station. The Square.. Parton. Whitehaven. Tel: 01946 590941.
Strand. 37, New Lowther Street. Whitehaven. Tel: 01946 65770.
Stump. 50, High Road. Kells, Whitehaven. Tel: 01946 693365.
Sun Inn. Main Street, Hensingham. Tel: 01946 695149.
Sunny Hill, Victoria Road, Whitehaven.
Taylors Tavern. Tangier Street. Whitehaven. Tel: 01946 65133.
Travellers Rest. Whitehaven Road. Whitehaven, Tel: 01946 01900 602064.
Vine Hotel. Market Place. Whitehaven. Tel: 01946 693632.
Welsh Arms, Tangier Street, Whitehaven.
Wheatsheaf Inn, 30, Birls Road. Whitehaven Tel: 01946 811904.
White House, Strand Street. Whitehaven. Tel: 01946 592029.
Whittington Cat. 21, Lowther Street. Whitehaven. Tel: 01946 67170.

LEISURE CENTRES.
Copeland Athletics Stadium. Hensingham,Whitehaven. Tel: 01946 67093.
Whitehaven Sports Centre. Flatt Walks. Whitehaven. Te; 01946 695666. (see advert)

NIGHT CLUBS & DISCO's
Cap'n Sennys. Senhouse Street. Whitehaven. Tel: 01946 62222.

WHITEHAVEN
Heapodrome. Tangier Street. Whitehaven. Tel: 01946 693357.
The Park. Strand Street. Whitehaven. Tel: 01946 67773.
NURSING & RETIREMENT HOMES.
Anchor Housing Assn, Briarwood, Yewbarrow Close, Whitehaven. Tel: 01946 590071.
PONY TREKKING.
Tutehill Farm Pony Trekking Centre. Whillimoor, Pica. Tel: 01946 833502.
Spout House Stables. Sandwith. Tel: 01946 63505.

POST OFFICES.
Market Place Post Office. Whitehaven. Tel: 01946 693088.
Moresby Park Post Office. Moresby Stores. Moresby Park. Tel: 01946 63477.
Parton Post Office. 3, Main Street. Tel: 01946 692804.
Sandwith Post Office. Aikbank Cottage. Tel: 01946 695771.
Tangier Street Post Office. 12 Tangier Street Whitehaven. Tel: 01946 692080.
Whitehaven Post Office Counter. 70, Lowther Street. Tel: 01946 693454.

PUBLIC LIBRARIES.
131 Main Street. Harrington. Tel: 01946 832649.
Daniel Hay Library. Lowther Street. Whitehaven. Tel: 01946 695611.
Hensingham Library. Richmond Hill Road. Whitehaven. Tel: 01946 693971.
Howgill Toy Library. The Play Centre. 15, Howgill Street. Whitehaven. Tel: 01946 694242.
Kells Library. High Road. Whitehaven. Tel: 01946 693755.
Mirehouse Library. Meadow Road. Whitehaven. Tel: 01946 693367.
Thornhill Library. Thornhill School. Ehen Road. Thornhill. Tel: 01946 8233383.

PUBLIC PARKS.
Castle Park. Whitehaven.
South Beach. Whitehaven.
St Nicholas Gardens. Whitehaven.
Trinity Park. Whitehaven.

RESTAURANTS & CAFES
Akash Tandoori Restaurant, 3 Tangier Street. Whitehaven. Tel: 01946 691171.
All Taj Indian Restaurant, 34 Tangier Street Whitehaven. Tel: 01946 693085.
Bruno's Restaurant, 10 Church Street, Whitehaven. Tel: 01946 65270.
A Cross. 59 Roper Street. Whitehaven. Tel: 01946 695774.
Georgian Coffee House. Unit 3, Roper Street. Whitehaven. Tel: 01946 692282.

Globe Kitchen Cafe. Duke Street Whitehaven Tel: 01946 695141.
Haven Cafe. 57 Lowther Street. Whitehaven. Tel: 01946 66224.
Howgate Hotel. Howgate. Tel: 01946 66286.
Market Cafe. 35 James Street. Whitehaven Tel: 01946 691430.
New Espresso Cafe. 22 Market Place. Whitehaven. Tel: 01946 591548.
Past Time. 21 Duke Street. Whitehaven Tel: 01946 692620.
Sagar Indian Restaurant, Low Corkicle. Tel: 01946 592862.

RIDING SCHOOLS.
Spout House Stables. Sandwith, Whitehaven. Tel: 01946 63505.

SCHOOLS & COLLEGES.
Arlecdon County Primary. Arlecdon Road. Arlecdon.Tel: 01946 861409.
Bransty School. Morna Road. Whitehaven. Tel: 01946 693348.
College House Tutorial Centre. Flatts Walk, Whitehaven. Tel: 01946 695008.
Distington Infant School. Church Road, Distington. Tel: 01946 830526.
Garth School, Coronation Drive. Salterbeck. Tel: 01946 830340.
Harrington Infants School. Harrington. Tel: 01946 830390
Harrington Junior School. Harrington. Tel: 01946 830423.
Harrington St Marys Roman Catholic School. Holden Road. Salterbeck. Tel: 01946 830433.
Hensingham Infants School. Main Street Whitehaven. Tel: 01946 692106.
Hensingham Junior School. Main Street Whitehaven. Tel: 01946 693623.
Jericho Primary School. Windsor Court. Whitehaven. Tel: 01946 694505.
Mayfield School. Moresby Road, Whitehaven. Tel: 01946 692395.
Monkwray School. Monkwray Brow. Whitehaven. Tel: 01946 693425.
Montreal Church of England Junior School. Ennerdale Road. Tel: 01946 810346.
Moresby School. Moresby Parks. Whitehaven. Tel: 01946 692748.
Royal College of General Practitioners. Cumbria Faculty. West Cumberland Hospital. Hensingham Road. Whitehaven. Tel: 01946 590169.
St Begh's Roman Catholic Junior School. Coach Road. Whitehaven. Tel: 01946 693015.
St Benedicts Roman Catholic High School. Red Lonning. Whitehaven. Tel: 01946 694688.
St Bridgets Church of England School. Main Street Parton. Tel: 01946 693874.
St Gregorys & St Patrick Roman Catholic Infant School. Esk Avenue. Whitehaven. Tel: 01946 692945.
St James Church of England Infant School. High Street Whitehaven. Tel: 01946 693698.

WHITEHAVEN
St James Church of England Junior School. Whitehaven Street. Whitehaven. Tel: 01946 693854
St Marys Roman Catholic School. High Street, Kells.Whitehaven. Tel: 01946 692247.
Thornhill School. Ehen Road. Thornhill. Tel: 01946 820402.
Valley Infants School. Whinlatter Road. Whitehaven. Tel: 01946 694400.
Valley Junior School. Whinlatter Road, Whitehaven. Tel: 01946 692820.
West Cumbria College. Flatt Walk. Whitehaven Tel: 01946 692261.
The Whitehaven School. Cleator Moor Road. Hensingham. Tel: 01946 694444.

SELF CATERING ACCOMMODATION.
Grey Abbey Properties, Coach Road, Whitehaven. Tel: 01946 693346.

SNOOKER.
Whitehaven Snooker Club. 28, Roper Street. Whitehaven. Tel: 01946 66500.

SPORTS CLUB & ASSOCIATIONS.
Kells Rugby League Club. Arrowthwaite. Tel: 01946 693985.
Lowca Rugby League Club. Tel: 01946 692122.
Moresby Rugby Union Football Club. Tel: 01946 695984.
Wath Brow Hornets RLFC Tel: 01946 811101.
Whitehaven Rugby League Football Club. Tel: 01946 692719.
Whitehaven Rugby League Supporters Club. Tel: 01946 693003.
Whitehaven Rugby League.Tel: 01946 66756.

SPORTS GROUNDS.
Copeland Athletic Stadium Trust. Hensingham. Whitehaven. Tel: 01946 67093.
Whitehaven Rugby League Football Club. Coach Road. Whitehaven. 01946 592869.

SWIMMING POOLS.
Copeland Swimming Pool. Cleator Moor Road. Whitehaven. Tel: 01946 695021.
Village Inn Nethertown. Tel: 01946 823005.

TAXIS.
Abbey Cabs. 53 Lakeland Avenue. Whitehaven. Tel: 01946 63000.
Ajax Taxis. 45 Copeland Avenue. Whitehaven Tel: 01946 695000.
Alan's Taxis. 64 Ullswater Avenue. Whitehaven. Tel: 01946 693006.
Amber Taxi's 26 Loop Road North. Whitehaven. Tel: 01946 63942.
Brass Cabs. Sneckyeat Road Ind Estate. Whitehaven. Tel: 01946 67070.

Cameo Taxis. 30 Tomlin Avenue. Mirehouse. Whitehaven. Tel: 01946 693344
Eric's Taxis. 14 Copeland Avenue. Whitehaven. Tel: 01946 65435.
GM Cabs. 132 Windermere Road. Whitehaven Tel: 01946 67780.
L & G Taxis. Armier Emmerdale Terrace. Whitehaven. Tel: 01946 66644.
Ron's Taxis. 20 The Close, Bransty. Whitehaven. Tel: 01946 694455.
Suns Cabs. 22 Rannerdale Drive. Whitehaven. Tel: 01946 66663.
White Line Taxis. 58 Buttermere Avenue. Whitehaven. Tel: 01946 66111.

THEATRES.
Civic Theatre. Whitehaven Tel: 01946 67575.
Rosehill Theatre, Moresby. Tel: 01946 692422. (see advert)

TOURIST INFORMATION CENTRES.
Cumbria Tourist Board, Ashleigh, Holly Road, Windermere. Tel:015394. 44444.
Market Hall, Market Place, Whitehaven.

TRAVEL AGENTS.
AT Mays, 62 Lowther Street, Whitehaven. Tel: 01946 66307.
Co-op Travelcare, 15 Roper Street, Whitehaven. Tel: 01946 592455.
Going Places. 15, Duke Street, Whitehaven. Tel: 01946 66333.
Lunn Poly Ltd., 9 King Street.Whitehaven. Tel: 01946 693151.
The Travel Group, 48 Roper Street. Whitehaven. Tel: 01946 691441.

WALKING.
Rambling Club of Whitehaven. Tel: 01946 64441.
West Lake Way. (Whitehaven to Millom via Scafell ,Pillar, and Black Coombe)

YOUTH HOSTELS.
Y.M.C.A. Irish Street. Whitehaven. Tel: 01946 693599.

RegentLane Publishers & Printers

are a refreshing new concept in quick-printing.

RING NOW FOR A QUOTATION

01229 770444

FAX: **01229 770339**

CUMBRIA'S WESTERN LAKES & COAST.

WORKINGTON & THE SOLWAY COAST

WORKINGTON & SOLWAY COAST

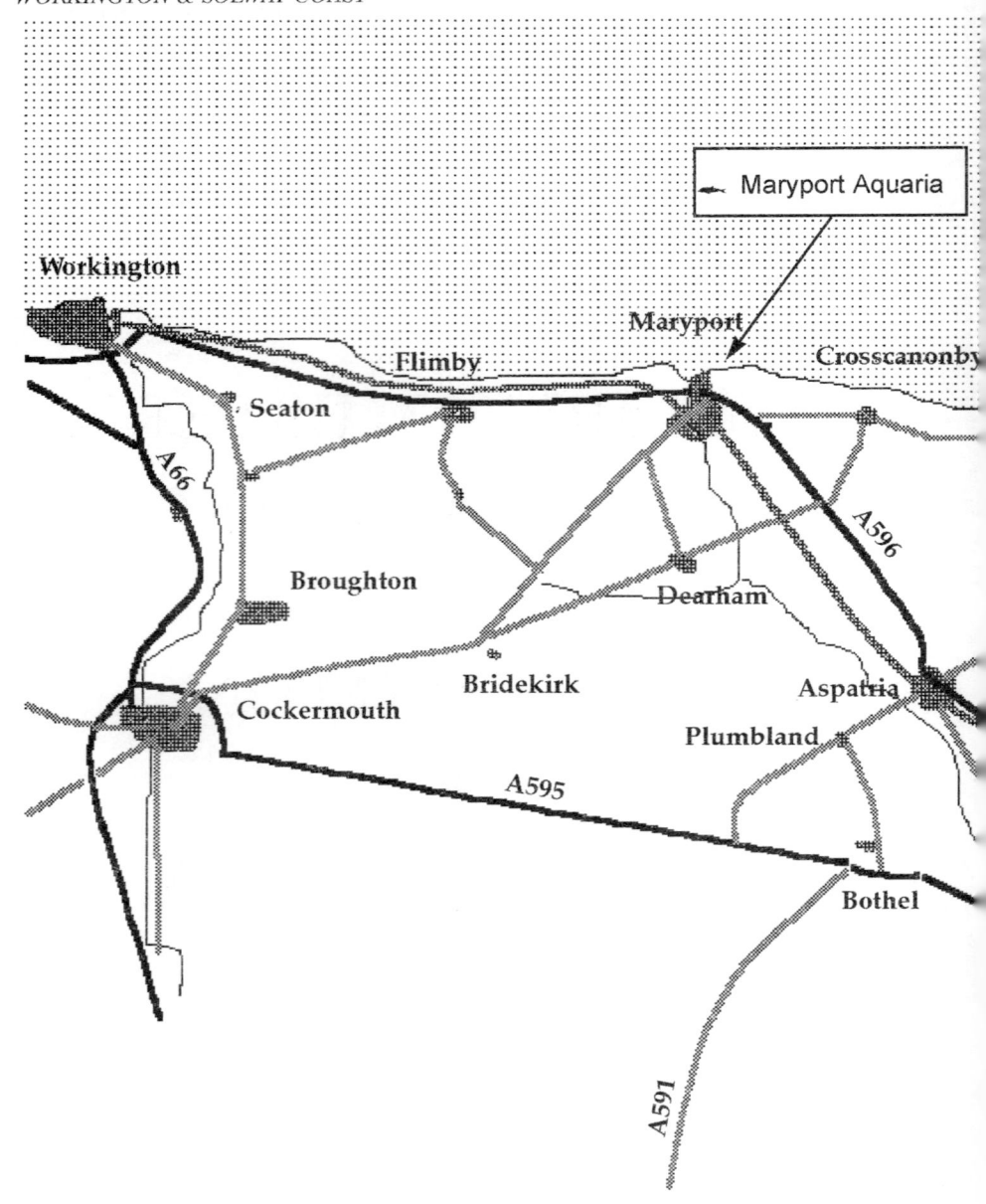

WORKINGTON & SOLWAY COAST

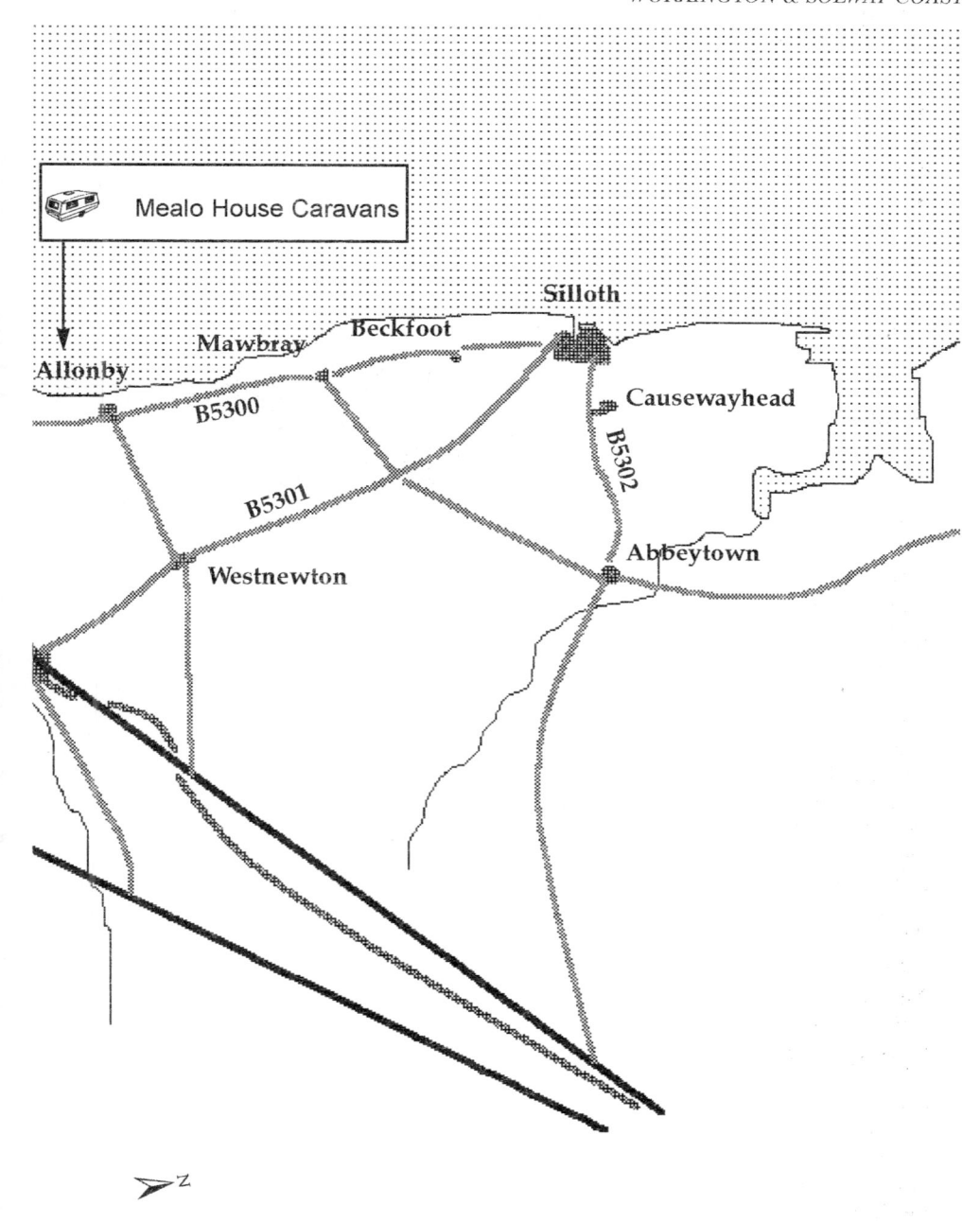

Travellers' Guide to Cumbria's Western Lakes & Coast 119

WORKINGTON & THE SOLWAY COAST.....COASTAL RESORTS

Allonby. A quiet farming area bordered by six miles of slightly muddy sand with patches of rock, which has been a popular local bathing place since the mid 18th century. There are many access points from the B5300. The unspoilt village of Allonby was a notorious smuggling centre in the 1700's. Very strong illicitly distilled whisky was shipped from Scotland and the Isle of Man, loaded on to ponies and taken inland.

Beckfoot. A broad band of gently sloping shingle leads to a beach of muddy sand which runs north to Silloth and south past Mowbray to Allonby Bay. The sea retreats more than a mile at low tide, leaving many pools round the scattered outcrops of boulders and shingle known locally as 'scars'.

Lowca. Although an unremarkable semi-suburban village bordering on industrial Workington, Lowca has one curious claim to fame. In 1915 it became the first land target ever to be attacked by a submarine. The German U-24 surfaced at dawn, sailed close inshore and opened fire on a chemical works. Before evacuating the building, the night shift set fire to a drum of benzole and opened the gas valves to release impressive but harmless flames. After firing 55 ineffectual shots the U-24 sailed away.

Maryport was a workaday town under a different name when the Romans climbed its steep streets, mounting on both sides of a bold ridge radiating to all parts of (then) Cumberland. For some years Maryport has been a depressed area but comparatively recently new factories have brought life back to the town, and the harbour, which was once a hive of dockside commercial activity has now been completely re-built and besides being an attractive area, houses many pleasure craft berthed in its marina. The Maritime Museum located close by in the premises is also occupied by the Tourist Information Centre, and clearly outlines Maryports interesting history. (see editorial feature)

Silloth. Little more than 100 years old, Silloth is a holiday resort and a port for coasters which supply the towns dockside flour mill.

The streets are broad, cobbled and neatly laid out. The beach is sandy, with muddy patches and a strip of shingle above the high-water mark. Strong currents sluicing out of the Solway Firth's upper reaches make bathing dangerous when the tide is ebbing, but conditions are safe at other times.

A promenade cum sea defence provides superb views of the Scottish hills across the Firth. The 1868 feet high Criffell is the tallest of these and looks particularly impressive at sunset.

Skinburness. The original town was engulfed by a flood in 1303, shortly after its harbour had been used as a base for Edward I's attacks on Scotland. The west beach is of mud-patched sand, but the shore beyond Grune Point is muddy and backed by salt marshes on which sheep and cattle graze. The right to graze a certain number of sheep on the marsh is known as a 'stint' from which comes the expression 'doing a stint'. The marshes have never been treated with any pesticides or artificial fertiliser and produce good crops of mushrooms.

Grune Point, on which there is a footpath, is an important migration centre for birds. The Firth is noted for wildfowl, geese and are hunted on the marshes. The Lonh House at Skinburness is where Bonnie Prince Charlie is said to have met local Jacobites during the ill-fated uprisings in 1745. It has been converted into cottages, each one named after one of Sir Walter Scotts novels.

Workington. More than 60 acres of parks and playing fields provide a background for this sprawling industrial town, which has been a centre for coal-mining and exporting for at least 350 years. Harrington, now joined to Workington by industrial and residential developments, was once a small but busy port and still has an industrial character. However the harbour has now been developed as a boating centre and is the headquarters of a sailing club. The muddy-sand beach is scattered with shingle and small rocks. Indoor fresh water swimming pool close by is open all year.

Abbeytown

Centuries ago, Abbey Town was one of the most important places in the North of England. It is a crossroads village and stands on the Solway Plain, almost midway between Wigton and Silloth, in the parish of Holm Cultram.

The village formerly a market town, is a hotch-potch of homes with its main claim to fame being the church of St Mary, known as Holm Cultram Abbey. The Abbey was built in the 12th century originally as a Cistercian monastery, and enjoyed great power for many centuries, even entertaining Edward I on two occasions, until the Dissolution in the reign of Henry VIII. It is actually one of the few monasteries to survive as a parish church, though only a small portion of the original building remains. The church itself is made from what was at one time the nave of the Abbey. Within a century of the Dissolution, Abbey Town had regretfully proved itself unworthy of the great church left in its care, and by the 17th century it was already a ruin. The 18th century saved what could be saved, the 19th century restored it, and the great Tudor porch is now a little museum of old things rescued. The museum itself has one of the finest pieces of Norman architecture in Cumbria, the magnificent west doorway, with its five moulded arches and its eight pillars with carved capitals. It is 16 feet high and stands in a wall eight feet thick.

To be seen also is a relatively modern inscription to the man who was the last Abbot, and then the first Rector, and another to Joseph Mann, who on his farm hereabouts did a great service to farmers when he invented the first crude reaping machine, one of the primitive fore-runners of the first reaper invented by Cyrus McCormick a year or two later.

In the graveyard will be found the tombstone of the father of Robert the Bruce who was buried here in 1294. (25 years in fact before Robert himself sacked the Abbey)

Many of the buildings associated with the monastery are still inhabited today, one of them being Mill Grove dating from 1664, which originally was the infirmary... along with cottages belonging to the Abbey which have been transformed into a library and offices. At one time the village had no less than five public houses, but nowadays this is reduced to one, along with a post office, and two additional shops. The oldest business in the village is the blacksmiths which has been trading as the original smithy since 1925.

Amateur archaeologists will no doubt discover the moated mound (probably a burg) just north of the church. Also nearby is the Raby Cote Farm, the sixteenth century seat of the Chambers family.

Aspatria

This former mining town straggles along the A596 for about a mile. Its name is supposed to mean (St.Patrick) Ash, but other derivations have been suggested.

In the market square is an ornate memorial fountain to 'Watery Wilfred' as his political opponents called Sir Wilfred Lawson, a local landowner who spent his forty years as an M.P. crusading for the temperance movement together with international peace. Medallions on either side of the monument symbolise these causes...a bronze relief portrait of Sir Wilfred is on the front, and above them stands a fine statue of St.George slaying the dragon. The inscription says Sir Wilfred believed in the brotherhood of man and defended his somewhat unpopular ideas with 'gay wisdom and perseverance. He was, of course, a great teetotaller, and no man in his day made more people laugh at temperance meetings. He lived in the big park of Brayton Hall, later burned down.. Here Sir Wilfred Lawson lived out his long life, dying early in this century

The church here only dates from 1846, but incorporates two Norman arches of an earlier building. There are also some tenth and eleventh century carved stones, including a wheel-head cross, a hog-back stone, and a grave cover with a swastika on it. In the churchyard is a holy well probably indicating that St.Kentigern, to whom the church is dedicated, baptised his converts there. It is now known as the Bishops Well. Also in the churchyard is a magnificent memorial carved by the man who lies in the grave close by it. He was the well known archaeologist W.S.Calverley, who was vicar here, and the memorial they have set up to him is a copy of the Gosforth Cross, one of the best surviving anywhere.

Bridekirk

Bridekirk means 'Church of St Bride' (or St Bridget) and relates to the 6th century Irish St Bride. The Norman church of the same name is a dominant feature of the village.

The church is known as St Bridgets and amongst its many interesting features is the 12th century font reputed to be one of the finest pieces of Norman sculpture in the country. This famous font would almost certainly have been used at the baptism of two particular men on Bridekirk's roll of fame, both sons of vicars and both born at the vicarage in the 17th century. One was Sir Joseph Williamson who became Secretary of State in 1674 and four years later, in the scare of a Popish Plot was shut up in the Tower of London by Parliament, only to be let out again by the King a few hours later. He gave Bibles and prayer books together with plate to his father's church and £500 for the poor of Bridekirk. The other vicar's son was Thomas Tickell, friend of Addison, whose works he edited. He is particularly remembered for his lines on the death of Addison.

Bridekirk keeps alive the name and fame of St Bridget (or St Bride). Legend is told that when Bridget was a girl she went to

Palestine and became a serving maid in the Inn at Bethlehem. She would have been there when Joseph and Mary arrived, and would have seen the shepherds and the wise men, together of course with the donkey in the stable.

On the outskirts of the village one time stood Wood Hall. Today only the acres of beautiful parkland originally surrounding it remain. Thoroughbred race-horses are a familiar sight here.

Camerton

Camerton is a parish on the Derwent, in a hollow, with three mains roads leading into it...each consisting of a steep hill; some four miles north of Workington, and five miles from Cockermouth. Originally a mining village.

Camerton's best known building is it's ancient parish church of St.Peters which goes back to the 11th century, though in fact there was a church here for many years before that.

Inside the church there is a sandstone effigy of a warrior which has been painted black, and is known locally as 'Black Tom of the North'. He was a direct descendant of the Curwen family of Curwen Hall at Workington. He was apparently a direct descendant of the Curwen family of Curwen Hall, Workington. There is much evidence to show that he was a smuggler with a reputation akin to Robin Hood...i.e. stealing from the rich and giving to the poor. He died in about 1500 and today is still very much a source of discussion, particularly at the 'Black Tom Inn'. The statue of him came to the church around 1500 though he himself is reputed to be buried in Shap Abbey. He makes a bold figure in his black armour, with his long hair resting on a crested helmet, and holding a mighty double-handed sword.

Near to St Peter's is a grassy field with a bridge at one end connecting Camerton to the village burial ground. The bridge is known as 'Miser's Bridge' after a Joseph Parkin who died in 1800 and was the first person to be buried there. He was nick-named thus due to his reputation for hoarding money.

On the outskirts of the village is Seat House Farm where the well-known strain of Clydesdale horses are bred.

Visitors cannot fail to notice Camerton Hall the large house situated on the outskirts of the village. Designated a building of historic and architectural interest, it is reputed to have been designed by Inigo Jones.

The property has been built on the site of a 14th century pele tower.

Causewayhead

Causewayhead lies just over a mile south-east of Silloth and is dominated by the church of St.Paul...erected in 1845.

Of note is the fact that the Earl of Lonsdale donated a piece of land for burial purposes in 1893. Today this graveyard has graves of some of the airmen killed during the Second World War.

Cross Canonby

Cross Canonby is a village three miles north east of Maryport.

Crosby, Birkby, Ellengrove, Allerby Hall, Kirkby, together with part of Bulgill combine as a township...first recorded in the 11th century.

Crosby and Kirkby are villages in the parish, which was given by Alan, second Lord of Allerdale, to Carlisle Priory...and served by the Canons...hence the name Cross Canonby.

Many of the buildings are built of sandstone, probably from large slabs hewn from Cross Canonby quarry, and manhandled to site. Sandstone in fact from a much earlier church was used to build St.Johns, an 11th century church, which can be seen with its Roman chancel arch along with two stone statue alcoves. Recent excavations here have brought to light relics over 1,700 years old including a 2nd century fortlet.

Many historical features in the church, all well displayed. In the graveyard is a Viking Hog-back gravestone..shaped to imitate a little house.. Another stone is a tall cross with a very crude human figure, thought to be St Lawrence.

The area is one where the Solway views and sunsets combine with the panorama of the Cumbria mountains.

Flimby

A 12th century village on the coast two miles south of Maryport.

It was the monks of Holm Cultram Abbey who were the first visitors to the piece of land, way back in 1279. They were apparently happy here until the Reformation when Henry V111 granted the village to one Thomas Dalston of Carlisle.

He in turn sold the land to a John Blennerhasset who resided at the newly built Flimby Hall until 1772, when the property was subsequently sold to Sir James Lowther.

.......these days Flimby Hall is a farm.

Flimby as a parish was separated from Camerton in 1546. The present parish church of St Nicholas was re-built in 1794 (on the site of a previous church).

Maryport

Maryport is a small industrial town on the west coast. Though already a port in Roman times, the town and port were first properly planned and developed in the 1750's by Humphrey Senhouse, owner of Netherhall, and the Manor...with the intention of making it a rival to the hugely successful port of Whitehaven...just down the coast. The town incidentally was named after Senhouse's wife..Mary.

It soon became an important port..shipping coal and iron. One local man who made his mark was a Thomas Henry Ismay who founded the White Star Line..the livery of which is still plainly visible on the wreck of the Titanic in 1985 when cameras photographed it on the sea bed.

The main docks were built in the 1850's and 1880's and some of the local publications of the time show how the narrowness of the river meant that broadside launchings had to be made...with the ensuing swamping of watching crowds, including the schoolchildren given the day off to watch the event. The harbour was finally closed to shipping in 1961.

Nowadays the South Quay has been remodelled to provide a broad esplanade. The 'Greyhound' sailing ships which once weighed anchor have now given way to pleasure craft berthed in the modern marina.

After a visit to the harbour and port, complete with its Maritime Museum....why not visit the hill on which the Roman Museum stands, and which provides an ideal viewpoint of the transformation of Maryport

A Roman fort Alauna, north of the Ellen, was first excavated in 1766 and again in the 1960's. It was occupied in the 5th century South of the town is a conspicuous mote...an 11th or 12th century castle, of which virtually nothing is known..

The Netherhall mansion, once the home of the Senhouses, is still there today, though frankly little remains..Originally a pele tower of the middle ages with extensive 19th century re-building.

Many of Maryport's finest sons have been seafarers. One remarkable centenarian was Joseph Peel who died in 1790 aged

---

MEALO HOUSE
ALLONBY, MARYPORT,
CUMBRIA CA15 6PB
TELEPHONE: ALLONBY 881210

FULLY SERVICED CARAVAN SITES AVAILABLE
NEW & USED CARAVANS FOR SALE

- TOURERS ALWAYS WELCOME. ELECTRIC HOOK-UPS AVAILABLE
- 120 PITCHES FOR STATIC HOLIDAY VANS
- FREE SHOWERS AND TOILETS
- LAUNDERETTE ON THE PARK
- PUBLIC TELEPHONE AVAILABLE ON THE SITE
- CHILDREN'S PLAY AREA
- DOGS ARE WELCOME BUT MUST BE KEPT ON A LEAD.

Situated on a quiet farm site and adjacent to the beach.
Mealo House offers the visitor many attractions.

Maryport Aquaria
Cumbria's Newest Indoor Attraction
Opening May 26th

Maryport **Aquaria** is Cumbria's underwater window on the amazing sealife found around the British Isles Seas and Coasts. **Aquaria's** dramatic displays show off sea creatures from the estuaries out to the depths of the Ocean. Opportunities to see and hear crashing waves pounding over rock pools, close encounters with creatures from the deep, and touch pools for the less squeamish makes this a great day out for all ages.

- Come eye ball to eye ball with congers, rays and octopus and explore an underwater world you never thought existed.

- **Aquaria** offers tourists a unique opportunity to explore an undiscovered water world beneath the waves. The tour takes approximately from 45 minutes to one and a half hours.

- **Aquaria** offers superb in the quayside Cafe, with seating for 60-70 people, with stunning uninterrupted views over the Solway to Scotland and the Harbour area.

- A well stocked tourist shop founds off a fascinating visit.

- A sea air walk following the "Harbour Trail" taking in the sights and sounds of harbour life and a visit to the Maritime Museum makes for an excellent day out.

How to find us: Follow the signs in the town to the Harbour -- Aquaria is on the South Quay.

Opening Daily (Except Christmas Day) 10.00am - 5.00pm

Adults	£3.50
Senior Citizens	£3.00
Children	£2.50
Family 2+2	£11.00

Maryport Aquaria, South Quay, Maryport, Cumbria CA15 8AB
Tel/Fax 01900 817760

106. In his youth he had sailed in the same ship as Alexander Selkirk...the original Robinson Crusoe, when that unfortunate was marooned on his Pacific Island. Peel is buried in the parish churchyard.

Seaton

Seaton is the largest village in Cumbria, though at one time it was just a small mining community with brickworks and a few farms; though today the mines and brickworks have disappeared.

Villagers will tell you that in 1752 John Wesley, the founder of Methodism, preached a sermon on the village green and proclaimed he was standing on the greenest turf in the country.

In the centre of the village stands the parish church. St Paul's which celebrated its centenary in 1982. It is built of local stone, in Gothic style.

Its an attractive spot with many excellent views. Seaton Mill Farm, for example, is situated on the banks of the River Derwent and has an old mill wheel.

Silloth

Silloth...the name derives from 'Sealathe'...meaning a barn for the storing of grain, ...and was the port used by the monks of nearby Holm Cultram Abbey for the export of wool.

Until 1857 Silloth was a tiny fishing hamlet. it was then that work commenced on building a port, to be served by a branch railway from Carlisle...the port being planned originally to rival Whitehaven.

No difficulty in finding financial backers in those days..one of the foremost being J.D.Carr, a major bakery owner of the region...and now of course a household name...Today the dock covers six acres and the expanse of water roughly measures 600 feet by 400 feet. Visitors will normally find one or two ships tied up here.

When the rail link with Carlisle opened in the 1850's a competition was held to design a new town, which was won by a Liverpool firm of architects.

Consequently, Silloth retains its Victorian 'spa' style atmosphere with an attractive sea-front and purpose built docks.

Many parts of Silloth are as attractive as any Cumbrian town...the street with the fish dealers...all the buildings red brick and Victorian...the fine parish church. It is an attractive district overlooking the Solway and Scotland in the distance with a great expanse of beach.

Silloth is much favoured by the Cumbrians on fine summer weekends. It never became another Blackpool, but it does have what the more popular resorts lack...a fine green between the buildings and the promenade.

The 18 hole golf course beside the shore here was the home course of Miss Cecil Leitch (1891-1978) the most celebrated woman golfer of all time. Other famous players were the late Duke of Kent, and Kathleen Ferrier, the great contralto. A plaque on the wall of the National

Westminster Bank in Eden Street, marks the place where her short married life in the town was spent.

Westnewton

Westnewton is a small rural village three and a half miles from the Solway coast at Allonby and eight miles west of the market town of Wigton. Recent excavations have shown that at one time the village was occupied by the Romans. Certainly a Roman road went through the village, and their are the remains of a Roman fort.

In more recent years the village has had its own castle (or Manor House) but little remains of it today and historical evidence is regretfully non-existent.

Most of the houses around are inclined to be 19th century and onwards, though the beautifully restored Yew Tree Farm is dated 1672.

A native of the village John Todd having made his money as a Manchester merchant, invested a great deal of his time and money in the village in the mid 1800's. He provided the wherewithal for the building of St Matthew's church, along with the school, school house, vicarage and four alms houses.

Westnewton was Cumbria's best kept small village in 1990, 1991, and 1993 and also the winner of the small village section of the Britain in Bloom competition in 1991.

Westward

Somewhat of a scattered village, close to Abbey Town near to the west coast of Cumbria. It stands where the land begins to rise from the Solway Plain to the high fells of Lakeland, its farms are scattered on the hills or hiding in trees with the church and the school in a deep valley of the Wiza beck. From the road above the village we have the majestic mass of criffell towering beyond Solway Firth, and a sight of Carlisle and Dumfries.

At Church Hill stands the church of St Hilda...which is the mother church of the parishes of Westward, Rosley and Welton. Visitors should look for the 1648 brass memorial tablet to one Gentleman Richard Barwise...late of Islekirk though thought to be a corruption of Hilda's Kirk)

Nicknamed Giant Barwise, early records show that he was a man of great strength...and it is said that he could walk around his courtyard carrying at arms length his wife on the one hand, and an enormous stone of great weight on the other.

St Hilda's it is recorded was preceded by a chapel near the River Waver thought to have been near Islekirk Hall, and which had been built by the monks from Holm Cultram Abbey nearby at Abbeytown. In the ravine just below St Hilda's church is a rebuilt house once a farmhouse and Inn still known today as Church Hill Farm, and dating back to the early 19th century.

WORKINGTON & SOLWAY COAST

During these days of the Resurrectionists the churchyard readily lent itself to these ghoulish marauders (or grave robbers to give them another name)

The Innkeeper, together with local residents were forced to form a guard around a recent burial site and keep watch nightly for at least 9-10 nights after a funeral. At one time when many believed in ghosts and the supernatural, it wouldn't have been the most pleasant of tasks.

Most famous residents of the village were undoubtedly Sir William Henry Bragg (1862-1942) who was born at Stoneraise Place, and his son Sir Lawrence Bragg, who jointly shared the Nobel Prize for physics.

Workington

Workington is a busy town and deep-water port.

It began life as a fishing village, the estuary and the river Derwent which flows through the town was famed for its salmon.

Until mid-Victorian times, the town was long and narrow..not at all the creation which visitors will see today. In its development since Tudor times as port and market centre it was quite different to near neighbour and rival Whitehaven. A planned 17th and 18th century town of regular appearance.

The port was largely dependent on the coal and coastal trade, especially to Ireland, the Isle of man, and Solway ports.

Prosperity really came with the exploitation of the coal fields in the area. When deeper mining became possible in the 18th century, there were at one time 14 mines in the area and the port had some 160 ships averaging 130 tons each, operating a thriving export trade. By the later 18th century in addition, there were two major blast furnaces, a number of smaller ones, and a thriving foundry. Even the production of cannons was a speciality here. The town received its charter as a municipal borough in 1888.

The contraction of the coal and the iron and steel industries in much later years brought problems to Workington. Signs of its early prosperity can be seen in a walk around Portland Square, where the 18th century buildings give a special charm.

The Helena Thompson Museum housed in an 18th century house illustrates very clearly much local history. The house was bequeathed to the people of Workington in 1940 by local philanthropist Miss Helena Thompson. There are displays here of pottery, silver, glass, furniture, women's and children's dresses from the 18th to early 20th century together with accessories and jewellry. It also has an interesting local history gallery.

Workington Hall, built around a 14th century pele tower. This striking ruin was at

Travellers' Guide to Cumbria's Western Lakes & Coast

WORKINGTON & SOLWAY COAST

one time one of the finest manor houses in the region, owned by the Lords of the Manor.It was a refuge for Mary Queen of Scots during her last night of freedom in May 1568,and also home for the Ghost of Galloping Harry Curwen, who was murdered in 1623...Mary at this time was just 25 years of age, and in the heyday of her loveliness, mistress of modern languages, a poet and writer of prose.Into ten years had been crowded triumph and tragedy enough for many lives...married at 16, Queen of France at 17, and a widow in a year. At 23 she had married Darnley and two years afterwards was privy to his murder by Bothwell, whom to the horror of the world, she married within two months of the crime. The country had certainly risen against her, and shattered her forces, and here she came flying to throw herself on the mercies of Elizabeth I.

Curwen Hall is the ruins of a 14th century castle built for the family of the same name. It has over the years been extensively altered and at one time by John Carr of York for John Christian Curwen, who as John Christian had married the Curwen heiress Isabella Curwen.

A unique Workington football game played between the 'uppies' and the 'downies' (inhabitants of the upper town and lower town) over Easter still flourishes today.

The pitch covers about a mile of the grass flat near the harbour, the ball about the size of a small schoolboys football, only a good deal heavier.and the objective is to get the ball by any means from end of the pitch to the other, throw it up three times and catch it. About a hundred players take part and a high degree of physical fitness is essential.

St Michael's Church is a refashioned building with a massive tower and lofty arcades, but it has a list of rectors going back to 1150, and one or two things that the first rector on the list may have seen. There is a simple Norman arch in the tower, a Norman capital, and a Norman font bowl no longer used. There are fragments of ancient crosses with interlaced work, and several mediaeval coffin stones.

RegentLane Publishers & Printers

are a refreshing new concept in quick-printing.

RING NOW FOR A QUOTATION

01229 770444

FAX: **01229 770339**

ACTIVITY/HOLIDAY CENTRES.
Annette Gibb Cookery, Mawbray, Nr Maryport. Tel: 01900 881356.
Newlands Adventure Centre. Tel: 017687. 78463.
Sea to Sea Adventure. (Cycling Holidays) Tel: 016973 71871.

ART & CRAFT SHOPS.
Callan & Kay. 1, Wampool Street.Silloth Tel: 016973 32699.
Ron Dickins. Branthwaite.Nr Workington. Tel: 01900 603814.
Danny Frost. Woodturner. Little Clifton. Nr Workington. Tel: 01900 871249.
The Flying Boat Model Shop. 58, Senhouse Street, Maryport. Tel: 01900 814443.
Helens Ceramic Studio. 84, Crosby Street, Maryport. Tel: 01900 813740.
Lakeland Studios, Maryport. Tel: 01900 818500.
The Pot Shop. 12a Oxford St, Workington Tel: 01900 66644.
Sculptured Coal Workshop. John Street Maryport. Tel: 01900 815380.
Sinclair's Gifts & China Shop. New Oxford St, Workington. Tel: 01900 602491.

ATTRACTIONS.
Jane Pit.
This striking piece of industrial archaelogy is a reminder of the coal industry that lay behind the growth of the town.It once houses a Watt-type pumping engine. Jane Pit itself was sunk in C1843 by H.Curwen. The engine house is unusual for being oval shaped and crenellated, perhaps a reflection of the Curwen's home Workington Hall. Jane Pit is on the road from Workington to Harrington (B5296)

Mansion Demonstration Garden, Workington. Tel: 01900 605085.

Maryport Maritime Museum, Maryport. Tel: 01900 813738.
The museum houses a wealth of objects, pictures, models and paintings that illustrate Maryport's proud maritime tradition. Exhibits range from a whale's tooth to telescopes and tools. There is a display about Fletcher Christian, leader of the mutiny on the Bounty who came from a local family. Also featured is Thomas Henry Ismay, born in Maryport who built the White Star Line, owners of the ill-fated Titanic

Outside will be found The Flying Buzzard, a 1951 Steam Tug lovingly restored together with Vic 96, a naval supply ship of the 1939-45 war era. She still has her original (and still working) coal-fired engine. In the hold a relatively new fun display has been created for all the family where visitors can raise and lower sails on the model schooner, tie ships knots, and find out how blocks and tackles increase your muscle power...there is even the opportunity of trying a sailor's hammock.

Maryport Aquaria, South Quay, Maryport. Tel: 01900 817760. (see advert)
Discover the amazing underwater life of Cumbria's seas and coasts. Set in the heart of the refurbished Maryport Harbour, the new purpose-built Aquaria contains over 30 creative displays. Here you can come face to face with creatures from the deep including thornback rays, and 'Ollie' the octopus.

WORKINGTON & SOLWAY COAST

Senhouse Roman Museum, Maryport. Tel: 01900 816168.

This former Naval Reserve Battery (built around 1885) now houses sculpture and inscriptions from the Roman fort at Maryport (which lies next to the Museum). The collection begun by John Senhouse of Netherall in the 1570's in the oldest in Britain. Here you can see the largest collection of Roman altars from a single site in Britain, together with many fine religious sculptures including the mysterious Serpent stone. There is a reconstruction of a shrine from the Fort's headquarters, plus interpretive panels describing the Fort, the Roman coastal defences and the Senhouse family.

Helena Thompson Museum, Workington. Tel: 01900 62598.

The museum is housed in a fine, listed mid-Georgian building. It was bequeathed to the people of Workington in 1940 by local philanthropist Miss Helena Thompson. There are displays of pottery, silver, glass, furniture, women's and children's dresses from the 18th to early 20th century together with accessories and jewellry, and a local history gallery. There is also a programme of special and touring exhibitions.The 'Georgian' room highlights the taste and style of nearly 200 years ago.

West Coast Indoor Karting, Workington.Tel: 01900 816472.

Workington Hall. Tel: 01900 604351.

The ancient seat of the Curwen family for over 600 years is now open to the public. The Hall was built up around a pele tower dating from the 14th century, to become one of the finest manor houses in the region. Mary Queen of Scots spent her last night of freedom here in May 1568, after fleeing from Scotland across the Solway Firth. The present ruin even has its own ghost 'Galloping Harry' Curwen, who was murdered in 1623.

AUCTIONEERS.

Thomson Roddick & Laurie, 20 Curzon Street, Maryport. Tel: 01900 812091.

Thomson Roddick & Laurie, 25 King Street, Silloth. Tel: 016973 32018.

BAKERS & CONFECTIONERS.

M Armstrong, 46 Senhouse Street, Maryport. Tel: 01900 812307.

Bells of Lazonby, 10 The Arcade, St Johns Precinct, Workington Tel: 01900 602735.

Bells of Lazonby, Co-op Superstore, St John's Precinct, Workington Tel: 01900 603810.

Bells of Lazonby, 42 Pow Street, Workington Tel: 01900 871990.

Berry & Sons. 5 Caldew Street, Silloth. Tel: 016973 31386.

A & M Gray, 1 Garner Street, Grasslot, Maryport. Tel: 01900 814049.

A & M Gray, 38 Curzon Street, Maryport. Tel: 01900 818841.

A & M Gray, 67 Senhouse Street.Maryport. Tel: 01900 813087.

A & M Gray, 101 Senhouse Street, Maryport. Tel: 01900 814229.

Cottage Pie, 50 Maryport Road, Dearham, Maryport. Tel: 01900 817003.

Fultons, 54 Curzon Street, Maryport. Tel: 01900 812463.

W S Graham, 5 King Street Aspatria. Tel: 016973 20284.
Kandy Shop. 14 Criffel Street, Silloth Tel: 016973 31331.
Maureen's, 89 Harrington Road, Workington Tel: 01900 61598.
Minshaw's, 93-95 Corporation Road, Workington Tel: 01900 603200.
Pat a Cake, 293 Moss Bay Road, Workington Tel: 01900 61824.
Pat a Cake, 5 Station Road, Workington Tel: 01900 67784.
Pattinsons Biskies. 11 Oxford Street Workington Tel: 01900 603278.
Rea's Bakers, 90 Main Road Seaton Tel: 01900 68023.
Rea's Bakers, 49 Pow Street, Workington Tel: 01900 65533.
Rea's Bakers, 134 Westfield Drive, Moor Close Roundabout Workington Tel: 01900 67435.
Thorntons 8 St Johns Arcade, Workington Tel: 01900 870225.

BANKS.
Midland Bank plc. 3 Pow Street. Workington. Tel: 01900 68136.
Midland Bank plc. 50 Senhouse Street, Maryport. Tel: 01900 812668
Midland Bank plc. Station Road, Silloth Tel: 016973 31328.
National Westminster. 31 Pow Street, Workington. Tel: 01900 65767.
National Westminster. 115 Senhouse Street, Maryport. Tel: 01900 812784.
National Westminster. 9 Eden Street, Silloth. Tel: 016973 31336.

TSB 21-23 Murray Road, Workington. Tel: 01900 602623.
TSB 109 Senhouse Street, Maryport. Tel: 01900 812880.

BOARDING KENNELS.
Abbey Lein Boarding Kennels & Cattery. St Helena. Causewayhead. Silloth. Tel: 016973 31848.
Glyndale Kennels. Castle Gardens Workington. Tel: 01900 602959.
Newcroft Kennels & Cattery. Haliforth Mawbray, Maryport. Tel: 01900 881270.

BOATING & SAILING.
Bassenthwaite Sailing Club. Bassenthwaite. Tel: 017687. 76341.
Water End Farm, Loweswater. Rowing boats. Tel: 01946. 861465.
West Coast Sailing Ltd, Maryport Marina. Tel: 01900 813331.

BOOKSELLERS.
The Bookshop. 89, Crosby Street, Maryport. Tel: 01900 812363.
Derwent Book Shop. 10. Finkle Street, Workington Tel: 01900.62503.

WORKINGTON & SOLWAY COAST
BOWLING.
Eden Street, Silloth. Flat Green.
Vulcan Park, Workington. Flat Green.
St Mungo Park. Aspatria..Flat Green.

BOWLING CENTRES.
Maryport Bowling Club, Netherton Toad, Maryport. Tel: 01900 813782.
Miami Superbowl 4, Derwent Howe Ind Estate, Workington. Tel: 01900 810310.

CAR HIRE.
Dobies Car Hire. Lillyhall West.Workington Tel: 01900 872853.

CARAVAN & CAMPING SITES.
Beeches Caravan Park, Gilcrux. Tel: 016973 21555Blue Dial Caravan Park. Allonby. Tel: 01900 881277.
Broughton Farm Caravans Ltd. Skinburness, Silloth. Tel: 016973 31121.
Calf Lonning, Plumbland Aspatria. Tel: 01965. 20258.
Dickson Place. Caravan Site. Allonby. Tel: 01900 84321.
Hylton Park Holiday Centre. Eden Street, Silloth Tel: 016973 31707.
Manor House Caravan Park, Edderside, Allonby. Tel: 01900 84326.
Mayfair Caravan Park. Beckfoot, Silloth Tel: 01965. 31382.
Mealo House, Allonby. Tel: 01900 84210. (see advert)
Midtown Farm Camping, Skinburness.
Moordale Caravan Park. Beckfoot, Silloth. Tel: 016973 31375.
Rowan Bank Caravans, Blitterlees.
Seacote Caravan Park. Skinburness Road, Silloth. Tel: S. 31121.
Solway Village.Skinburness Drive.Silloth. Tel: 016973 31236.
Spring Lea Caravan Park. Allonby. Tel: 01900 881331.
Stanwix Park Holiday Centre. Greenhow, Silloth Tel: 31671.
Tanglewood Caravan Park. Causewayhead. Silloth. Tel: S 31253.
Vicarage Field Caravan Park. Beach Road. Allonby.
Westville Caravan Park. Allonby.Tel: 017687. 78442.

CATTERIES.
Bridgefoot Holiday Home for Cats. Marron Lane, Bridgefoot. Tel: 01900 824654.
Posh Paws Boarding Cattery. 1 Church Road.Harrington. Tel: 01229. 832296.

WORKINGTON & SOLWAY COAST

CHEMISTS.
Boots the Chemists 29, Murray Road, Workington. Tel: 01900.602405.
Bowmans Chemists.(Carlisle) Ltd. 1, Station Road, Silloth Tel: 016973 31394.
H S Dobie. 29, Curzon Street, Maryport Tel: 01900 812662.
A F Norman. 55, Senhouse Street, Maryport. Tel: 01900 812615.
W Gourlay, 25-27, Oxford Street, Workington Tel: 01900 603258.
Health Centre Pharmacy, South William Street, Workington Tel: 01900 66919.
National Co-Operative Chemists. 15, Murray Road, Workington Tel: 01900 602102.
P M Roberts 56, King Street Aspatria. Tel: 016973 20236.
Sandham Chemists., Alamo, 64, Harrington Road, Workington Tel: 01900 872876.
JH Sandham, 64, Harrington Road, Workington Tel: 01900 602044.
JS Urwin. 91, Main Road, Seaton, Tel: 01900 67679
FC Whelan, 72, John Street Workington Tel: 01900 603332.

CHURCHES.
All Souls Church of England, Netherton. Tel: 01900 812200.
Christ Church of England, Allonby. Tel: 01900 814192.
Christ Church of England, Maryport. Tel: 01900 813077.
Christ Church, Waverton. Tel: 016973 20261.
Church of Jesus Christ Latter Day Saints, Workington Tel: 01900 871479.
Clifton Methodist. Tel: 01900 602468.
Distington Methodist. Tel: 01900 602214.
Harrington Methodist. Tel: 01900 602214.
Holme Cultram. St Cuthberts Church of England, Abbeytown Tel: 016973 61246.
Holme Cultram St Mary Church of England, Abbeytown. Tel: 016973 61246.
Holy Trinity Church of England. West Seaton Tel: 01900.602162.
Kingdom Hall of Jehovah's Witnesses, Maryport. Tel: 01900 823682.
Kingdom Hall of Jehovah's Witnesses, Wigton. Tel: 016974 76414.
Kingdom Hall of Jehovah's Witnesses, Harrington Rd, Workington. Tel: 01900 603734.
Methodist Church, Maryport Tel: 01900 812614.
Our Lady & St Patricks Roman Catholic, Maryport. Tel: 01900 812157.
The Priory Roman Catholic, Workington. Tel: 01900 602114.
Seaton Methodist. Tel: 01900 602468.
Salvation Army. 56 Corporation Road, Workington. Tel: 01900 605888.
St Cuthbery Church of England. Plumbland. Tel: 016973 20255.
St Gregory's Roman Catholic. Westfield. Tel: 01900 603800.
St John Church of England, Cross Canonby. Tel: 01900 814192.
St John Church of England, Workington. Tel: 01900 602383.

Travellers' Guide to Cumbria's Western Lakes & Coast

WORKINGTON & SOLWAY COAST
St Luke Church of England, Clifton Tel: 01900 603886.
St Mary Church of England, Gilcrux. Tel: 016973 20255.
St Marys Church of England, Maryport. Tel: 01900 813077.
St Mary Church of England. Westfield. Tel: 01900 603227.
St Michaels Church of England Stainburn. Tel: 01900 61169.
St Michael Church of England, Workington. Tel: 01900 602311.
St Mungo Church of England, Bromfield. Tel: 016973 20261.
St Mungo Church of England, Dearham. Tel: 01900 812320.
St Nicholas Church of England, Flimby Tel: 01900 812386.
St Oswald Church of England, Dean. Tel: 01900 603886.
St Peter Church of England, Camerton Tel: 01900 602162.
Trinity Methodist, Workington Tel: 01900 602468.
United Reformed Church, Workington. Tel: 01900 871004.
Westnewton Church of England. Tel: 016973 20261.

CINEMAS.
Rendezvous Twin Cinema. Oxford St.Workington. Tel: 01900 602505.

CITIZEN ADVICE BUREAUX
Vulcans Lane, Workington. Tel: 01900 604735.

CLIMBING & MOUNTAINEERING.
West Coast Adventure. Tel: 01900 605290.

CLUBS & ASSOCIATIONS.
Blue Star Social Club. Wood Street, Maryport. Tel: 01900 812032.
Catholic Men's Club, John Street Workington Tel: 01900 603587.
Conservative Club. New Oxford Street, Workington Tel: 01900 603737.
Dearham Social Club. Craika Road. Dearham, Maryport. Tel: 01900 813432.
Ellenborough Socila Welfare Centre. Church Terrace, Maryport. Tel: 01900 812060
Flimby Working Mens Social Club, Chapel St Flimby. Tel: 01900 812852.
Grasslot Working Mens Club. Main Road, Maryport. Tel: 01900 812367.
Great Clifton & District British Legion Club, Great Clifton Tel: 01900 602810.
Gunner Club. 28 Fisher Street, Workington Tel: 01900 602897.
Labour Club, William Street Workington Tel: 01900 61037.
Maryport Labour Club. 41, Senhouse Street Maryport. Tel: 01900 812412.
Moss Bay Working Mens Club. 6, Salisbury Street, Workington Tel: 01900 604196.
Opera Bingo & Social Club. Pow Street Workington Tel: 01900 602026.

RAFA West Cumbria. New South Watt Street, Workington Tel: 01900 604707.
RAFA West Cumbria. Petteril Street, Silloth. Tel: 016973 31567.
R A O B Club. 1, Fleming Place, Maryport. Tel: 01900 812885.
Rotary Club, Maryport. Thursdays 12.30pm. The Waverley Hotel.. Tel: 01900 812115.
Rotary Club, Workington. Wednesdays 12.45pm. Westland Hotel. Branthwaite Road. Tel: 01900 604544.
Rotary Club, Workington Derwent. Mondays 6.45pm. Hunday Manor Hotel, Workington Tel: 01900 61798.
Royal British Legion Clubs:
Mealpot Road, Maryport. Tel: 01900 812304.
Princess Hall Low Seaton Seaton Tel: 01900 602751.
Royal Naval Association. South Quay.Maryport. Tel: 01900 812301.
St Johns Court Jane Street Workington Tel: 01900 604662.
St Gregorys Catholic Social Centre. Moor Close, Workington Tel: 01900 603025.
Seaton Boys Club. 81, Main Road, Seaton. Tel: 01900 870848.
Senhouse Street Working Mens Club, 154 Senhouse St Workington Tel: 01900 603500.
Siddick Social Club & Institute, Workington Tel: 01900 602638.
Silloth Community Hall. Wigton Road, Silloth Tel: 016973 31816.
Silloth Social Club. Waver Street, Silloth. Tel: 016973 31582.
Stewart Club, 1-3 Stewart Street, Workington Tel: 01900 602221.
Trades Hall Social Club, 41, Brow Top, Workington Tel: 01900 603102.
Twinames Social Club. Low Road Brigham. Tel 01900 825345.
Workington Bridge Club. 3, Banklands, Workington Tel: 01900 603349.
Workington Royal British Legion. St Johns Court, Workington. Tel: 01900 66834.
Workington Working Mens Club 45/47 Station Road, Workington Tel: 01900 603989.

COACH & COACH HIRE.
Robert Benson. 7 Main Road, Seaton. Tel: 01900 62902.
Bridge Mini Coaches. 2, Gavel Street, Maryport. Tel: 01900 812406.
Carr's Coaches. Central Garage. Waver Street.Silloth. Tel: 016973 31276.
E,R Travel. 37, Douglas Road, Workington. Tel: 01900 66816.
John Hoban King Street Garage, Workington Tel: 01900 603579.
Keith Kabs. of Maryport Tel: 01900 818686.
McKenzie Travel. 15, Minster Close Workington Tel: 01900 603069.
R Smith. 33, Midtown, Dearham, Maryport. Tel: 01900 813938.
West Cumbria Community Transport. Tel: 01946.592787.
West Cumbria Community Transport. Tel: 01900 871611.

WORKINGTON & SOLWAY COAST

CRAFT WORKERS.

Danny Frost, Masons Farm, Hunday Lane Little Clifton, Workington. Tel: 01900 871249.Furniture designer

Gilcraft. West Park Cottage. Gilcrux. Aspatria. Tel: 016973 20741. Pyrography.

Heartbeat. Unit 8. Carbegie Design Centre. Finkle Street Workington. Tel: 01900 872808. Designer pram and cot ware.

Hedgerows. Galefield Farm, Dean, Workington. Tel: 01946. 861930. Hand-painted metalwork.

Helen's Ceramic Studio. 84, Crosby Street, Maryport. Tel: 01900 813740.

Jonathon Robinson & Patricia Dunn. 17, Seaton Park, Seaton.Workington.Tel: 01900 604120. Artists.

Magpie Crafts. 18, Moorfield Avenue Workington Tel: 01900 .823691. Hand-made jewellry

Memories. 44, Furnace Road, Maryport. Tel: 01900 815380. Coal sculptures.

Malcolm Stilwell 18, Moorfield Avenue, Workington Tel: 01900 66757.Photography

Matt Finish Beck Grove. Lamplugh, Workington Tel: 01900 01946. 861549.Hand-woven goods.

Moricambe Crafts. 9, Moricambe Park. Skinburness.Silloth. Tel: 016973 31107. Dried flower arrangements.

Pamela Bush 2a, Whitestiles, High Seaton, Workington Tel: 01900 872223. Scented gift items

Solway Wood Carving. 8, Whinbarrow Lane Aspatria. Tel: 016973 21622. Wood carving.

CYCLE SHOPS & HIRE.

Eric Hindmoor. 18, Wood Street, Maryport. Tel: 01900 812231.

New Bike Shop. 18-20 Market Place, Workington. Tel: 01900 603337.

Traffic Lights Bike Shop. 35, Washington Street, Workington. Tel: 01900 603283

DENTISTS

Kenneth Archer, 4, Belvedere Street, Workington Tel: 01900 603866.

F Buchanan. 3,Alma Terrace, Silloth. Tel: 016973 31270.

I Steele. 28, Esk Street, Silloth. Tel: 016973 32042

Trotter, Smith & Vernon. 18, Nook Street, Workington Tel: 01900 603869

Out of hours emergency numbers: Trotter. 01946. 861458

Smith. 01900 63219.

Vernon. 01900 822178.

Bannister 01946. 862113.

Robinson. 019467. 28988.

Steele, Sykes & McBride. 6. King Street Aspatria. Tel: 016973 22900.
Steele, Sykes & McBride. 9 Curzon Street.Maryport. Tel: 01900 812109.
M J Davison. 25, Station Road, Workington Tel: 01900 604279.
AM Thompson. 67, John Street Workington Tel: 01900 65217.
Trotter & Smith, 18, Nook Street, Workington. Tel: 01900 603869.

DOCTORS.
Burgol, Jones, Howarth, McGreevy, Shaw & Hemingway. James Street, Workington Tel: 01900 62241.
Gourlay, Butler, Macbeth & Shaw. 20 Oxford Street, Workington Tel: 01900 604522.
Joy & Rao. 11 Roper Street Workington Tel: 01900 602997.
Maryport Group Practice. 12a, Selby Terrace, Maryport. Tel: 01900 8155544.
Workington Helath Centre, South William Street, Workington Tel: 01900.605258
Mujahed, Crosby, & Steel, Workington Health Centre, South William Street, Workington Tel: 01900 603985.
Ross, Jones & Macmillan, Silloth Group Medical Practice. Lawn Terrace, Silloth Tel: 016973 31309.
Wilmott, Jackson & Jones. Beechwood Group Practice. 57, John Street Workington Tel: 01900 64866.
Wilmott, Jackson & Jones. Beechwood Group Practice. 79, Main Road, Seaton. Tel: 01900 603231.

ESTATE AGENTS.
Bairstow Eves North West. 29, Finkle Street, Workington. Tel: 01900.68363
Cumberland Estate Agents.21, Pow Street, Workington. Tel: 01900 872001.

General Accident Property Services.58, Pow Street, Workington. Tel: 01900.62258

Mitchells Lakeland Properties,1, St Johns Arcade, Workington. Tel: 01900 604249.
Thomas Roddick & Laurie. 8, Station Road, Silloth. Tel: S 32018.

FISH FARMS.
Marron Fish Farm. Mill House Branthwaite, Workington. Tel 01900 605089

GARDEN CENTRES.
B & Q Garden Centre. Derwent Drive, Derwent Howe Workington. Tel: 01900 68585
Law's Nurseries. Central Dearham, Maryport. Tel: 01900 812680.
Rose Garden Crafts Unit B Reedlands Road, Clay Flatts, Workington Tel: 01900 871755.

Travellers' Guide to Cumbria's Western Lakes & Coast

WORKINGTON & SOLWAY COAST

GIFT SHOPS.
Callan & Kay. 1, Wampool Street, Silloth Tel: 016973 32699.
J & B Henderson. 29, Eden Street Silloth. Tel: 016973 31555.

GOLF COURSES
Maryport Golf Club. Tel: 01900 812161.
Silloth on Solway Golf Club. The Clubhouse Station Square.Silloth Tel: 016973 31304.
Workington Golf Club. Branthwaite Road, Workington. Tel: 01900.603460.

GUEST HOUSES AND B&B
1 Selby Terrace, Maryport. Tel: 01900 817131.
Aikhurst, Distington Village
Mrs Bates, 10 Selby Terrace, Maryport. Tel: 01900 813595.
Boston Guest House, 1 St.Michaels Road, Workington. Tel: 01900 603435.
Bothel Parks Farm. Bothel. Tel: 016973 20567.
Brampton House, 29 Park End Road,Workington. Tel: 01900 603230.
Castle View Guest House, 30 Curwen Street, Workington. Tel: 01900 604891.
East Farm, Crosscanonby, Maryport. Tel: 01900 812153.
Fernleigh House, 15 High Seaton, Workington Tel: 01900 605811.
Hayes Castle Farm, Distington.
Mrs Lauder, 4 Pine Terrace, Silloth. 016973 31794.
Lawns Hotel, 20 Belle Isle St, Workington. Tel: 01900 602633.
Mrs Marshall, 3 Hylton Terrace, Silloth. Tel: 016973 31257.
Morningside, Plumbland, Nr Aspatria. Tel: 016973 21126.
Morven Hotel, Siddick Road, Workington Tel: 01900 602118.
Nith View Licensed Guest House, 1 Pine Terrace, Silloth. Tel: 016973 31542.
Nook Farm. Beckfoot, Silloth. Tel: 01900 881279.
Osborne House, 31 Brow Top, Workington. Tel: 01900 603400.
Park View Guest House, 118 Vulcans Lane, Workington. Tel: 01900 60487
Mrs Renac, 11 Selby Terrace, Maryport. Tel: 01900 817150.
Riversleigh Guest House, 39 Primrose Terrace, Harrington. Tel: 01900 830267.
Sandmans, 123 John Street Workington. Tel: 01900 605763.
Silverdale. 17 Banklands, Workington. Tel: 01900 61887
Stanbeck, Carlton Road, Workington.
Sundawn, Carlisle Road, Bridekirk. Tel: 01900 822384.
Three Chimneys, Allonby. Tel: 01900 881215.
Wampool Street, Silloth Tel: 016973 32026.
Winder Farm House. Main Street. Dearham. Nr Maryport. Tel: 01900.816746.

GUIDED TOURS.
Jeeves Tours 01900 603016.

HILL TARNS.
There are many hill tarns in the Lake District which offer free fishing for brown trout and perch. The trout tend to be small but the perch are often numerous and sometimes big. These hill tarns vary in size and depth, but they seldom exceed 15 acres in area. The fishing in these tarns is unlikely to be scintillating but anglers who appreciate solitude and wide open spaces will enjoy the challenge they offer. The hill tarns have one thing in common, and that is they all require fell walking to reach them.

HOLIDAY CENTRES.
Hylton Park Holiday Centre. Eden Street Silloth. Tel: 016973 31707.
Solway Village. Skinburness Drive, Silloth. Tel: 016973 31236.

HOSPITALS & CLINICS.
Aspatria Clinic. St Mungo's Park, North Road, Aspatria. Tel: 016973. 20295.
Community Mental Health Centre.Park Lane, Workington Tel: 01900 872122.
Cumbrian Independent Hospital, Branthwaite Road, Workington Tel: 01900 67111.
Silloth Clinic. Lawn Terrace, Silloth. Tel: 016973 31325.
Victoria Cottage Hospital. Ewqanrigg Road, Maryport. Tel: 01900 812634.
Workington Infirmary, Infirmary Road, Workington Tel: 01900 602244.

HOTELS.
Balmoral Hotel, Criffel Road, Silloth. Tel: 016973 32550.
Baywatch Hotel, Allonby. Tel: 01900 881398.
Cumberland Hotel, Belle Isle St, Workington. Tel: 01900 64401.
Ellenbank Hotel, Ellenbank, Maryport. Tel: 01900 815233.
Golden Lion Hotel, Senhouse Street, Maryport. Tel: 01900 812663.
Golf Hotel, Criffel Street, Silloth. Tel: 016973 31438.
Grapes Hotel, Market Square, Aspatria. Tel: 016973 22550.
Green Dragon Hotel, Portland Square,Workington. Tel: 01900 603803.
Hall Park Hotel, Carlton Road, Workington. Tel: 01900 602968.
Hunday Manor Hotel, Hunday, Workington. Tel: 01900 61798.
Lawns Hotel, 20 Belle Isle Street, Workington.
Melbreak Hotel & Restaurant. Little Clifton, Workington Tel: 01900 606589.
Morven House Hotel. Siddick Road, Workington. Tel: 01900 602118.
New Westlands Hotel, Branthwaite Road Workington. Tel: 01900 604544.
Old Mill Inn. The Rowbeck. Dearham, Maryport.Tel: 01900 813148.

WORKINGTON & SOLWAY COAST
Queens Hotel, Park Terrace, Silloth Tel: 016973 31373
Riverside Guest House. 10, Selby Terrace, Maryport. Tel: 01900 813595.
Royal Victoria Hotel, John Street, Maryport. Tel: 01900 818495.
Ship Hotel, Allonby.
Skinburness Hotel. Skinburness.Silloth. Tel: 0016973 32332.
Viaduct Hotel, Falcon Street, Workington. Tel 01900 603733
Washington Central Hotel Washington St, Workington. Tel: 01900 65772.
Waverley Hotel, Gordon Street, Workington Tel: 01900.. 603246
Waverley Hotel. 57 Curzon Street Maryport. Tel: 01900 812115.

INNS & PUBLIC HOUSES
Albion Inn. Eden Street, Silloth. Tel: 016973 31321.
Appletree Inn. 31,Finkle Street Workington Tel: 01900 61577.
Blue Bell Inn, King Street Workington. Tel: 01900.604025.
Bounty Inn. Victory Crescent. Netherton Maryport. Tel: 01900 812520.
Broom Vaults. High Street, Maryport. Tel: 01900 813152.
Bush Inn, Tallentire. Tel: 01900 823707.
Captain Nelson Tavern. South Quay, Maryport. Tel: 01900 813109.
Castle Inn, Distington. 01900 830417
Coachman Inn 43, High Seaton. Seaton Tel: 01900 603976.
Coastguard Inn. Henry Street Workington Tel: 01900 603976.
Commercial Inn Maryport Road. Dearham Tel: 01900 818040.
Commercial Inn Market Place Workington Tel: 01900 603981.
Criffel Cafe Bar Criffel Street Silloth. Tel: 016973 31764.
Crown Inn. Ellenborough.Maryport. Tel: 01900 813374.
Crown Inn, 61, Senhouse Street, Maryport. Tel: 01900 812904.
Cumberland Inn, Silloth. Tel: 016973 31431.
Elliot's Pub Ladies Walk Workington Tel: 01900 601107.
George the Fourth Inn, 29 Stanley Street Workington Tel: 01900 602266.
Globe Inn Church Street Dearham. Tel 01900..813849.
Golden Lion, Senhouse Street, Maryport.
Grapes Inn Pinfold Street Workington Tel: 01900 604938.
Henry Curwen, Bridge Street, Workington. Tel: 01900 603765
Horse & Jockey Inn. Parsonby. Aspatria. Tel: 016973 20482.
Huntsman. Eden Street, Silloth Tel: 016973 32111
Huntsman. 43, Main Street Tel: 01900 826560.
Kellys Bar. Siddick, Workington Tel: 01900 871649.
Lamplugh Tip, Lamplugh. (see advert)

Last Man Inn, Plumbland.
Lifeboat Inn. Shipping Brow, Maryport. Tel: 01900 813916.
Lonsdale Inn. Lonsdale Terrace. Crosby Villa, Maryport. Tel: 01900 818421.
Mall 45, Washington Street, Workington Tel: 01900 601777.
Market Cross Inn. 7 Hunter Bank Great Clifton. Tel: 01900 602914.
Mermaid Tavern. 63 Derwent Street Workington Tel 01900 66002.
Miners Arms, Main Road, Fothergill, Flimby, Maryport. Tel: 01900 812720.
Miners Arms Guard St Workington. Tel: 01900 67216.
Moorclose Hotel, Newlands Lane South Workington Tel: 01900 605494.
Nags Head, 65 Derwent Street Workington Tel: 01900 602974.
Oily Johnnies, Windscales, Harrington. Tel: 01900 603217.
Pack Horse Inn, 10 Low Seaton, Workington Tel: 01900 603618
Ploughman, Main Road, Dearham, Maryport. Tel: 01900 814748.
Princess Royal, Main Road. Flimby, Maryport. Tel: 01900 813311.
Raffles, 15 Wilson Street, Workington Tel 01900 602952.
Red House, King Street, Workington Tel: 01900 603396.
Royal Oak Inn, 25 Pow Street Workington. Tel: 01900 603950.
Royal Oak, 49 Main Road. Seaton. Tel: 01900 62920.
Royal Victoria, John Street, Maryport. Tel: 01900 817757.
Sailors Return, 111 Church Street Workington Tel: 01900 604104.
Sailors Return, King Street, Maryport. Tel: 01900 813124.
Stag Inn, Crosby, Maryport. Tel: 01900 812549.
Station Inn, Main Road, Maryport. Tel: 01900 812094.
Steam Packet Inn, 51 Stanley Street Workington Tel: 01900 62186.
Sun Inn, Central Road, Dearham. Tel: 01900 812383.
Swan Inn, Westnewton. Tel: 016973 200627.
Swann, Main Street, Ellenborough, Maryport. Tel: 01900 813151.
Sylvesters, 19 Senhouse Street, Maryport. Tel: 01900 812300.
Travellers Rest Whitehaven Road, Workington Tel: 01900 602064.
Westfield Hotel, Wastwater Avenue. Salterbeck. Workington Tel: 01900 602087.
Wild Duck Inn, Branthwaite, Workington Tel: 01900 602487.
Yankees Bar, 37 Washington Street Workington Tel: 01900 65644.

KARTING.
West Coast Indoor Karting, Solway Trading Estate, Maryport. Tel: 01900 816472.

LEISURE CENTRES.
Arrival Leisure Centre, 33 Senhouse Street, Maryport. Tel: 01900 813216.

WORKINGTON & SOLWAY COAST

Workington Sports & Leisure Centre. Newland Lane, Moorclose, Workington Tel: 01900 61771.

MUSEUMS.

Helena Thompson Museum. Park End Road, Workington. Tel: 01900 62598.
Maryport Steamship Museum. South Quay, Maryport. Tel: 01900 815954.
Senhouse Roman Museum. The Battery, Sea Browse, Maryport. Tel: 01900 816168.

NATURE RESERVES.

Harrington Reservoir Nature Reserve. Tel: 01900 735414.
Siddick Pond Workington. Tel: 01900 830651.
Please Note: Additional nature reserves will be found at:
Crimpfield Marsh, Glasson Moss National Nature Reserve and Fingland Wood National Nature Reserve, Drumburgh.

NIGHT CLUBS & DISCO'S.

The Forum, New Westlands Hotel Brainthwaite Road Workington Tel: 01900 604544.
Goldies. Golden Lion Hotel, Maryport. Tel: 01900 812663.
The Grove. 6, Criffel Street, Silloth Tel: 016973 31014.
Madison's Night Club. New Oxford St, Workington. Tel: 01900 871043.
Sachas, Silloth. Tel: 016973 31014.
The Sunset. Stanwix Park Holiday Centre, Silloth Tel: 016973 31671.
Washington Central Hotel, Workington Tel: 01900 65772.

NURSING & RETIREMENT HOMES.

Branthwaite Nursin Home. Branthwaite Road, Workington. Tel: 01900 66830.
Newlands, Newlands Park, Workington. Tel: 01900 872257.
Silloth Nursing Home, Silloth. Tel: 016973 31493.

PONY TREKKING.

Stanwix Park Holiday Centre, Silloth. Tel: 016973 31671.

POST OFFICES.

Broughton Moor Post Office. Seaton Road, Maryport. Tel: 01900 816412.
Camerton Post Office. Silver Dawn. Tel: 01900 604876.
Flimby Post Office, Brook Street. Tel: 01900 813168.
Maryport Post Office. High Street. Tel: 01900 812321.
Moor Post Office. 1, Skiddaw View. Tel: 01900 822473.

Moor Row Post Office. 1, Church Street. Tel: 01946 810322.
Moor Close Post Office 4, Moorclose Precinct,Workington. Tel: 01900 603290.
Moss Bay Post Office. 203, Moss Bay Road, Workington. Tel: 01900 603859.
Netherton Post Office. 19,Rydal Avenue, Tel: 01900 812618.
North Side Post Office. Northside,Workington. Tel: 01900 603219.
Workington Post Office Counter, 1, Finkle Street. Tel: 01900 603545.
Seaton Post Office,89, Main Road, Seaton Tel: 01900 602031.
Silloth Post Office. 4, Esk Street. Tel: 01697 32146
Station Road Post Office, 29, Station Road. 01900 602010.

PUBLIC LIBRARIES.
The Brandraw,Aspatria Tel: : 016973 20515.
131,Main Street, Harrington. Tel: 01946.832649.
Lawson Street, Maryport. Tel: 01900 812384.
Moorclose New Library. Southfield School, Needham Drive Workington Tel: 01900 870231.
Seaton Library. Main Road Seaton. Tel: 01900 604598.
Silloth Library. Eden Street. Tel: 016973 31620.
Thornhill Library. Thornhill School. Ehen Road, Thornhill. Tel: 01946 823383.
Workington Library. Vulcans Lane, Workington. Tel: 01900 603744.

PUBLIC PARKS.
Curwen Park, Workington.
The Green Silloth.
The Green. Allonby.
Sea Brows, Maryport.
St Mungo, Aspatria.

RESTAURANTS & CAFES
Alamin Restaurant. 39, Jane Street Workington. Tel: 01900 64106.
Appetite. 47, South William Street Workington Tel: 01900 63340.
The Briery, Stainburn Road, Stainburn Tel: 01900 603395.
Carnegie Colour Cafe. Finkle Street,Workington Tel: 01900 605743.
Dannys Ices. Solway Ind Estate, Maryport. Tel: 01900 816492.
Di-Anns Cafe Unit 6g, Buddle Road, Clay Flatts Ind Estate.Workington Tel: 01900 605443.
East House, Main Road, Allonby..
Friendlys, 2 Station Road, Silloth Tel: 016973 31319.

WORKINGTON & SOLWAY COAST

Harbour View Restaurant. 2 South Quay, Maryport. Tel: 01900 817573.
Impressions 173 Vulcans Lane, Workington. Tel: 01900 605446
Neens Coffee Shop, Distington.
Old Town House, 3 Portland Street,Workington. Tel: 01900.871332.
Palace Cafe. Market square. Aspatria. Tel: 016973 20215.
Pats Place, 30, St John's Precinct, Workington Tel: 01900 605587.
Retreat Restaurant. Birkby, Maryport. Tel: 01900 814056.
Ritz.31, Murray Road, Workington Tel: 01900 603426.
Riverside Inn, Workington. Tel: 01900 602520.
Romano's Restaurant. Ladies Walk, Workington. Tel: 01900 66257.
South Quay Restaurant, 2 South Quay, Maryport. Tel: 01900 817573
Susanna's Pantry. 14/16 Eden Street.Silloth. Tel 016973 32541.
Tasters, Windermere Buildings Peart Road, Workington Tel: 01900 63275.
H & R Tognarelli, 46 Pow Street Workington Tel: 01900 602317.
Treats Tearoom, 26 Finkle Street, Workington. Tel: 01900 871752.
Townhouse Cafe, 97 Senhouse Street, Maryport. Tel: 01900 812839
Waverley Hotel, 57 Curzon Street, Maryport. Tel: 01900 812115.
West Winds, Allonby. Tel: 01900 830232.

RIDING SCHOOLS.
Allonby Riding School. The Hill, Allonby, Maryport. Tel: 01900 881273.

SAILING, SEA
Launching facilities are available at Allonby, Beckfoot, Harrington, Maryport & Workington.
Vanguard Sailing Club, Workington. Tel: 01946 725152.
West Coast Sailing Ltd, Maryport. Tel: 01900 813331.

SCHOOLS & COLLEGES.
Ashfield Infants School. Newlands Lane, Workington Tel: 01900.603997.
Broughton Moor School. Tel: 01900 812433
Crosscanonby St Johns Church of England School. Crosyby Maryport. Tel: 01900 812326.
Dearham Primary School, Dearham. Tel: 01900 812518.
Derwent Vale Primary School. Great Clifton. Tel: 01900 602070.
Eaglesfield Paddle School. Eaglesfield. Tel: 01900 823355
Ellenborough Nursery School. Main Street Maryport. Tel: 01900 813588.
Ewanrigg Infant School. Victory Crescent, Maryport Tel: 01900 812931.

Ewanrigg Junior School Ennerdale Road, Maryport. Tel: 01900 812330.
Fairfield Junior School, Gallowbarrow. Tel: 01900.822052.
Flimby Primary School. Rye Hill Road, Flimby, Maryport. Tel: 01900 812264.
Grasslot Infants School. Main Road, Maryport. Tel: 01900 812268.
Holme Cultram Abbey Church of England School. Abbey Town. Tel: 016973 61267.
Holme Coltram Abbey Infant School Abbey Town. Tel: 016973 61261.
Maryport Church of England Infant School. Camp Road. Tel: 01900 812074.
Maryport Church of England Junior School. Camp Road. Tel: 01900 812209.
Netherhall Pool School. Netherhall Road, Maryport. Tel: 01900 812161.
Netherhall School. Netherhall Road, Maryport. Tel: 01900 812709.
Northside Primary School. Northside Road, Northside. Tel: 01900 603823.
Oughterside School. Oughterside Aspatria. Tel: 016973 20579.
Plumbland Church of England School. Parsonby Aspatria. Tel: 016973 20628
Richmond Hill School. Queen Street Aspatria. Tel: 016973 20650.
St Gregory's R C Primary School. Furness Road, Workington Tel: 01900 62401
St Joseph's R C Comp. School. Harrington Rd, Workington Tel: 01900 604688.
St Matthews Church of England School. Westnewton. Tel: 016973 20545.
St Michael's Infant School. Station Road, Workington Tel: 01900 602192.
St Michael's Tutorial Centre, Station Road, Workington Tel: 01900 604967
St Patricks R C Primary School. Derwent St, Salterbeck. Tel: 01900 603138
St Patricks Roman Catholic School. Ennerdale Road, Maryport. Tel: 01900 812582.
Seaton Infants School. High Seaton, Workington Tel: 01900 603370.
Seaton Junior School, Seaton Park, Seaton. Tel: 01900 602944.
Silloth Primary School. Liddel Street, Silloth. Tel: 016973 31243.
Solway Community School. Liddel Street, Silloth. Tel: 016973 31234.
Stainburn School, Stainburn Road, Workington. Tel: 01900 68383.
Victoria Infant School.Islay Place, Workington Tel: 01900 602748.
Victoria Junior School, Victoria Road, Workington Tel: 01900 602296.
West Cumbria College, Park Lane, Workington Tel: 01900 64331.
West Cumbria College, Lillyhall Construction Centre, Hallwood Road, Workington Tel: 01900 66646.
Westfield Infant School, Nilsson Drive, Westfield, Workington Tel: 01900 603315.
Westfield Juinior School, Nilsson Drive, Westfield, Workington. Tel: 01900 602700.
Workington Sixth Form Centre. Neddham Drive, Workington Tel: 01900 602119.

SNOOKER.
J R's Snooker Club. Peter Street, Workington. Tel: 01900 605915.

WORKINGTON & SOLWAY COAST

SPORTS CLUB & ASSOCIATIONS.

Ellenborough Rugby League Football Club. TeL: 01900 814567.
Flimby Amateur Rugby League Football Club. Tel: 01900 817278.
Glasson Rangers A R L F C Tel: 01900 812840.
Maryport Boys Club. Tel: 01900 813390
Netherhall R U F C Tel: 01900 813845.
Seaton Rugby League Club. Tel: 01900 604136.
Silloth RUFC Tel: 016973 32299.
Town Rugby League Promotions Tel: 01900 872883.
Workington A F C. Tel 01900 602871.
Workington Cricket Club. Tel 01900 605515.
Workington R U F C. Tel 01900 602625.

SPORTS GROUNDS.

Maryport Rugby League Club. The Mealpot, Maryport. Tel: 01900 815506.
West Cumberland Stadium. Lonsdale Park, Workington. Tel: 01900 602464.

SQUASH COURTS.

Maryport Squash Club, 16, Senhouse Street,Maryport. Tel: 01900 814791.
Silloth Squash Courts. Tel: 016973 31944.

SWIMMING POOLS.

Netherhall School Swimming Pool, Maryport. Tel: 01900 812161.
Skinburness Hotel Leisure Centre, Silloth. Tel: 016973 32332.
Solway Village Holiday Centre, Silloth. Tel: 016973 31236.
Spring Lea Leisure Centre. Allonby.Tel: 01900 881331.
Workington Sports & Leisure Centre. Tel: 01900 61771.

TAXIS.

A to B Private Hire. 3, Rydal Avenue, Maryport. Tel: 01900 816336.
AJ Cabs. 6,Cain Street, Workington. Tel: 01900 870576.
Ace Cabs. 36, Blackburn Street.Workington. Tel: 01900 62844.
Ace Line Cabs. 7-8 Duke Street, Workington. Tel: 01900 62392.
B Cabs 40, Bowflatts Great Clifton, Workington. Tel: 01900 65968.
B & P Taxis 3, Ling Road Seaton. Tel: 01900 63839.
Bea's Cabs 33, Pearl Road, Workington Tel: 0860 771587.
Brysons Chauffeur Drive Service. 28 Hawkshead Ave Workington Tel: 01900 603016.
Cable Cabs 48, Crummock Road, Workington Tel: 01900 601122.

WORKINGTON & SOLWAY COAST

Coles Private Hire. 26, Wyndham Row. Broughton Moor. Tel: 01900 813443.
D Cabs 154 Corporation Road, Workington Tel: 01900 66108.
Dial a Cab. Annsmere, Northside Road, Workington. Tel: 01900.605766
Geoffs Cabs. 13, Bradbury Avenue, Maryport. Tel: 01900 816767.
J.M.Hoban 22 King Street, Workington. Tel: 01900 603579
J & E Taxis. 3, Barnes Road, Workington Tel: 01900 603713.
JT Cabs 50 Broadacres. High Harrington. Tel: 01900 871200.
Jacks Taxis Moor House Farm Winscales. Tel: 01900 605789.
Keiths Kabs. 48, High Street Maryport. Tel: 01900 817297.
LMB Travel 29,Ashton Street, Workington Tel: 01900 65939.
Lynda's Taxis. 3, Mobet Building Peart Road, Workington Tel: 01900 870945.
McKenzie Taxis 15, Minster Close Workington. Tel: 01900 872073.
Max Cabs. 7 Peart Road, Derwent Howe, Workington Tel: 01900 601006
Seaton Taxis 3, Cape Road, Seaton. Tel: 01900 603927.
Silloth Taxis. 4/6 Station Road, Silloth Tel: 016973 31508.

THEATRES.
Carnegie Theatre & Arts Centre, Workington Tel: 01900 602122.
Maryport Civic Hall. Lower Church Street.Maryport. Tel: 01900 812652.
Monroes Bar. Finkle Street Workington Tel: 01900 612122.
Theatre Royal Workington. Tel: 01900 603161.
Workington Playgoers. Theatre Royal Washington St Tel: 01900 603161.

TOURIST INFORMATION CENTRES.
Cumbria Tourist Board, Ashleigh, Holly Road, Windermere. Tel: 015394. 44444.
Maritime Museum. 1, Senhouse Street,Maryport. Tel: 01900 01900 813738.
The Green, Silloth. Tel: 016973 31944
The Green, Silloth. Tel: 016973 31944.

TRAVEL AGENTS.
A.T.May 23 St John's Precinct, Workington Rel: 01900 602144.
Craig Travel, 38 Finkle Street, Workington Tel: 01900 64916.
Craig Travel, 35 Murray Road, Workington Tel: 01900 67169.
Grahams Travel Service, 37 Jane Street, Workington Tel: 01900 62222.
Grahams Travel Service, 44 Pow Street Workington Tel: 01900 68371.
Grahams Travel Service, 113 Crosby Street.Maryport. Tel: 01900 814541.
Let's Travel. 90 Senhouse Street, Maryport. Tel: 01900 815599.
Wayfarers UK Brayton. Aspatria. Tel: 016973 22383.

Travellers' Guide to Cumbria's Western Lakes & Coast

WORKINGTON & SOLWAY COAST
WALKING.
Allerdale Ramble. Tel: 01900 604351.
Blue Badge Guides. Tel: 017683. 62233.
Holiday Plans Cumbria. Tel: 016973 21999.
Jeeves Tours. Tel: 01900 603016.
Mountain Goat Tours Tel: 017687. 73962.
Rambling Club of Workington. Tel: 01900 62548.
Waling Centre. (Holiday Fellowship) Tel: 01900 827327.
West Cumberland Heritage Walks. Tel: 016973 21999.

CUMBRIA'S WESTERN LAKES & COAST.

COCKERMOUTH & AREA

COCKERMOUTH & AREA

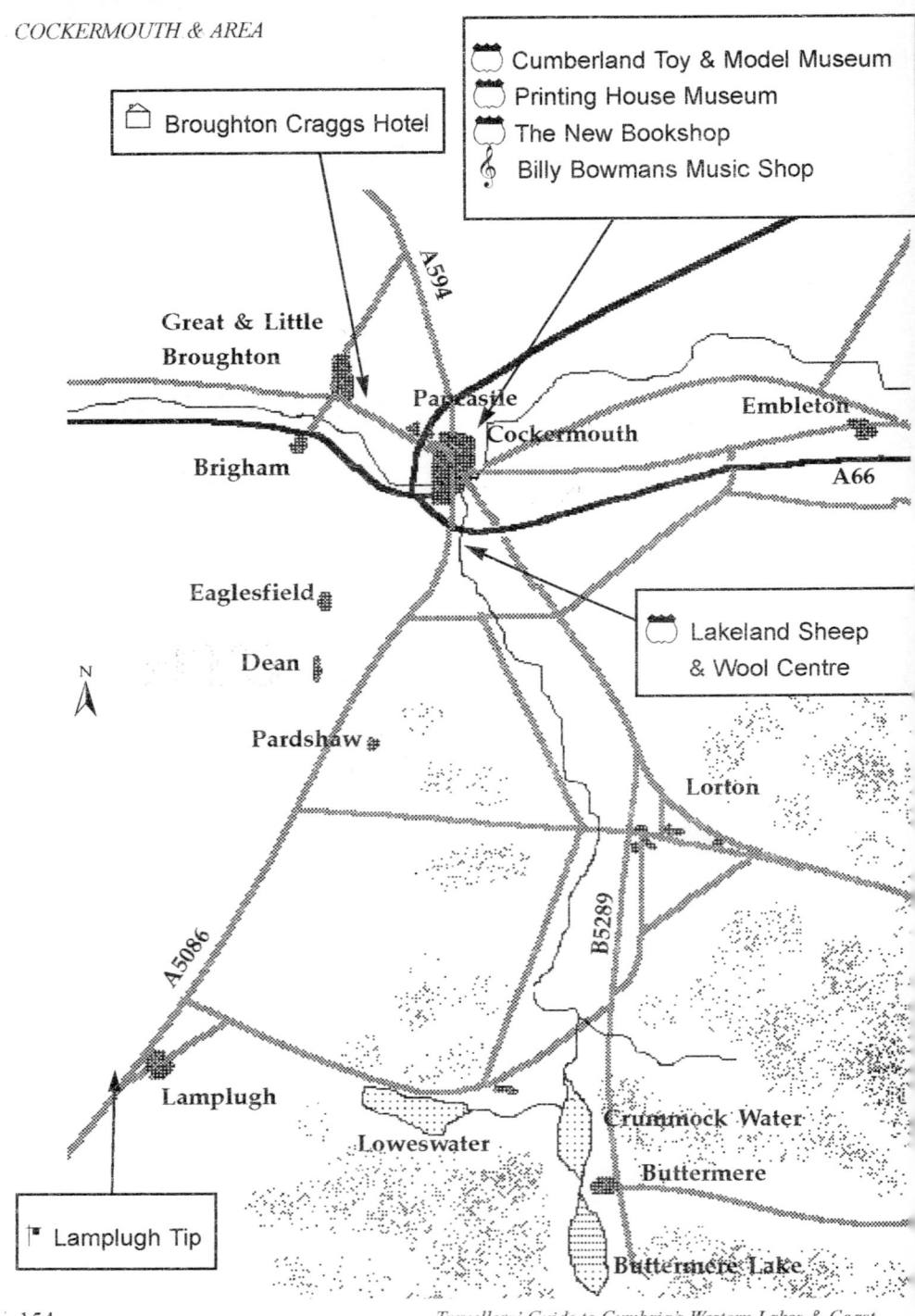

- Cumberland Toy & Model Museum
- Printing House Museum
- The New Bookshop
- Billy Bowmans Music Shop

- Broughton Craggs Hotel
- Lakeland Sheep & Wool Centre
- Lamplugh Tip

Great & Little Broughton
A594
Pardcastle
Cockermouth
Embleton
A66
Brigham
Eaglesfield
Dean
Pardshaw
Lorton
A5086
B5289
Lamplugh
Loweswater
Crummock Water
Buttermere
Buttermere Lake

154   *Travellers' Guide to Cumbria's Western Lakes & Coast*

COCKERMOUTH & AREA

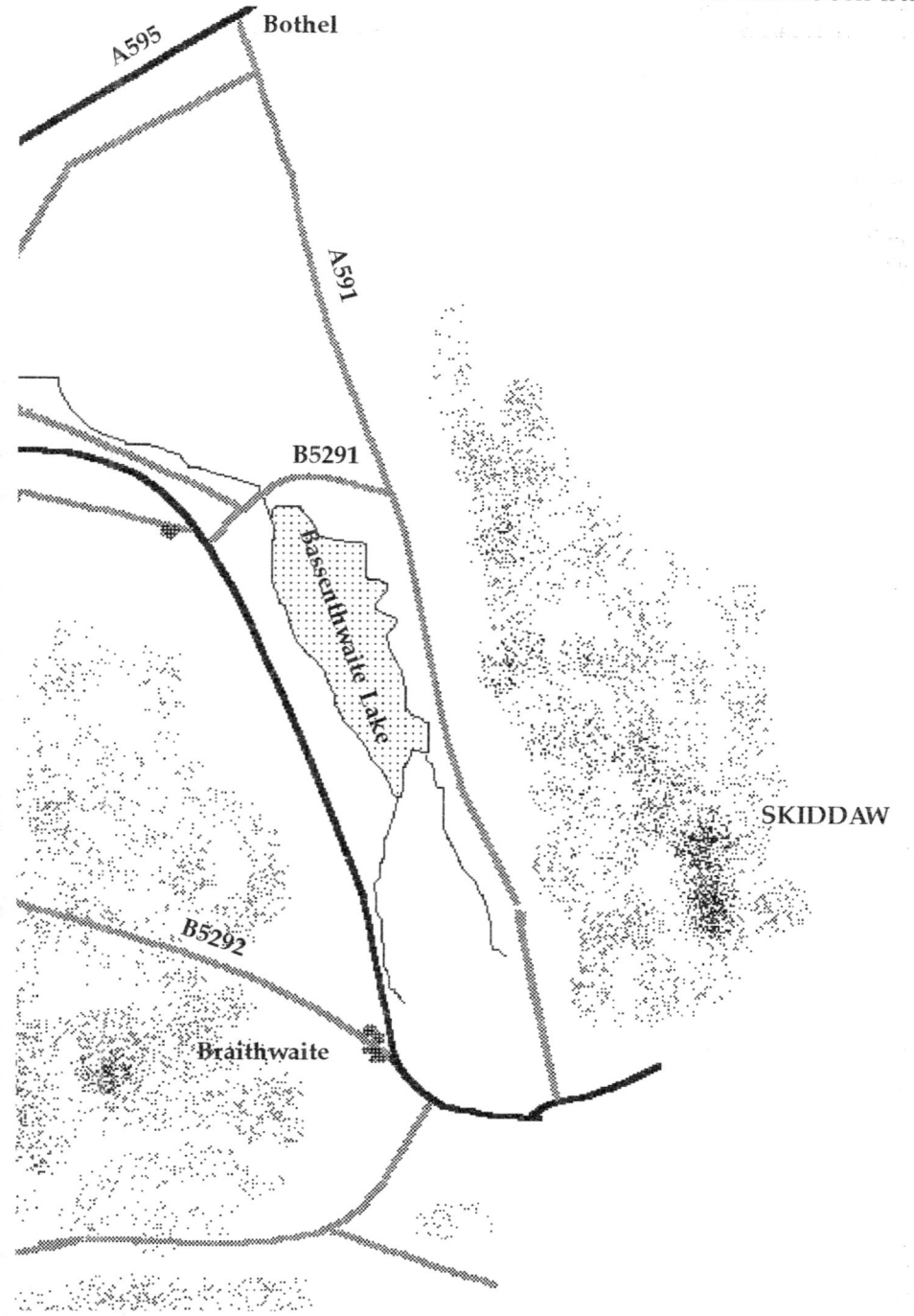

Bothel
A595
A591
B5291
Bassenthwaite Lake
B5292
Braithwaite
SKIDDAW

Bothel

Bothel...from the name 'Bot-Hill', signifying the beacon on the hill...in fact in mediaeval times the inhabitants were required to perform a service called 'seawake'. or seawatch, such duty entailing lighting fires as warnings which could then be seen for many miles across the Solway. Today's visitors are not expected to perform such duties but they will nevertheless enjoy the fine views across the Solway to Criffel and southern Scotland.

These days Bothel is separated from its neighbour Torpenhow by the busy A595 Whitehaven-Carlisle road, but nevertheless is inextricably linked by the circa 1120 Norman church of St Michael, which was built during the reign of William Rufus or in the reign of Henry I. Most of this early church remains, namely the western end of the chancel, the Chancel arch and masonry adjoining, along with the walling above the Nave arcades.

One of the most interesting features of the church is the nave ceiling, adorned with conventional flowers and gildings. Of interest is the fact that a Priest-in-Charge of the parish between 1735-1757, while a former Dean of Carlisle was Vicar, was a Reverend Ralph Brocklebank, the father of the Founder of the Brocklebank (later Cunard) Steamship Line.

Up until some 60-70 years ago the village would have been very different to what the visitor will see today. Bothel Parks farm for example had its own water wheel which allowed the farmer to grind his own grain. The grinding stones are now a feature of the farms garden.

St Bathan's Lodge, Park View farm, and Greenfell Cottage have all been pubs at one time or another over the years. The only pub these days is the one known as the "Greyhound Inn'.

Brigham

'Brigham' meaning 'homestead or enclosure by a bridge'.

Brigham lies near Cockermouth, with a great quarry abandoned in its very midst, but trees hide the scars and near the busy road to Workington a stone arch leads to the church with a 13th century tower rather spoiled by a little gabled roof. In side the tower is vaulted and are displayed fragments of ancient stones.

The restorers have taken distinction from the church as well as from its tower, but they have left the three Norman arches, with carved capitals separating a fine 14th century aisle. This aisle was the chantry of Thomas de Burgh, who was rector before he died in 1348, and in it he sleeps. His tombstone is carved with an elaborate cross, a chalice, and a missal, and lies beneath a beautifully traceried arch in the wall. Next to it are three sedilia and a pretty piscina from which three faces look out.

Many old carved stones lie in the church, some believed to be fragments of a church standing here before the Normans came. One is the base of a cross 900 years old, carved with twinning patterns. The font is 13th century, and let into the wall is an old coffin stone bearing a fine cross. The glass of the east window is in memory of Wordsworth's son John, who was vicar here for 40 years, but does not come into fame in any other way.

To the north three arches of the bridge span the Derwent on its way by sea to Workington.

Buttermere

Tucked in between Crummock Water and its own lake of Buttermere, this small village lies in all the splendour of Lakeland scenes, with little but a church and an inn to turn our thoughts from nature back to man.

Yet the Fish Inn has a poignant memory, for it was the home of a Cumberland girl whose fame once went all over England and found its way into verse and drama. She was Mary of Buttermere, known everywhere for her beauty and the cruel tragedy of her marriage. Her story really belongs to Caldbeck, where she lies in the same churchyard as John Peel.

The small plain church of of St James at Buttermere is very attractive, with mucgh fine woodwork. The font cover was given by the children: the ceiling has 16 angels looking down, the altar rails are delicately carved, the pulpit has traceried panels and a vine frieze, and there is a reading-desk given by the old boys of a Southampton headmaster who died on his way to this church.

Small as it is though, the village serves for the two beautifully-placed lakes of Buttermere and Crummock Water. It is the only place hereabouts where there is room for a village, so immediately and steeply do the mountains rise from the shores of the lakes. Between lake and lake is about two-thirds of a mile of flat ground, caused by material brought down by rushing streams being deposited and built up as delta to such an extent that it eventually bisected the original large lake, and over the level strip Buttermere Lake sends its outlet waters by a brook's course to Crummock Water, and Crummock sends them on by the River Cocker to the Derwent.

There is so much of beauty and interest about these close by neighbouring lakes that it is impossible to see them adequately in a few hours. Everyone compares them. Buttermere, the smaller, is much the better wooded on both sides, and its woods give it a softer charm. Both are

Travellers' Guide to Cumbria's Western Lakes & Coast

hemmed in by mountains close at hand, but Crummock Water seems the more overhung, though with one exception ...the Buttermere mountains are higher.

The general views over Buttermere are the more extensive and the best. They include the Buttermere Fells, Hinster Crag, and the descent from the pass; and southward over the lake the bold summits Red Pike, High Style, and High Crag. Down Red Pike come the white, tumbling, vociferous waters of Sour Milk Gill, seen from afar. Red Pike, after a rugged climb, has the best view from these Buttermere hills, and over that way, under High Crag, goes the walking path to the central cone of English mountains, Scafell Pike and his peers.

Buttermere possibly has the preference over Crummock Water, for Crummock looks harder, with Mellbreak, a most aggressive hill for its height, rising abruptly from the shore on one hand, and Whiteless Pike and massive Grasmoor, farther back, frowning wild and rugged. But Crummock Water takes on a softer beauty at its lower end and the shoreline is more varied, while from its upper end tracks lead to Gale Fell where Scale Force leaps 120 feet sheer, one of the grandest waterfalls in the Lake District. And then, of course, there are the attractions of the mountains on either side of Newlands Vale seen to advantage from Buttermere.

Cockermouth

The ancient market town of Cockermouth, as its name implies, is located at the mouth of the river Cocker, where it joins the river Derwent.

The town is probably most famous for being the birthplace of the Lakeland poet, William Wordsworth. On Main Street will be found the 18th century house in which he was born, in 1770 and lived there until his mother died. The house is open to the public ...seven rooms are open to view all furnished in 18th century style, along with several of the poet's personal effects; even his childhood garden with its terraced walk.

Beside the house is a little lane leading down to the riverside with views of the castle and brewery. Wordsworth's father John Wordsworth is buried in the churchyard of All Saints Church. He was Steward to Sir James Lowther...who owned most of the nearby Cumberland coalfields.

Cockermouth has been a market town since 1226, and today cattle auctions are held here each Monday and alternate Wednesdays...with additional sheep sales on Fridays in the autumn. Mondays is for the stalled market held (logically enough) in Market Place...which in the summer months is announced by the traditional ringing of the 'Butter Bell'.

The first historical mention of Cockermouth is made in the year 1069, when the then County of Cumberland formed part of Scotland. It was gifted to Ranulph des Meschines, and subsequently added to England. Later it came into the possession of Waltheof, First Baron of Allerdale, who, it is said, built the

158 Travellers' Guide to Cumbria's Western Lakes & Coast

COCKERMOUTH & AREA

The Printing House Museum

Working Museum of Printing
Open 10am-4pm Mon-Sat

Working Museum of Printing
Open 10 am - 4 pm. Mon - Sat.
Picture Framing, Stationery,
Quality Colour Photocopying,
Artist's Material, Books,
Antiquarian Prints.

102 Main St. Cockermouth Cumbria
Tel: 01900 824984 Fax: 01900 823124

THE NEW BOOKSHOP

A large selecton of books for all the family. Any queries will be dealt with by our experienced staff.

42/44 Main st. Cockermouth, Cumbria. Tel: 01900 822062.

"If music be the food of love"
learn to play an instrument

At Billy Bowman's Music Shop you can buy or hire first class instruments, both secondhand and new! Choose from flutes, clarinets, trumpets or saxophone. If you prefer something less woodwind or brass oriented there is a choice of pianos, traditional or electric keyboards. Plus a wide range of Guitars - electric and acoustic - Folk instruments - Drums - Sheet music etc. In fact all things musical.
**Come in, walk around,
It costs nowt to look!**

BILLY BOWMAN'S MUSIC SHOP

For more details call in at the shop;
5 Lowther Went, Cockermouth,
Cumbria CA13 9RT
or Telephone: (01900) 826708
Fax: (01900) 825984

Travellers' Guide to Cumbria's Western Lakes & Coast

COCKERMOUTH & AREA

Norman castle, with most of the stone coming from the Roman fort at Papcastle.

Most of what we see was built in the 13th and 14th centuries, and the structure is divided into two wards by a group of buildings in the middle. The lower ward has the flag tower and the great gatehouse, with its barbican walls seven feet thick, and its arms of famous families. The ruined walls of the upper yard are shaped like the bows of a mighty ship, with three storeys of windows at the tip looking out over the Derwent far below. The central buildings include a inner gatehouse and a roofless tower with two storeys. The upper storey was the kitchen and still has two wide fireplaces. The lower seems to have escaped damage and is the best complete room in the ruins, with a finely vaulted ceiling supported by a single column in the middle. There are also two little vaulted dungeons.

In 1221, the Sheriff of Westmorland was bidden by the King to besiege and destroy the castle. The lower part of the western tower shows traces of this siege.

The Castle was again besieged some 400 years later during the Civil War, and subsequently relieved on the 29th September 1648 by Parliamentary troops, sent out by Cromwell from Lancashire...Regretfully thereafter the building was partly dismantled and allowed to fall into decay..in fact much as it stands today...with the exception of one wing re-built during the last century. Mary Queen of Scots was one of the famous visitors who stayed there in 1658,after with 16 followers from her defeat near Glasgow, and here she was received by the wealthy merchant Henry Fletcher, who gave her 16 ells of rich crimson velvet to replace the poor clothes in which she stood.With Darnley murdered, Bothwell taking refuge far away, her throne gone, and her cause lost,her visit here would have been amongst her last days of freedom before the long years of imprisonment ahead.

The castle nowadays is rarely open to the public (being lived in by the Egremont family) and even then only to groups or parties by appointment.

The oldest part of the town is at the bottom of Castlegate. Percy House was built in 1598 by Henry Percy, Ninth Earl of Northumberland. Originally the home of the Earls bailiff, though now converted to

Winner of the 1995 National Heritage Shoestring Award for achieving the best results with limited resources.
The museum exhibits a wide selection of mainly British toys from c1900 to the present in adjoining carefully restored late 18th Century buildings, one a former hat factory and the other a joiner's workshop.
There are many visitor operated displays and buttons to press.

TIMES OF OPENING
1st February to 30th November every day, 10.00 to 17.00.
December and January vary. Please phone for details or ask at a Tourist Information Centre.
Banks Court, Market Place, Cockermouth, Cumbria, CA13 9NG
Tel: (01900) 827606

COCKERMOUTH & AREA

Lakeland Sheep & Wool Centre

Here is a real hands-on opportunity to meet Cumbria's most famous residents. Visitors are guaranteed a wonderfully woolly experience as we bring you face-to-face with 19 different breeds of live sheep during our indoor presentation (four times daily).

In the theatre you will discover many surprising facts about each breed - and witness the skill of the sheep shearer at work. This is especially popular and visitors are afterwards invited on stage for an even closer encounter.

And the entertainment doesn't stop there, because in our 300-seat arena, we will also show you how highly-trained sheepdogs can skilfully handle a flock. Entertaining, yes... but also both fascinating and educational.

There are other displays and exhibits to look at, before and after the presentation. And to round-off your visit, enjoy a coffee, bar meal or snack in our licensed restaurant. We also have a shop selling high quality woollen goods and gifts, some with a distinctly sheepish theme.

At the Lakeland Sheep and Wool Centre you will come closer to the real Cumbria... with help from those who really do know it best.

CUMWEST offers an insight into the individuality of this most famous of all English counties. Enjoy the spectacular visual show and various exhibits showing local attractions to discover what this area has to offer you.

CUMWEST Exhibition gives you an opportunity to discover why the Western Lakes & Coast is a very special part of Cumbria with its own distinctive character, history, landscape and culture. Through the spectacular visual show and different exhibits, we introduce you to life in the countryside, the towns and villages, the industry and the famous people and places with which West Cumbria is associated, including many in which you play an active part. Try your hand at sheepdog trials with our computer game and our computerised information point.

The Lakeland Sheep & Wool Centre and CUMWEST Exhibition are open all year round.
Sheep Show Times: 10.30am, 12 noon, 2.00pm & 3.30pm
From Mid February to Easter - 4 Shows Daily Wednesday to Sunday (no shows Monday or Tuesday)
From Easter to Mid November - 4 Shows Daily 7 days a week.
Shows daily over Christmas school holiday.

Egremont Road, Cockermouth, Cumbria CA13 0QX

Tel & Fax: 01900 822673

Travellers' Guide to Cumbria's Western Lakes & Coast

COCKERMOUTH & AREA

three shops. One of the upstairs room's, even today, bears the coat of arms of the 'Percys;.

The churchyard is a place of many memories. It has the grave of Wordsworths father. John, along with Fearon Fallows. As a boy friends sent him to develop his genius at Cambridge, and by 1820 he became the first Astronomer Royal at the Cape of Good Hope. He planned the first observatory there and saw it built...he made a catalogue of southern stars;and he died far from home at the early age of 43.

The town has several links with famous people...apart from the Wordsworth's John Dalton the mathematician and chemical philospher was born nearby in 1766. He was the inventor of atomic theory. A little known fact is that he was a child prodigy, even teaching at Pardshaw Hall school at the early age of 13 years!!

Turner stayed here in 1809, and his painting of the castle now hangs in the Turner Room at Petworth. Robert Louis Stevenson was another visitor staying in the town in 1871.

Fletcher Christian, the leader of the 'Mutiny on the Bounty' was born at Moorland Close in 1764. He was educated at the old Grammar School...now the site of the church rooms. Many people think that he is buried in the churchyard here...where an elaborate tombstone records members of his clan. If he had returned to England then he could easily have been the inspiration for S.T Coleridge's 'The Ancient Mariner' More accurately however is the fact that he is buried on the Pitcairn Islands, and where todays his descendants populate the islands.

A common visitor to Cockermouth was the singer Bing Crosby on his regular fishing visits.

Other attractions in Cockermouth is the Cumberland Toy and Model Museum, situated in Market Place, and Jennings Brewery close to the castle. It is of interest to know that the well which originally served the castle with water is now used to produce beer and those people who tour the brewery can sample the Sneck Lifter, together with other Jennings fine ales.

In the old brewery buildings is now also housed the vehicle exhibition, 'Aspects of Motoring'. One of the best attractions to come to Cockermouth is the Lakeland Sheep and Wool Centre at the junction of the A66 and the Egremont Road. In addition to an excellent static display there are also live demonstrations involving sheep as well as a well-stocked store of various kinds of woollen goods and clothing. There is also the "Cum-West" exhibition where visitors approaching from the direction of Keswick and the M6 can find out all about the entire Western Lakes area.

Dean

A parish one mile east of the river Marron, at Branthwaite, and consists of five small villages which lie between the western lakes and the sea.

At Branthwaite, steep hills descend to what can loosely be described at the centre of town. Branthwaite Hall with its well preserved 14th century pele tower is on the edge of the village, in a very picturesque setting.

There is a legend hereabouts that in the early 17th century a headless female corpse was found in the old barn attached to Neuk Cottage. The ghost is reputed to appear in white wandering about and wailing...looking for her head!. Watch out for the 'Branthwaite Boggle'

The little church of St Oswald's is in a picturesque setting at the edge of the village and is partly 12th century, although the preaching cross is believed to be much older. Many gargoyles and several ancient gravestones are in the churchyard.

One of the villages here is Pardshaw, and is where in the 17th century George Fox, the founder of the Quaker movement held his first meeting on Pardshaw Craggs. 'Fox's Pulpit' as it is locally known is actually two blocks of limestone.

Another village, Ullock, is set back from a stream. This is spanned by a pack-horse bridge, and eventually joins the river Marron.

Embleton

Embleton is a scattered parish east of Cockermouth in one of the Lakeland's most attractive hamlets.

The name is derived from Eanbald's Tun...meaning farmstead or land belonging to Eanbald. It was a Norman manor, but a community existed here in Brigantian times. There is no centre to the village as such.

The church of St Cuthbert is built on the spot of a further site where the saint's body rested. It was in Embleton that an iron sword was discovered in the 19th century, thought to have belonged to a Brigantian of the first century AD. In the churchyard a tombstone will be found that reads' Sacred to the memory of Ann Sewell whose life was terminated by the hand of an assassin whilst in the discharge of her humble duties on the 26th March 1860 aged 26 years.' She had worked at Beckhouse Farm and had been stabbed to death by a farmworker named Cass, for Ann's purse. Cass was hanged at Carlisle.

Embleton is closely linked with the small hamlet of Wythop. It has its one church, St Margaret's. Branching off the Embleton valley is the lovely Wythop valley...or the secret valley as referred to in one of Wainwright's guide books.

In this valley lies the ruins of an early church dating back to the 16th century. Also here is the ancient Wythop Hall and beyond that the ruins of the silica works.

Wythop Mill here was originally owned by the Wythop Estate. It was used originally to provide timber for the repair of estate property. It has been fully renovated, and today is back in full working order.

Gt & Lt Broughton

Broughton...meaning 'farmstead by a brook'.

Truthfully.. Great and Little Broughton.... two rather grey hamlets actually, of winding ways set pleasantly on the slopes of a hill above the scurrying Derwent, here being crossed by a fine old stone bridge. From the road above the valley are some wonderful views over the Solway to Criffell.

Just one mile away a stone marks the site of the ancient church which has vanished like the mill which at one time stood beside it. In the fields between the two parts of the village is a 19th century church with little to show of its own, but it does have a splendid view of the Cumbrian mountains.

Over two hundred years ago the almshouses here were founded for four poor women, and over three hundred years ago the Baptists built a chapel here, along with the Quakers who built a meeting house.

It is Little Broughton which can boast it's greatest son, for it was here that Abraham Fletcher was born in 1714. Of his early education it is said that this cost just ninepence...and certainly the only thing that he did not have to pick up for himself was his father's trade of tobacco pipemaking. Reading, writing and arithmetic he taught himself, and it was the lure of arithmetic which drew him up a rope to the cottage loft at the end of the day in his father's workshop, where he would study until he could no longer keep his eyes open.

By the age of 30 he was a schoolmaster with a gift for mathematics, and a wife who discouraged learning as an unprofitable thing. However he was able to turn learning to profit by studying the medicinal properties of plants and selling herbal mixtures till all the people spoke of him as 'Doctor' Fletcher.

His proudest moment was when he held in his hands the first of his two mathematical books, called the Universal Measurer, a survey of every theory of measurement. He died at 78, having many years before accurately predicted his length of life to within 16 days.

Broughton Craggs
HOTEL AND RESTAURANT

Set in 3 acres of delightful gardens overlooking the Derwent Valley, 3 miles west of Wordsworth's Cockermouth and 7 miles to the Solway Coast. The Hotel provides the ideal base for a variety of holiday activities, most of which can be arranged from the hotel.

Our renowned restaurant caters for all tastes and our chefs prepare outstanding cuisine using all local produce.

The 14 bedrooms including a four poster are all en-suite and are complete with telephone, colour TV, tea and coffee making facilities and have recently been refurbished. The Hotel is licensed to hold the solemnization of marriage ceremony. Meeting and conference rooms available. Short breaks available all year except Christmas and new Year. Roaring fires in lounges in winter.

Write or call for a brochure and tariff.
**Broughton Craggs Hotel & Restaurant, Great Broughton, Cockermouth, Cumbria, CA13 0XW.
Telephone: (01900) 824400 Fax: (01900)825350**

RAC★★★ AA★★★ ETB 4 Crowns Commended

Travellers' Guide to Cumbria's Western Lakes & Coast

Lamplugh

Lamplugh is a parish some two miles east of the Marron valley. The parish extends for about six miles from the north to south, and three miles from east to west.

The church has been dedicated to St. Michael, and stands on the site of an old chapel. The vestry here was previously part of the Lamplugh family mortuary chapel.

The church however has been much renewed, but some of it can be seen to be some 600 years old, and there is a charming little window with two carved faces. One of the old memorials is to Thomas and Francis Lamplugh, the other being to their daughter who was born in 1693 and died within a few months of her wedding.

In 1747 one Richard Brisco of Lamplugh Hall bequeathed a yearly rental of £12 payable out of Skelsmoor lands...to be distributed amongst poor widows and the school. These days, Lamplugh Hall, now a farmstead still has an ancient feature at its entrance...an archway bearing the Lamplugh family crest with the date 1595.

The row of houses at Cross gates originally housed the navvies who constructed the reservoir at Cogramoss. A building near Brook House housed Lamplugh's first school. Later the school was used to house the local hearse, and somewhat naturally became known as 'Hearse House'. These days the building is used to store hay.

THE LAMPLUGH TIP

LAMPLUGH
WORKINGTON, CUMBRIA, CA14 4SB
TEL: 01946 861232

'*The Lamplugh Tip*', so called because of the sheep auctions that took place here many years ago and known locally as 'The Tip'.

Charming 'Olde Worlde' village pub.
Good home cooked food - extensive menu.
Warm, friendly atmosphere
Children Welcome - Ample Parking
Large selection of Wines, Beers and Spirits.

OPEN EVERY EVENING
6.30 - 9pm for meals
12 - 2pm for lunches

Lorton

'Lorton' meaning 'farmstead on a stream'. Its river is the Cocker, which flows from Crummock Water down the beautiful Lorton Vale, and its little place in poetry is by Wordsworth who wrote...

a living thing
Produced too slowly ever to decay:
Of form and aspect too magnificent
To be destroyed.

These are the words he wrote in 1803, and the great yew of which he wrote is flourishing still...even though many of its branches are broken. This same yew is the one where George Fox preached the gospel of Quakers, to a great crowd of people, many of whom were Cromwell's soldiers. In fact it was said at the time that so many people were sitting on its branches that it was in danger of falling down.

The chief beauty of the church is its richly coloured window showing the group of figures round the empty tomb of Jesus. It has little other interest, but what it lacks is found among the graves outside. Here lies Thomas Fisher, who ministered in Lorton for 59 years and saw the first 26 days of the 19th century; his son John was vicar of Kirkoswald for 57 years, so that father and son served the church for 116 years.

The Vale of Lorton extending to Cockermouth is good agricultural land and like the Vale of Eden is open to the north. A good general view of it, up and down, can be seen from the road at Swinside between the Whinlatter Pass and the village of Loweswater.

Papcastle

Papcastle is a village one mile north-west of Cockermouth. Here was the Roman fort of 'Derventio'...now nearly obliterated by buildings and the road...worth looking for though..

The barrack block and commandants bath house were excavated in 1961-2 and the large fort of just over six acres appears to have housed a cavalry unit. Regretfully stones from the fort have been plundered over the years for building in the surrounding areas...Cockermouth Castle is a good example of that.. To date the fort has never been fully excavated.

Papcastle village is much the same as it was some 200 years ago. The name originates from 'Pips Castle'...namely the castle built here by one Gilbert Pipard...though no trace of the castle now exists.

A mile off the line of the Roman road to Maryport is a marked footpath known locally as 'Wet Lonning'.

RegentLane Publishers & Printers

are a refreshing new concept in quick-printing.

RING NOW FOR A QUOTATION

01229 770444

FAX: **01229 770339**

ANTIQUES.

Antique Market. Main Street, Cockermouth Tel: 01900 824346.

Bridge House Antiques, 1, The Courthouse, Main Street, Cockermouth. Tel: 01900 824283.

CG's Curiosity Shop. 14, South Street, Cockermouth Tel: 01900 824418.

Cockermouth Antiques. 5, Station Street.Cockermouth. Tel: 01900 826746.

Holmes Antiques. 1, Market Place, Cockermouth.Tel: 01900 826114.

Memory Lane Antiques. 84, Main Street, Cockermouth. Tel: 01900 828562.

ART & CRAFT SHOPS.

Castlegate House & Art Gallery. Cockermouth.Tel: 01900 822149.

Cockermouth Craft & Gift Centre. 5, Crown Street. Cockermouth. Tel: 01900 824662.

Fagan's, 51, main Street Cockermouth. Tel: 01900 823223.

Fig Tree Craft Centre. 32, Market Place. Cockermouth Tel: 01900 822297.

Lakeland Ceramics. 5, Old Kings Arms. Main Street.Cockermouth. Tel: 01900 827296.

Ken Longcrake.Blindcrake,Cockermouth. Tel: 01900 824474.

Nikiski Notions. 4, Old Kings Arms Lane, Cockermouth Tel: 01900 825666

Panache ,Northam House, Main Street, Cockermouth Tel: 01900 823549.

Pipkin Puppets.Cockermouth. Tel: 01900 828867.

Printing House. 102, Main Street, Cockermouth Tel: 01900 824984.

Riverside Craft Studio, Market Place, Cockermouth. Tel: 01900 828867.

Skylark Studio. 9, South Street.Cockermouth. Tel: 01900 823521.

ART GALLERIES.

Castlegate House Gallery.Castlegate.Cockermouth Tel: 01900 822149. (see events, festivals)

ATTRACTIONS.

Aspects of Motoring, The Western Lakes Motor Museum. Cockermouth Tel: 01900 824448.

Motoring from the early years of the century to present day design and development. From vintage racer to dune buggy and from speedway to formula three, Aspects of Motoring will certainly entertain the whole family. Many of the exhibits are displayed in tableau settings which create a unique atmosphere inside the Old Maltings. Several of the exhibits will be of special interest to children and are designed to be educational and informative.

Around forty cars and many motorcycles are displayed with texts relating to their history and construction amongst these exhibits are the answers to a quiz which all the family can enjoy. Also to be enjoyed is an amazing collection of over 400 incredible detailed models built over the last forty years.

COCKERMOUTH & AREA

Video presentations and a computer quiz are also included in the museum and a welcome in the Pit Stop coffee and souvenir shop is assured. A unique opportunity will be presented to visitors to be photographed....seated in a formula racing car.

Bitter End Brewery & Pub. Cockermouth. Tel: 01900 828993.

Castlegate House. Tel: 01900. 822149.

This listed Georgian House and garden, built in 1739 and situated opposite the entrance to Cockermouth Castle is the setting for stunning displays of modern paintings and sculpture, ceramics and glass. There are open fires in winter giving an atmosphere of warmth and friendliness. The walled Secret Garden is open from time to time in the summer.

Between March and December there is a changing programme of monthly exhibitions, The gallery which is privately owned specialises in showing the work of Northern and Scottish artists which includes Cumbrian painters Sheila Fell, Percy Kelly, Bill Peascod and Michael Bennett among many others.

Cumberland Toy & Model Museum. Cockermouth. Tel: 01900. 827606 (see advert)

The Museum exhibits mainly British toys from C1900 to the present. There are many visitor operated displays including vintage tinplate trains, Scalextric cars, Lego models and even a helicopter to fly. Famous names include Hornby trains, Meccano, Triang, Sutcliffe boats, Lego, JEP, Bayco, Minic, Airfix, Pedigree, etc. There are prams, dolls houses, a railway in both a 'loft' and a garden shed.

There is a family quiz to do and small children can find the little teddy bears or play with the wooden bricks. Whether you are eight or eighty there should be something to remind you of your childhood.

Jennings Brewery. Cockermouth.Tel: 01900. 823214.

Jennings Brothers have been brewing traditional beers for over 160 years and still use today the same traditional methods that were used by their founder, as long ago as 1828 in the village of Lorton.

Jennings Castle Brewery is in the quaint market town of Cockermouth, sited in the shadow of historic Cockermouth Castle at the confluence of the rivers Cocker and Derwent. The water for the brewing process is still drawn from the traditional well source which supplied the Castle with pure water around the time of the Norman Conquest. The one and a half hour tour takes visitors around the Jennings Brewery explaining such intriquing brewery expressions as "Hop Back" and "Mash Tim".

Lakeland Sheep & Wool Exhibition. Cockermouth Tel: 01900 822673. (see advert)

This is a real 'hands on' opportunity to meet Cumbria's most famous residents. Visitors here are guaranteed a wonderful woolly experience as you are brought face to face with 19 different breeds of live sheep during the daily presentation. Also here is the Cumwest Exhibition which gives visitors the opportunity to discover why the Western Lakes & Coast is a very special part of Cumbria with its own distinctive character, history, landscape and culture.

Minerals & Fossils Museum. Cockermouth. Tel: 01900 828301.

Mining for minerals in Lakeland and Northern England dates back to Roman times. These minerals and rocks which include Andesite, Shap Granite, Garnet and Cumberland Green Slate come in many beautiful shapes and colours. The Creighton

Mineral Museum comprises a collection of Northern England Minerals and includes the late Wm. Shaw's mineral collection. Also on display are miners lamps, tools, old photographs, and a show of fluorescent minerals in the 'Aladdins Cave'. The Museum shop stocks minerals and fossils for sale, also jewellry, original paintings, photographs, and crafts.

Printing House Museum. Cockermouth Tel: 01900 824984. (see advert)

Here at last visitors can have the opportunity of visiting a working museum of printing. Set in a building specially extended for the purpose. Here you can see a varied and interesting range of printing presses and equipment brought together from all over Britain. Walking round the Museum takes the visitor on a fascinating journey through time. Starting with a display describing the history of printing from its origins in the 15th century and onwards to the use of automated machinery. The composing room is the first stop on the tour of the museum, where you can see type set by hand and then see what sort of a 'fist' you can make of the job. Your effort will be proofed on one of the Museum presses...time permitting. The range of historical iron presses comes next, impressive and massive in all their glory, they represent the first step forward in the printing revolution at the beginning of the 19th century when the wooden presses, which had ruled supreme for 300 years were made redundant. The range of presses on show include an Imperial press, two Colombians, two Albions, a Jones press, Cropper Minerva, an Arab, Heidleberg and Wharfedale. The Museum aims to cater for many tastes, the large varied and ever-changing displays will appeal to both the young and old alike.

Wordsworth House, Cockermouth. Tel: 01900 824805.

Wordsworth House is a fine Georgian town house built in 1745 for the Sheriff of Cumberland.

It later passed into the ownership of Sir James Lowther (1st Earl of Lonsdale) who let it to his Estate and Law-Agent, John Wordsworth. Here all five Wordsworth children were born, including the Poet Laureate, William, on 7th April 1770, and his sister Dorothy on Christmas Day 1771.

Recently restored Georgian garden which features the famous Terrace Walk.

Wythop Mill. Embleton. Tel: 017687 76394.

AUCTIONEERS.

Mitchell's Auction Co.Ltd. Fairfield House. Station Road, Cockermouth. Tel: 016973 822016.

BANKS.

Barclays Bank. 30, Main Street, Cockermouth. Tel: 01900 823120.
Midland Bank 1, Main Street, Cockermouth. Tel: 01900 822055.
National Westminster. 23, Station Street, Cockermouth. Tel: 01900 822831.
TSB 50, Main Street, Cockermouth Tel: 01900 822129.

COCKERMOUTH & AREA
BOARDING KENNELS.
Thorne Dyke Kennels. Pardshaw. Cockermouth. Tel: 01900 825990.

BOATING & SAILING..Lakes.
Water End Farm. Loweswater. ...Rowing boats. Tel: 01946 861465.

BOOKSELLERS.
New Bookshop. 42/44 Main Street, Cockermouth Tel: 01900 822062. (see advert)
DR & AP Winkworth. 102, Main Street, Cockermouth. Tel: 01900 824984 (see advert)

BOWLING.
Harris Park, Cockermouth. Flat Green.

CARAVAN & CAMPING SITES.
The Beeches Caravan Park. Gilcrux. Nr Cockermouth. Tel: 016973 21555.
Dougienook Caravan Park. Lamplugh
Inglenook Caravan Park. Lamplugh. Tel: 01946 861240.
Skiddaw View Caravan Park. Sunderland. Tel: 019673 20919.
Violet Bank Caravan Park. Simonscales Lane. Cockermouth Tel: 01900 822169.
Wheatsheaf Inn. Lorton. Tel: 01900 85268.
Whinfell Caravan Park. Lorton. Cockermouth
Wyndham Caravan Park. Cockermouth. Tel: 01900 825238 & 822571.

CHEMISTS.
JWW Allison. 31, Main Street. Cockermouth. Tel: 01900 822292.
Boots the Chemists. 56-58, Main Street , Cockermouth. Tel: 01900 823160.

CHURCHES.
All Saints Church of England. Christchurch.Tel: 01900 823269.
Cockermouth Methodist Church. Tel: 01900 823273.
Kingdom Hall of Jehovah's Witnesses, Maryport. Tel: 01900 823682.
St Bridget Church of England. Brigham. Tel: 01900 825383.
St Cuthberts Church of England. Embleton. Tel: 01900 823269.
St Josephs Roman Catholic. Cockermouth. Tel: 01900 822121.
St Margarets Church of England. Wythop. Tel: 01900 823269.
St Marys Church of England. Ennerdale Bridge. Tel: 01946 861310.
St Michael Church of England. Lamplugh Tel: 01946 861310.

St Phillip Church of England, Mosser. Tel: 01900 825383.

CLUBS & ASSOCIATIONS.

Anchor Club. Challoner Street. Cockermouth Tel: 01900 823688.

Derwent Railway Society. Lynwood Redmain.Cockermouth Tel: 01900 826968.

Harris Park Bowling Club. Harris Park. Cockermouth Tel: 01900 826541.

Rotary Club. Cockermouth. Meetings Fridays 12.30.p.m. The Globe Hotel. Main Street. Tel: 01900 822126.

Main Street, Great Broughton. Cockermouth Tel: 01900 824684.

COACH & COACH HIRE.

Daglish Coaches. Glenrose Pasture Road, Rowrah, Lamplugh. Tel: 01946 861940.

Ken Routledge. 1a, St Helens Court, Cockermouth Tel: 01900 822795.

Simpsons Coach Hire. 20, Whiteside Avenue. Cockermouth Tel: 01900 828414.

CRAFT WORKERS.

Gild the Lily. Skylark Studio. 9, South Street.Cockermouth. Tel: 01900 823521.

E M Lee, 16, Harrot Hill, Cockermouth Tel: 01900 828761. Corn Dollies.

Mike Eye Cards, Riggs House, Routenbeck, Wythop, Cockermouth Tel: 017687 76458. Printed postcards.

Neville Mills.Jeweller. Scales Farm, Lorton, Cockermouth. Tel: 01900 85301.

Pipkin Puppets. Riverside Craft Studio. Cockermouth Tel: 01900 826417. Glove & String Puppets.

Nigel E A Scopes. Sunnyside. Blindcrake, Cockermouth. Tel: 01900 828628. Greetings cards.

Kathleen Usher, Highside Bungalow, Blindcrake. Cockermouth Tel: 01900 824055. Crochet.

The Woolly Workshop. The Fig Tree Craft Centre. 32, Market Place, Cockermouth Tel: 01900 822297. Knitting wools from Cumbrian Sheep.

CRUMMOCK WATER.

Crummock Water lies between Buttermere and Loweswater, near Keswick. This lake has depths in excess of 100'. The lake contains brown trout and some salmon and sea trout enter the lake when they come upriver to spawn. The perch are plentiful, and there are also a few pike. In the deeper water there are also char. 1st April to 31st October (salmon), 3rd April to 31st October (sea trout), 20th March to 14th September (brown trout) and 16th June to 14th March (coarse fish)

CYCLE SHOPS & HIRE.

Derwent Cycles. 4, Market Place. Cockermouth. Tel: 01900 822113.

COCKERMOUTH & AREA

DENTISTS.

MC Bell. St Helens Surgery. Market Place. Cockermouth Tel: 01900 826210.

Bird & Sanderson. Rudds Bank House. Windmill Lane. Cockermouth Tel: 01900 826905.

AJ & BL Rigby. 59, Kirkgate. Cockermouth. Tel: 01900 823467.

DOCTORS.

Drouet, Mason, Pearson & Eldred. Derwent House Surgery. Wakefield Road. Cockermouth Tel: 01900 822345.

Holloway, Lees, Dickson & Cowan, The Surgery, South Street, Cockermouth Tel: 01900 822393.

Townend & Taylor. 24, Fitz Road. Cockermouth. Tel: 01900 822790.

ESTATE AGENTS.

Cumberland Estate Agents. 2, Station Street, Cockermouth Tel: 01900 825900.
General Accident Property Services. 41, Main Street. Cockermouth Tel: 01900 826955.
Mitchells Lakeland Properties. 49, Station Road, Cockermouth Tel: 01900 827292.
Reeds Rains Estate Agents. 3, Station Street. Cockermouth Tel: 01900 825114.
Smeatons Estate Agents. 39, Station Street. Cockermouth. Tel: 01900 825918.

FISHING (Stocked Tarns)

Cogra Moss, Lamplugh, (Permits available in village)

FOOD.

Delicatessens.

Country Kitchen. 1a, Station Street, Cockermouth Tel: 01900 824247.
Number Seventeen. 17, Station Street. Cockermouth. Tel: 01900 822622.

Confectionery.

Sweets & Treats. 9, Main Street, Cockermouth. Tel: 01900 828390.

Bakers & Confectioners.

John Bryson, Tye House. Main Street, Cockermouth Tel: 01900 822114.
D Martin. 2, Market Place. Cockermouth. Tel: 01900 823400.
Rea's Bakers. 78, Main Street, Cockermouth. Tel: 01900 822012.

GARDENS.

National Gardens Scheme. Properties open all year upon request.

Greystones. Nr Cockermouth. Tel: 017687. 76375.
Palace How. Loweswater. Tel: 01900 85648.
Woodall. Nr Cockermouth. Tel: 01900 823585.

GARDEN CENTRES.
Firns, 4, Station Road. Cockermouth Tel: 01900 823123.
Oakhurst Garden Centre. Lamplugh Road. Cockermouth. Tel: 01900 822180.

GIFT SHOPS.
Lakeland Ceramics.. 6, Old Kings Arms Lane. Main Street. Cockermouth Tel: 01900 827296.
Panache Northam House. Main Street. Cockermouth. Tel: 01900 823549.

GOLF COURSES.
Cockermouth Golf Club. Tel: 017687. 76223.

GUEST HOUSES AND B&B
Albany House. Wordsworth Terrace. Windmill Lane. Cockermouth.Tel: 01900 822757.
Applegarth Tallentire. Nr Cockermouth Tel: 01900 827466.
Benson Court Cottage. 10, St Helens Street, Cockermouth. Tel: 01900 822303.
Birk Bank.Brandlingill. Nr Cockermouth. Tel: 01900 822326.
Briscoe Close Farm, Scales Moor, Lamplugh. Tel: 01946 861633
Brook Farm, Thackthwaite. Loweswater. Tel: 01900 85606.
Castlegate Guest House. 6, Castlegate Cockermouth Tel: 01900 826749.
Cornhow Farm. Loweswater.Cockermouth Tel: 01900 85200.
Crag End Farm, Rogerscale. Lorton Tel: 01900 85658.
Cragg Farm, Buttermere, Nr Cockermouth Tel: 017687 70204.
Croft House Guest House. 8, Challoner Street Cockermouth Tel: 01900 822532.
Dairy Farm, Greysouthen, Nr Cockermouth. Tel: 01900 825466.
Dalegarth.Buttermere.Nr Cockermouth Tel: 01900 017687.
Ellerbank Farm & Fishery. Brigham. Nr Cockermouth. Tel: 01900 825268.
Emoh Ruo, 2, Willow Lane. Cockermouth. Tel: 01900 822951.
Evening Hill House. Brigham Road, Cockermouth Tel: 01900 827980.
Friars Walk. Papcastle. Cockermouth Tel: 01900 823729.
Graythwaite. Loweswater, Nr Cockermouth. Tel: 01946 861555.
Highcroft Farm. Tallentire. Cockermouth Tel: 01900 822351.
High Stanger Farm, Cockermouth. Tel: 01900 823875.
Hope Farm, Lorton, Nr Cockermouth. Tel: 01900 85226.

COCKERMOUTH & AREA
Lime Tree House. Dovenby. Cockermouth. Tel: 01900 824923.
Low Hall Country Guest House. Brandlingill Cockermouth Tel: 01900 826654.
Manor House, 23, St Helens Street, Cockermouth Tel: 01900 822416.
Meadow Bank. High Lorton. Nr Cockermouth.Tel: 01900 85315.
New House Farm, Lorton, Nr Cockermouth. Tel: 01900 85404.
Old Coach House. Leagate Pardshaw Nr Cockermouth Tel: 01900 828082.
Old Vicarage. Lorton Road. Cockermouth Tel: 01900 828505.
The Old Vicarage. Church Lane, Lorton. Nr Cockermouth Tel: 01900 85656.
Pardshaw Hall. Pardshaw. Nr Cockermouth. Tel: 01900 822607.
Rose Cottage. Lorton Road. Cockermouth Tel: 01900 822189.
Stanger Farm, Cockermouth Tel: 01900 824222.
Sundawn.Carlisle Road, Bridekirk.Cockermouth. Tel: 01900 82238
Sunny Corner. Pardshaw. Nr Cockermouth. Tel: 01900 824015.
Terrace Farm, Lorton, Nr Cockermouth Tel: 01900 85278.
Winder Hall. Low Lorton. Cockermouth Tel: 01900 85107.

HILL TARNS
There are many hill tarns in the Lake District which offer free fishing for brown trout and perch. The trout tend to be small but the perch are often numerous and sometimes big.These hill tarns vary in size and depth, but they seldom exceed 15 acres in area. The fishing in these tarns is unlikely to be scintillating but anglers who appreciate solitude and wide open spaces will enjoy the challenge they offer. Thehill tarns have one thing in common, and that is they all require fell walking to reach them.
Ellerbeck Farm & Fishery. Brigham, Cockermouth Tel: 01900. 825268.

HOSPITALS & CLINICS.
Cockermouth Cottage Hospital. Isel Road. Cockermouth Tel: 01900 822226.
Dovenby Hall Hospital. Dovenby. Cockermouth Tel: 01900 823369.

HOTELS.
Allerdale Court Hotel. Market Square, Cockermouth. Tel: 01900 823654.
Bridge Hotel. Buttermere. Nr Cockermouth. Tel: 017687 70252.
Broughton Craggs Hotel. Cockermouth (see advert)
The Bush, Main Street,Cockermouth Tel: 01900 822064.
Globe Hotel. Main Street.Cockermouth.Tel: 01900 822126.Fax. 01900 823705.
The Grange Country House Hotel. Loweswater. Nr Cockermouth. Tel: 01946 861211.
Hundith Hill Hotel. Lorton Vale. Cockermouth Tel: 01900 822092.
Lakeland Sheep & Wool Centre. Egremont Road. Cockermouth.Tel: 01900 822673.
Lime Kiln Inn, Low Road. Brigham Cockermouth Tel: 01900 825375.

COCKERMOUTH & AREA

Link House. Bassenthwaite. Cockermouth Tel: 017687 76291.
Pheasant Inn, Bassenthwaite Lake, Cockermouth Tel: 017687 76898.
Ship Inn. 14, Market Place. Cockermouth Tel: 01900 823091.
Stork Hotel. Rowrah Road, Lamplugh Tel: 01946 861213.
Trout Hotel. Crown Street.Cockermouth. Tel: 01900 823591.
Winder Hall. Low Lorton. Tel: 01900 85107.
Wordsworth Hotel. Main Street.Cockermouth. Tel: 01900 822757.

INNS & PUBLIC HOUSES

Bitter End Brew Pub. 15, Kirkgate. Cockermouth. Tel: 01900. 828993.
Black Bull. 17, Main Street, Cockermouth Tel: 01900 824071.
Black Cock Inn, Eaglesfield. Cockermouth. Tel: 01900 822989.
Bowling Green Inn. St Hewlens Street Cockermouth Tel: 01900 826992.
Brown Cow Inn, 37, Main Street, Cockermouth Tel: 01900 823174.
Fox & Hounds Inn, Ennerdale Bridge, Lamplugh. Tel: 01946. 861373.
Kingfisher Inn Crown Street. Cockermouth Tel: 01900 823449.
Kirkstile Inn. Loweswater. Nr Cockermouth. Tel: 01900. 85219.
Lamplugh Tip Inn, Lamplugh Tel: 01946. 861232.
Lime Kiln Inn, Low Road, Brigham, Nr Cockermouth. Tel: 01900 825375.
Old Posting House, Deanscales. Cockermouth. Tel: 01900 823278.
Rizzo's Bar, South Street, Cockermouth Tel: 01900 824404.
Roundabout, Bellevue. Cockermouth Tel: 01900 823518.
Royal Yew Inn, Dean, Tel: 01946 861342.
Ship Inn, Dovenby, Cockermouth Tel: 01900 828097.
Sun Dial Inn. Little Broughton. Cockermouth Tel: 01900 825252.
Sun Inn, Arlecdon, Frizington. Lamplugh. Tel: 01946. 862011.
Tithebarn Hotel. 41, Station Street, Cockermouth Tel: 01900 822179.
Volunteer Inn, Main Street, Great Broughton, Cockermouth Tel: 01900 824547.
Wheatsheaf Inn, Low Road, Brigham.Cockermouth Tel: 01900 825411.
Wheatsheaf Inn. Low Lorton. Nr Cockermouth. Tel: 01900. 85268.

LEISURE CENTRES.

Cockermouth Sports Centre. Castlegate Drive. Cockermouth Tel: 01900 823596.

MOUNTAIN RESCUE.

Cockermouth Moutain Rescue Team. Mountain rescue in the Buttermere, Ennerdale, Lorton and Loweswater. Available 365 deay a year. 24 hours per day. Secretary. Steve Brailey. Tel: 01900 827916.

Travellers' Guide to Cumbria's Western Lakes & Coast

COCKERMOUTH & AREA

MUSEUMS.

Cumberland Toy & Model Museum. Banks Court. Market Place. Cockermouth. Tel: 01900 827606.

The Printing House Museum. 102, Main Street, Cockermouth Tel: 01900 824984.

William Creighton Mineral Museum. 2, Crown Street, Cockermouth Tel: 01900 828301.

MUSICAL INSTRUMENT & MUSIC SHOPS.

Billy Bowman Music. 5, Lowther Went. Cockermouth. Tel: 01900. 826708 (see advert)

NIGHT CLUBS & DISCOS.

Moota Hotel, Moota, Nr Cockermouth. Tel: 016973 20681.

POLICE.

Cockermouth. Tel: 01900 823212.

POST OFFICES.

Arlec don Post Office. Arlecdon Road, Lamplugh. Tel: 01696 861215
Cockermouth Post Office. 18, Main Street. Tel: 01900 822277.
Lamplugh Post Office. High Mill. Ghyll Head. Tel: 01946 861531.
Lorton Post Office. Tel: 01900 85220.
Sandwith Post Office. Aikbank Cottage. Tel: 01946 695771.

PUBLIC LIBRARIES.

Main Street, Cockermouth. Tel: 01900 822467.

PUBLIC PARKS.

Harris Park, Cockermouth.
Memorial Gardens. Cockermouth.

RESTAURANTS & CAFES

Beatfords Country Restaurant. 7, Lowther Went. Cockermouth Tel: 01900 827099.
The Cockatoo Restaurant. 16, Market Place. Cockermouth Tel: 01900 826205.
Fairfield Restaurant. Station Street, Cockermouth. Tel: 01900 822037.
Knights of India. 7, The Old Kings Arms Lane, Cockermouth.Tel: 01900 822526.
Over the Top. 36, Kirkgate. Cockermouth Tel: 01900 827016.
Pack Horse House Restaurant. 5, Main Street, Cockermouth.Tel: 01900 823146.

Poets Corner. Olde King Arms Lane, Main Street. Cockermouth Tel: 01900 828676.
Quince & Pedlar Restaurant. 12, Castlegate. CockermouthTel: 01900 823579.
Riverside Inn. 2, Main Street Cockermouth Tel: 01900 823871.
Strawberry Fayre. Strawberry How Business Centre. Cockermouth Tel: 01900 828100.
Taste of India. 4-5 Heqadford Court. Main Street. Cockermouth Tel: 01900 822880.
Wythop Mill, Embleton. Tel: 017687 76394.

SCHOOLS & COLLEGES.

All Saints Church of England School.Slatefell Drive. Cockermouth Tel: 01900 822195.
Bridekirk Dovenby School, Dovenby. Tel: 01900 822359.
Broughton Primary School. Moor Road. Great Broughton. Tel: 01900 825436.
Cockermouth School, Castlegate Drive. Tel: 01900 823300.
Dean Church of England School, Dean. Tel: 01946 861408.
Fairfield Infant School. Gallowbarrow. Cockermouth Tel: 01900 822428.
Fairfield Junior School. Gallowbarrow. Cockermouth Tel: 01900 822052.
Lamplugh School. Lamplugh. Tel: 01946 861386.
Lowca School. Lowca. Tel: 01946 692213.
St Joseph's Roman Catholic School. Mountain View. Cockermouth Tel: 01900 822093.

SELF CATERING ACCOMMODATION.

Gallery Mews Cottages. Randlehow.Sossgill Road, Mockerin. Tel: Lamplugh 861018.
Pardshaw Methodist Holiday Centre. Pardshaw, Cockermouth Tel: 01900 626696.

SPORTS CLUB & ASSOCIATIONS.

Highfield (Cockermouth) Sports & Social Club. Tel: 01900 824956.
Maryport Boys Club. Tel: 01900 813390.

Travellers' Guide to Cumbria's Western Lakes & Coast

COCKERMOUTH & AREA

SPORTS GROUNDS.
Cockermouth Rugby Union F.C. Laithwaite Low Road, Cockermouth Tel: 01900 824884.

SQUASH COURTS.
Cockermouth Squash Club. Highfield Road. Cockermouth. Tel: 01900 822985.

SWIMMING POOLS.
Cockermouth Swimming Pool. Tel: 01900 823596

TAXIS.
Brigham Taxis. 7, The Hill, Brigham. Cockermouth Tel: 01900 824428.
Cockermouth Taxi Co. 17, Grassmoor Avenue. Cockermouth Tel: 01900 826649.
Cooters Cabs Brick Works Garage, Broughton Moor. Tel:01900 814141.
DB Taxis. 40,South Terrace..Great Broughton. Cockermouth. Tel: 01900 816071.
G & J Taxis.39,Ghyll Bank,Little Broughton. Cockermouth Tel: 01900 826307.
T Kirkpatrick.& Sons, Sibson House. 36, Main Street Great Broughton. Cockermouth. Tel: 01900 825346.
Ken Routledge Travel. 1a, St Helens Road, Cockermouth. Tel: 01900 822795.

THEATRES.
Kirkgate Centre. Cockermouth Tel: 01900 826448. (see events, festivals)
Victoria Hall. Cockermouth. Tel: 01900 822634.

TOURIST INFORMATION.
Cumbria Tourist Board, Ashleigh, Holly Road, Windermere. Tel:015394. 44444.
Cum West Exhibition, Lakeland Sheep & Wool Centre, Egremont Road, Cockermouth.
Town Hall, Market Street, Cockermouth Cumbria. Tel: 01900.822634.
West Cumbria Tourism Initiative. 5, Lakeland Business Park, Lamplugh Road, Cockermouth. Tel: 01900 829990.

TRAVEL AGENTS
Cockermouth Travel. 60, Main Street. Cockermouth Tel: 01900 822308.
Going Places. 37, Station Street Cockermouth. Tel: 01900 826444.

YOUTH HOSTELS.
Cockermouth Youth Hostel. Double Mills. Cockermouth. Tel: 01900 822561.
West Cumbria Field Centre. Rowrah Hall. Lamplugh.Tel: 01946 861029.

CALENDAR OF EVENTS 1997

Abbeytown. 13th Annual Fund-Raising Road Race. 1st June. Info: 016973 31944.

Abbeytown. Strawberry Teas. 5th-6th June. Info: 016973 31944.

Abbey Town. Wheyrigg Hall. Every Saturday. Live Music–Country & Western. 016973 61242.

Allerdale Activity Week. 18th-21st August. A week of activities for children and families in and around Keswick and the Borrowdale Valley. Information: 015394 46601.

Appleby Agricultural Show. Barley Field, Appleby Golf Course, Appleby. 14th August. Cattle, horses, sheep, goats, poultry, vintage and industrial classes. Competitions for BSJA jumping. Trade stands, craft tent and ring events. Open 1800-1700. Mrs Collinson. 01931 714571.

Biggest Liar in the World Competition. Bridge Inn, Wasdale, Santon Bridge, Holmrook. 20th November. Set in the beautiful western Lake District, boasting England's deepest lake (Wastwater), highest peak (Scafell Pike) smallest church and of course the WORLD'S biggest liar. Lots of tall tales on the night, plus traditional 'tatie pot' supper. Starts 1930. Information Mrs Graham. Tel: 01946 67575.

Bike Ride. (National Park) The History of Ennerdale Valley. 4th August. 015394. 46601.

Bike Ride. (National Park) Dunnerdale Fells. 14th September. Information 015394 46601.

Blencogo Village Bonfire. 5th November.

Bootle Seashore Search. National Park. 7th July. Information 015394 46601.

Bootle Seashore Search. National Park. 4th August. Information 015394 46601.

Bootle Seashore Search. National Park. 18th August. Information 015394 46601.

Bootle Seashore Search. National Park 1st September. Information 015394 4660

Braithwaite. Church Hall. Every Tuesday. West Cumbrian Lacemakers. Info: 017687 74000.

Braithwaite Discovery Walk. 6th June.Information 015394 46601.

Braithwaite Discovery Walk. Discovering Newlands. 13th October. Information 015394 46601.

Broughton Carnival. (50th) 19th July.

Broughton in Furness .Childrens Carnival. 21st June. Mrs Leach. Tel: 01900 826322.

Broughton in Furness. Victory Hall. Antique & Collectors Fair. 26th January.

Victory Hall.	ditto.	23rd February.
Victory Hall.	ditto.	30th March.
Victory Hall.	ditto.	27th April.
Victory Hall.	ditto.	25th May.
Victory Hall.	ditto.	29th June
Victory Hall.	ditto.	27th July.
Victory Hall.	ditto.	31st August.
Victory Hall.	ditto.	28th September.
Victory Hall.	ditto.	26th October.
Victory Hall.	ditto.	30th November.
Victory Hall.	ditto.	28th December.

Broughton in Furness. Whitsuntide fair. The Square. 26th May. Information 01229 716115.

Broughton in Furness.Mountain Bike Races. Wilson Park. 22nd June. 01229 716582.

Travellers' Guide to Cumbria's Western Lakes & Coast

EVENTS

Broughton in Furness. Charter Festival. 1st August. Information Tel: 01229. 716115.

Broughton in Furness Discovery Walk. 10th June. Information 015394. 46601.

Broughton in Furness Discovery Walk. From iron age to stone age. 9th September 015394 46601.

Calderbridge. Stanley Arms. 'Christmas Party'! 22nd March.

Calderbridge. Stanley Arms. 'The Good Old Days' Evening. 11th April.

Cleator Moor Sports & Kinniside Fell Race. 19th July. Info: 01946 695678.

Cockermouth. Castlegate House. 'Poets from the Emerald Isle.' 7th March.

Cockermouth. Castlegate House. Art Exhibitions. March 10-April 2. 'Jagdish'..Works in papier machee by an internationally known sculptor from India. 01900 822149.

A Family Affair. April 7th-30th April. A collection of work by Eileen Naismith and family of four srtist daughters. Info: 01900 822149.

Eliza Andrewes...paintings. Tessa Waite...Painting...John Gooding... Pots. May 5th- June 4th. Info: 01900 822149.

Peter Colquitt. Paintings & sculpture, Jessica Overy Painting, and Robert Bailey. Paintings. June 9th to July 2nd. Info: 01900. 822149.

Birthday Exhibition. July 7th-September 3es. A very special exhibition to cele brate the Gallery's 10th Birthday. Works include Sheila Fell, Bill Peascod, Percy Kelly, Peter Prendegast, Julian Trevellyan, William Tillyer, Mary Fedden, Marj Bond, Charles Oakley, Len Tabner, Michael Bennett, Anne Redpath, and various gallery artists. Sculpture in the garden.

September 8th to October 8th. Enid Foote Watts..paintings, Douglas Davies, paintings and pots, Laurence Simon. Sculpture. 01900 822149.

October 13th to November 12th. Connie Simmers ..paintings, David Herrod... photographs...Rene Gunstone...drawings and sculpture. 01900 822149.

November 16th to December 24th. Christmas at the Gallery. small paintings, pots, glass jewellry. Info: 01900. 822149

Cockermouth Carnival 14th June. Memorial Gardens.

Cockermouth Cumbria Classic Caper & Canter. 21st June.

Cockermouth Christmas Lights 23rd November to 5th January. Grand Gala day followed by switch on of Christmas lights by a celebrity. Lights remain on until January 5th. Information from Mr Bertram. Tel: 01900 823608.

Cockermouth & District Agricultural Show. 2nd August.Cockermouth

Cockermouth The Kirkgate Centre. 'The Magic of the Middle East' talk with slides. 13th February. Info:01900 826448.

Cockermouth. Isel Hall. Mondays. 'House open this afternoon (Main holiday season only) Information 1900 822634.

Cockermouth. Kirkgate Centre. 'The Great Divorce'. 13th February. Info: 01900 826448.

Cockermouth. Kirkgate Centre. 'Sailor Beware'. 20th-22nd February. Info: 01900.826448.

Cockermouth. Kirkgate Centre. 'The New Riverside Jazz Band'. 23rd February 01900 826448.

Cockermouth. Kirkgate Centre'. Dancing with the Devil. 28th February. Info: 01900 826448.

Cockermouth. Kirkgate Centre. Six Foot three with Robert Harbron. 1st March. 01900 826448

Cockermouth. Kirkgate Centre. Alex Pascall O.B.E. 9th March. Info: 01900 826448.

Cockermouth. Kirkgate Centre. Allerdale Mayor's Fund Raising Cumberland Neet. 15th March. Info: 01900 826448.

EVENTS

Cockermouth. Kirkgate Centre. Wildlife Talk. Animals in Lakeland. 18th March.
Cockermouth. Kirkgate Centre. African Caribbean Steel Band. 22nd March.
Cockermouth. Kirkgate Centre. Elsie & Norm's Macbeth'. 26th March. Info: 01900 826448.
Cockermouth. Kirkgate Centre. Black Voices. Capella Singing Group. 29th March.
Cockermouth. Kirkgate Centre. Jamma Jazz. 30th March.
Cockermouth. Kirkgate Centre. Spring Loaded. 2nd April. Info: 01900 826448.
Cockermouth. Kirkgate Centre. Wildlife Trust. Reserve Management. 15th April.
Cockermouth. Kirkgate Centre. Old King Coal. 18th April Info: 01900. 826448.
Cockermouth. Kirkgate Centre. Art Exhibition. Karen Degett. 28th Dec to 25th January. Info: 01900 826448.
Cockermouth. Kirkgate Centre. Snap Theatre. Tom Jones. 29th April.
Cockermouth. Kirkgate Centre. Art Exhibition. Traditional art from Rajastan. 31st January to 15th February. Info: 01900 826448.
Cockermouth. Kirkgate Centre. Art Exhibition. African-Caribbean Art. 21-30th March Info: 01900 826448.
Cockermouth. Kirkgate Centre. Art Exhibition. Cumbria Schools Art Competition. April 8th to 12th. Info: 01900. 826448.
Cockermouth. Kirkgate Centre. Northern Sinfonia. Young Persons Concert. 10th May.
Cockermouth. Kirkgate Centre. Zenith Hot Stompers. 17th May.
Cockermouth. Kirkgate Centre. Quicksilver Childrens Theatre. 100 million footsteps.
Cockermouth Kirkgate Centre. The Cumberland Artists Exhibition. 24th-26th May.
Cockermouth Kirkgate Centre. Songs from 'Fiddlesticks'. 4th June.
Cockermouth Kirkgate Centre. Ballet Gwent-Midsummer Nights Dream. 25th June.
Cockermouth Kirkgate Centre. Ralph Meanly. Edwardian Ballads. 3rd October.
Cockermouth Festival..Cockermouth 1st-31st July. An annual festival of art, theatre, music, exhibitions,,demonstrations, childrens shows and story telling. Information from Mr A Bertram 01900 82360
Cockermouth Round Table Donkey Derby. 25th August.
Cockermouth. Mitchells Auctions. Every Sunday. Car Boot Sale. Info: 01768. 64405.
Cockermouth Auction Rooms. Fine Art Sale. 22nd May.
Cockermouth. Auction Rooms. Fine Art Sale. 31st July.
Cockermouth Auction Rooms. Fine Art Sale. 9th October.
Cockermouth Auction Rooms. Fine Art Sale. 11th December.
Cockermouth Sheepdog Trials. 17th May.

Travellers' Guide to Cumbria's Western Lakes & Coast

EVENTS

Cockermouth Malcolm Wilson Rally. 1st March Info: Tourist Information Centre.

Cockermouth U R C Hall. RSPB AGM & Birds of Iceland.

Cockermouth URC Church. Music Society. SIRINU Early Music. 15th cent. Xmas. 11th Dec.

Cockermouth. Christ Church. Music Society. Members Concert. 29th April.

Cockermouth Christ Church Harmonic Soc. Festival Concert. 5th July.

Cockermouth Christ Church. Music Society. 'Ilya Itin ..Piano. 30th September.

Cockermouth. Christ Church. Music.Society. Joanne Freeland Clarinet. 21st October.

Cockermouth. Friends Meeting House. West Cumbria Lacemakers. 10th May.

Cockermouth Friends Meeting House. West Cumbria Lacemakers. 12th July.

Cockermouth. Friends Meeting House. West Cumbria Lacemakers.13th September.

Cockermouth. Friends Meeting House. Civic Society. Land Mines Advisory Group. 1st October.

Cockermouth Friends Meeting House. Civic Soc. Life in a Rescue Centre'. 3rd November.

Cockermouth Friends Meeting House. West Cumbrian Lacemakers. 8th November.

Cockermouth Friends Meeting House. Civic Society. Wild Birds of Fells. 3rd December.

Cockermouth Sports Centre. 10 Mile Road Race. 27th September.

Cockermouth. Tithe Barn. Every Thursday. Cockermouth Folk Club. Info: 01900 604765.

Cockermouth. All Saints Rooms. Every Thursday. Scottish Country Dancing. 01900. 828046.

Cockermouth. Sale Rooms. Every Thursday. Sale of Household furniture/effects. 01900. 822016.

Cockermouth. Church Hall. Every Thursday. W I Market. Info: 01900. 822654.

Cockermouth. Wordsworth House. National Trust Morning. (Sale of Plants.)17th May.

Cockermouth. Trout Hotel. Midsummer barbeque. 28th June.

Cockermouth. Trout Hotel. Braujolais Evening. 21st November.

Cockermouth Show Field. Festival of Sport Fell Races. 5th September.

Cockermouth Town Centre. Firework Display. 9th November.

Copeland Event /Activity Week. Various locations in Copeland District. 4th-8th August. A pro gramme of activities/events including outdoor pursuits, crafts, wAlks, talks and arts. Information Miss Morris. Tel: 015394. 46601.

Country Field Day, Ponsonby

Cumbria Brass Band Association Annual Open Event. Whitehaven Civic Hall, Lowther Street, Whitehaven. 2nd November. Brass Band contest involving sections of graded bands from all over the North of England and Scotland performing a piece of their own choosing and a test piece. Open 1000-1830. Information Mr Rooms. Tel: 01946. 61955.

Cumbria Riding Club. Gosforth. One Day Event.20th April.

Cumbria Riding Club. Gosforth. Gymkhana. 8th June.

Cumbria Riding Club. Gosforth. Combined Training. 20th July.

Cumbria Riding Club. Gosforth. Hunter Trials. 5th October.

Cumbria & North Lancs Dance Festival. Workington. Mid February.

Curwen Fair Workington. Workington Hall, Curwen Park, Workington. 24th May. Arena events and entertainment for children and families. Craft stalls, miniature railway, chil drens fun fair. Information Mr Sherwin. Tel: 01900 602122.

Dearham. Cockermouth Brow. 28th June. Hound Trails. Info: 01900. 81228.

EVENTS

Dearham. Craika Farm. 29th June. Midsummer fair./Gymkhana/Sheep Dog Trials. 01900. 81228.
Derwentwater Discovery Walk. 8th July. Information 015394. 46601.
Distington. West Cumbria Vintage Steam Rally. & Gymkhana. 6th July. Info: 01946. 832790.

Drigg Local Nature Reserve Special Event. 28th May. Info: 015394. 46601.
Drigg Local Nature Reserve Special Event. 24th June. Information 015394. 46601.
Drigg Local Nature Reserve Special Event. 5th August. Information. 015394. 46601.
Egremont Crab Fair.& Sports. Baybarrow, Orgill, Egremont. 13th-20th September. A fair with both traditional and unusual sporting events and competition. Greasy pole, street racing, wrestling, track events, terrier racing, hound trails, pipe smoking contest, applecart parade, martial arts display, fell racing, and finishing with the world-renowned Gurning. competition. Starts 1000.
   Information Mr Clements. Tel: 01946 821554.
Egremont Fur & Feather Annual Show. 8th November, 
Egremont. Lowes Court Gallery: Info: 01946. 820693. January 13th- February 7th. Scene by Wheel. A competition exhibition of photographs and sketches from our local cycleways.
   February 10th to March 14th. 'Inspiration'. Batiks and photographs produced by local secondary school students as a result of Lowe's Court Tanzanian Artists Residency in Visual Arts Year 1996.
   March 17th to April 25th. Judy Evans. Paintings, papers and silkscreen prints.
   April 28th to May 30th. 'Back from Africa'. Batiks and photographs produced by Tanzanian artists, Estomih Kirita and Baltazar Elimika, during their visit to Cumbria in 1996, as well as paintings by Philbert Mlay, Richard Wood and Ian Hinde will also show work influenced by a rcent visit to Tanzania, as part of Lowes Court's Copeland-Kilimanjaro Artists Exchange.
   June 2nd to July 4th. Trevor Green & Roger Newberry. Paintings Iain Denniss. Pots.
   July 7th to August 8th. Alistair Fletcher...Drawings, etchings aquaprints & Graeme Hopper Ironwork.
   August 11th to September 12th. Eosemary Morison. Paintings & Philip Bradley.. Baskets.
   September 15th to October `7th. David Herrod...Black & White photographs & Danny Frost...Turned Wood.

Travellers' Guide to Cumbria's Western Lakes & Coast

EVENTS

October 20th to November 14th. Open Exhibition...An opportunity for local artists and makers to display and sell their work in the annual non-selective exhibition.

November 17th to Christmas Eve. Crafts for Christmas. A fine selection of gift ideas by invited local makers.

Egremont. Wyndham School. 14th March. SASRA Music. Cambridge Scholars. 01946 25269.

Wyndham School. West Cumbria Ramblers. Evening Walk. 8th July. 01946 67121.

Wyndham School. SASRA Music. Sirimi. 12th december. Info: 01946. 25269.

Chapel Cross. West Cumbria Ramblers Evening Walk. 22nd July. Info: 01946. 67121.

Egremont. Egremont Cemetery. Ramblers . 24th June. Info: 01946. 67121.

Eskdale Fete. Outward Bound Mountain School. Eskdale. Holmrook. 24th August. A family day out with canoeing on the tarn, pony rides, climbing, zip wire, bouncy castles and children's corner, brass and folk bands, stalls, displays and sideshows. Open 12.30 to 1700 Information Mr Hall Tel: 019467 23319

Eskdale 'Tup' Show. 26th September.

Eskdale Show. Brotherilkeld Farm, Hardknott Pass, Boot, Eskdale. 27th September. Small country show in the beautiful Eskdale Valley with classes for Herdwick Sheep, foxhounds and terriers. With hound trails, local handicrafts, childrens sport events and fell races. Open 1000-1800. Information Miss Porter. Tel: 019467. 23269.

Eskdale Discovery Walk. The Trust and the Park. 5th August. Information 015394. 46601.

Eskdale. Guided Walk. The story of Eskdale. August 5th. Info: 01229. 716552.

Eskdale & Ennerdale Foxhounds Puppy Show. 13th September.

Firework Display. Memorial Gardens, Cockermouth. 9th November Spectacular firework display. Starts 1900. Information Mr Bentham Tel: 01900 823608.

Fletchertown. All Hallows Centre. 10th & 19th April. Major Road. 'Old King Coal'. Info: 01900 822314.

Flimby Carnival. 5th July. Info: 01900. 813738.Gosforth. Methodist Hall. 9th April. CWT 'Entomology'. Info: 019467. 28250.

Gosforth. Public Hall. 24th April. Embroider's Guild. Lectures. 'Her Majesty's Heralds. Info: 019467. 28764.

Gosforth Agricultural Show. The Showfield, Gosforth, Seascale. 20th August. Rural agricultural show with classes for cattle, sheep, goats, horses and ponies, horticulture, handicrafts, produce and vintage machinery. Featuring numerous trade stands selling a wide variety of goods and a rural craft display. Opens 0830. Information Mr Stewart. 019467 24652

EVENTS

Haverigg. 6th July. Raft Race. Info: 01946. 695678.

Irton Field Day. 3rd August. Craft Demonstrations, Vintage Machinery, Childrens Attractions Info: 01946. 820693. (Egremont T I C.)

Lamplugh. Inglenook Caravan Park. LDNP Talk Mountain Rescue. 'A Man in Lakeland. 28th March. & 4th May, 26th May, 25th August. Info: 015394. 46601.

Little Theatre Dance Festival. Workington. 2nd to 5th April.

Lorton. Church 5th April Concert. Trios, duets, & solos. Info: 01900. 85648.

Lorton Cass Howe. Sheepdog Trials & Hound Show. 26th July. Info: 01900. 85233.

Loweswater. Village Hall.10th May. Nuts in May Fell Race.Tel: 01900. 823961.

Loweswater. Village Hall. Cream teas.'Hospice at Home'. 8th June. Info: 01900. 85648.

Loweswater & Brackenthwaite Agricultural Society Annual Show. School Field, Loweswater. 18th September. Annual country show of livestock and poultry sections, sheepdog and hound trails. Includes industrial tent and craft fair.

Lowick & District Agricultural Show. 6th September Info; 01229. 587120.

Maryport. Senhouse Roman Museum. 25th March. Lecture..Cumbrian Industry.

Maryport Senhouse Roman Museum. 1st, 8th, 15th 22nd & 29th April. Lecture. Cumbrian Industry.

Maryport. Elizabeth Docks. The Blessing of the Boats. 4th May.

Maryport. Civic Hall. Queen of the Solway Dance Festival. 5th-10th May.

Maryport. Our Lady/St Patricks Church. 17th May. The Landolfi Ensemble.

Maryport & District Carnival. 12th July. Information: 01900. 813738.

Maryport & District Sea Anglers Club. 25th May. & 19th October.

Maryport. Civic Hall. Carols by Candlelight. 15th December. Info: 01900. 828097.

Maryport .Music Festival. All Souls Church. 20th-22nd June.

Maryport. The Netherhall Arts & Crafts Exhibition, McCarron Hall. Netherhall School. 3rd-5th May.

Melbreak Hunt Show .Lorton. 26th July.

Melmerby May Day. 10th May.

Midsummer Barbecue & Jazz Evening. Trout Hotel, Crown Street Cockermouth 28th June. An evening of jazz music provided by 'River City Jazz Band' in a marquee seating about 120 people on the hotel lawns. Information Ms G Blackah Tel: 01900 823591.

Millom & Broughton Agricultural Show. West Park, Broughton in Furness. 30th August. Agricultural show including horses, cattle, sheep, village industries, Cumberland and Westmorland wrestling and dog show. Open 0900 to 1800. Information Mr Maddock. Tel: 01229 772556.

Millom. Carnival. 12th July. Info: 01946 695678.

Millom Palladium. 14th February. County Rock Dance ,featuring The Fabulous Picasso Brothers Band. Info: 01229. 774733.

Millom Palladium. 8th March. 40's Dance & Cabaret evening. Info: 01229. 774733.

Millom Palladium. 3rd May. MAOS presents 'Oliver' by Lionel Bart. Info: 01229. 774733.

Millom Palladium. July (date to be announced in the local press. Les Bull's Festival Jazz Band.

Travellers' Guide to Cumbria's Western Lakes & Coast

EVENTS

Info: 01229. 774733.

Moresby. Rosehill Theatre. 8th February. Norma Winstone & Trio. Info: 01946 692422.

20th Feb & 21st Feb. Magic ...A Tribute to Freddie Mercury & Queen. 01946 692422

25th February. Lindisfarne. Info: 01946 692422.

28th February. 'It's a Grand Night for Singing'. Info: 01946 692422

2nd March. Geraldine McEwan's Jane Austen. Info: 01946 692422.

15th March. Camerata Roman. 15 piece orchestra. Info: 01946 692422.

17th & 18th March. 'The Owl who was afraid of the Dark. Info: 01946 692422.

20th March. The Lakeland Alphabet. A tape-slide presentation. Info: 01946 692422.

22nd March China Crisis. Hite band. Info: 01946 692422.

23rd March. Davey Arthur & Co. Hit band Info: 01946 692422

26th March. Brass Monkey. folk music. Info: 01946 692422.

4th April- 9th April (Not Sunday) 'Half A Sixpence'. Musical. Info: 01946 692422.

12th April. Ivan Drever & Duncan Chisholm. Scottish folk rock band. 01946 692422

21st April. The Wolves. Michael Punter's new play. Info: 01946 692422.

23rd April Patrick Street. Irish folk band. Info: 01946 692422.

26th April. Manchester Boys Choir. One of the finest childrens choirs in the world. Info. 01946. 692422.

'Art in the Foyer Gallery'. 1st February to 15th March. Keith McMean. Lakeland watercolours. Info: 01946. 692422.

'Art in the Foyer Gallery'. 17th March to 26th April. Tim Wood

'More of similar' or 'continuing to paint interesting buildings wherever I find them'. Further attractions throughout the year Tel: 01946. 692422 for latest information.

Mountain Rescue Open Evening. 28th March (Behind the scenes) Lamplugh. 015394 46601.

Mountain Rescue Open Evening. 1st April. Cockermouth. Info: 015394. 46601.

Mountain Rescue Open Evening. 10th April 'The History of Mountain Rescue'. Seatoller. Info: 015394 46601.

Mountain Rescue Open Evening 4th May. 'Mountain Rescue behind the scenes" Lamplugh. Info: 015394. 46601.

Mountain Rescue Open Evening. 26th May. Lamplugh Info: 015394 46601.

Mountain Rescue Open Evening. 27th May. Cockermouth. Info: 015394. 46601.

Mountain Rescue Open Evening. 29th May. The History of Mountain Rescue. Seatoller Info: 015394 46601.

Mountain Rescue Open Evening. 24th July. Mountain Rescue behind the scenes. Buttermere. Info: 015394 46601.

Mountain Rescue Open Evening. 29th July Cockermouth. Info: 015394 46601.

Mountain Rescue Open Evening. 31st July. 'Mountain Rescue behind the scenes. Buttermere.Info: 015394 46601

Mountain Rescue Open Evening. 7th August. Buttermere. Info: 015394.46601.

Mountain Rescue Open Evening. 12th August. Cockermouth. Info: 015394 46601.

Mountain Rescue Open Evening. 14th August. Buttermere. Info: 015394 46601.

Mountain Rescue Open Evening. 21st August. Mountain Rescue behind the scenes.

EVENTS

Buttermere.Info: 015394 46601.

Mountain Rescue Open Evening. 25th August. Mountain Rescue behind the scenes. Lamplugh. Info: 015394 46601

Mountain Rescue Open Evening. 28th August. Buttermere. Info: 015394. 46601.

Mountain Rescue Open Evening. 10th September. The History of Mountain Rescue. Seatoller. Info: 015394 46601.

Mountain Rescue Open Evening. 19th September. Sea & Mountain Rescue Course. Info: 015394 46601.

Mountain Rescue Open Evening. 28th October. Cockermouth. Info: 015394 46601.

Muncaster Castle. Ravenglass. Re-enactment of life in the 15th Century.3-5th May. Info: 01229 717614.

Muncaster Castle. Ravenglass. Muncaster 'Luck' Fell Race. 1st June. Info: 01229. 717614.

Muncaster Castle. Ravenglass. World Owl Trust 25 years Anniversary Celebrations. 20th July. Information: 01229. 717614.

Muncaster Castle. Ravenglass. Open Field Archery Competition. 23-24th August. Info: 01229 717614

Muncaster Castle. Ravenglass. Model & Family Fun weekend. 30-31st August. Info: 01229.717614.

Muncaster Country Fair& Sheepdog Trials. Muncaster, Ravenglass. 25th August. Sheepdog trials, archery, fly casting, dog show, sheep and goat show, sports, various trade stands, flower show. Rural craft tent. Cumberland & Westmorland wrestling, gundog, and falcony display. gundog scurry and poultry show. Open 0930 to 1800. Information Mr Smith Tel: 01229. 717608.

Nether Wasdale. Screes Hotel. 23rd April. Middlefell Fell Race. Info: 019467. 26262.

Nether Wasdale. Screes Hotel. 25th October. Info: 019467. 26262.

Pilgrimage..Cleator

Queen of the Solway Dance Festivals. Maryport. Whit week.Ravenglass & Eskdale Railway.
    'Northern Rock' 21st Birthday Celebrations. 3-5th May. Information: 01229. 717171.

Ravenglass & Eskdale Railway. Family Fun Day. 24th May.

Ravenglass & Eskdale Railway. Friends of Thomas the Tank Engine weekend. 18-19th October. Information : 01229.717171.

Ravenglass Charter Fair. Main Street ,Ravenglass. 15th June. Attractions include Barrow ACF Corps of Drums .Belfagan Ladies Morris, childrens fancy dress and best dressed bicycle, Cumberland Wrestling, Egremont Town Band, Fairly Famous Family, magic show, traction engines, vintage vehicles, water sports and West Lakes Dog training. Open 1100 to 1600 Information Mr Hallett. Tel: 01229 717373.

Ravenglass .Evening stroll by the Estuary. May 5th. Info: 015394 46601.
    May 12th. ditto
    May 19th ditto.

Travellers' Guide to Cumbria's Western Lakes & Coast

EVENTS

May 26th ditto.
June 2nd. ditto.
June 9th ditto
June 16th ditto.
June 23rd ditto.

Ravenglass. Muncaster Castle. Every Thursday. 'Dabble with Scrabble'. Info: 019467. 28329

Ravenglass. Muncaster Castle. Re-Enactment of Life in the 15th Century.

Rosley. Pentabus T.C. 'Dancing with the Devil'. The Village Hall 1st March. Info: Allerdale B.C.

Rowrah. (Between Cockermouth and Egremont) Kart Racing.

8th February.
9th March
6th April.
13th April.
11th May.
8th June.
13th July.
24th August.
25th August.
12th October.
9th November.
14th December.

Santon Bridge. Bridge Inn. 20th November. Biggest Liar in the World Competition. Info: 01946. 67575.

Sawrey Sheepdog Trials. Esthwaite How. Near Sawrey. 24th August. Competition trials display ing the skills involved in traditional sheepdog work. Starts 0900. Information Mr Mallett. Tel: 015394. 36450.

Sea & Mountain Rescue weekend. Buttermere Youth Hostel. Buttermere. Cockermouth. 19-21st September. Find out more about the amazing work of the local rescue services and the services they provide in the Lake District. Information Miss Morris. 015394 46601.

Seascale. Methodist Hall. Embroider's Guild..Tassel.s 24th March. Info: 019467. 28764.

Seascale. Methodist Hall. Embroider's Guild. Perforated Paper. 21st April.

Seascale. Methodist Hall. Embroider's Guild. Folip. 19th May.

Seascale Methodist Hall. Embroider's Guild. Stump Work. 16th June.

Seascale. Methodist Hall. Embroider's Guild. Ruskin Lace. 21st July.

Seascale. Methodist Hall. Embroiders' Guild Fans. 12th September.

Seascale. Methodist Hall. Embroider's Guild. Workshop. 13th September.

Seascale. Methodist hall. Embroider's Guild. AGM & Talk. ' One thing leads to another'

Seascale. Methodist Hall. Embroider's Guild. Gold Work. 17th November.

Seascale. Methodist Hall. Embroider's Guild. Christmas Ideas. 15th December.Silloth. Christ Church Hall. Butterfly Coffee Morning & Stalls. 29th march Info: 016973. 31944.

Silloth 1st June. North West Sea Angling Leaque Annual Silloth Open Championship. Info: 016973. 31944.

Silloth Celebrates World Ocean Day 8th June. Info: 016973. 31944.

Silloth. Christ Church. 13th June. Silloth Ladies Choir Concert. Info: 016973. 31944.

Silloth. Christ Church. 22nd June. Guided Church Tour. Info: 016973. 31944.

Silloth. OAP Hut. 6th July. Strawberry Teas. Info: 016973. 31944.

Silloth. 16th July. Seashell Safari. Guided Walk.

Silloth 16th July. Birds on the Sand Dunes. Guided Walk.

Silloth. Christ Church. 18th-20th July. Flower Festival Weekend. Info: 016973. 31944.

Silloth. 22nd July. Roman Defences. Guided Walk.

Silloth. 23rd July. Birds & Nature Guided Walk.

Silloth. 30th July. Birds on the Grune. Guided Walk.

Silloth 30th July. Seashell Safari. Guided Walk.

Silloth. 2nd August. OAP Hut. Annual Tea & Sale of work. Info: 016973. 31944.

Silloth. 3rd August. Church Tour St Pauls.

Silloth Cycle Sports Day (National Trust.) 3rd August. Info: 016973. 31944.

Silloth. 5th August. Discovering Romans Guided Walk.

Silloth. 6th August. Birds of the Solway. Guided Walk.

Silloth. Community Centre. 7th August. Slide & Ride with the British Trust for Conservation Volunteers Info: 016973. 31295.

Silloth. Christ Church Hall. 8th-10th August. Picture & Craft Display. Info: 016973. 31413.

Silloth. Silloth Docks. 9th August. Silloth Annual Trawler Race. Info: 016973. 31944.

Silloth. 13th August. Seashell Safari Guided Walk..

Silloth. 13th August. Birds on the Sand Dunes Guided Walk. .

Silloth. 20th August. Birds & Nature Guided Walk.

Silloth. Golf Club. 20th-22nd August. Ladies National Championshios. Info: 016973. 31304.

Travellers' Guide to Cumbria's Western Lakes & Coast

EVENTS

Silloth. Convalescent Home Summer Sale. 23rd August. Info: 016973. 31944

Silloth. The Green. Silloth Carnival. 25th August. Info: 016973. 31944.

Silloth. 27th August. Birds Around Moricambe Bay Guided Walk..

Silloth. 2nd September. Romans on the Solway. Guided Walk.

Silloth. 3rd September Birds & Nature Guided Walk.

Silloth. 10th September. Birds on the Grune Guided Walk.

Silloth. 17th September. Birds on the Sea Shore Guided Walk.

Silloth. 24th September. Birds on the Sea Shore Guided Walk..

Silloth Annual Trawler Race. Silloth Dock, New Dock, Silloth. 9th August. Local fishing boats, sponsored by local businesses and club race around a marked course off Silloth sea front. Boats and crews are judged in Silloth Dock prior to the race, for the best dressed. Starts 1500. Information Tourist Information Centre. Tel: 016973. 31944.

Silloth Carnival. Silloth Green, Criffel Street, Silloth. 25th August. Carnival procession through streets of Silloth with floats and fancy dress. Other attractions include sideshows, stalls and the crowning of the Carnival Queen on the village green. Cumberland and Westmorland wrestling. Starts 1100. Information Mr Marshall. Tel: 016973 31257.

Silloth Victorian Weekend. 21st-22nd June.

St Bees. Management Centre. Art Society. Paul Gaugin. 19th March

St Bees Management Centre. Art Society. Hidden Treasures of China'. 21st May.

St Bees. Priory. Christopher Herrick Recital. 15th July.

St Bees. Priory. James Vivian. Organ Recital. 26th August.

St Bees. Priory. Neil Cockburn. Organ. 16th September.

Tallentire.. The Bush Inn. 6th April. The Tallentire Olympics. Info: 01900 822634.

Uldale Shepherds Meet. 1st December.

Uldale Village Show. 13th-14th September.

Urswick Flower & Vegetable Show. Recreational hall. 27th September. Information Mrs Hornsby. Tel: 01229 463837.

Urswick Rushbearing. Urswick Church. Church Road, Urswick, Ulverston. 28th September. Colourful procession of Rush Queen and children decorated with garlands of flowers and carrying rushes later to be strewn on the church floor. Bunches of flowers are then placed on the grave of someone forgotton in a touching moment of this traditional ceremony. Followed by service at St Mary and St Michael Parish Church. Starts 1300.

Information Tourist Information Centre. Tel: 01229 587120

Vale of Lorton Sheepdog Trials. Lorton.19th July. \

Wasdale Head. Camp Site. 27th September. Scafell Pike Fell Race. Info: 019467 24263.

Wasdale Head Show. Wasdale Head. Seascale. 11th October. Show of Herdwick sheep and sheep dogs. Supported by hound trails, fell races, children's sports, Cumberland and Westmorland wrestling, terrier show, walling competition and other attractions of Cumberland origin and character. Information MrSmith. Tel: 019467 25340.

Wasdale Head Discovery Walk. (Smugglers Tales) 4th June. Information: 015394 46601.

Wasdale Head Discovery Walk. Smugglers Tales & Packhorse Trails. 25th July. Info 015394 46601.

Wasdale Head Discovery Walk. Smugglers Tales & Packhorse Trails. 2nd November. Info: 015394 46601.

West Cumbria Vintage Club Machinery Rally and Gymkhana. Hayes Castle Farm, Hayes Castle Road, Distington, Workington. 6th July. Rally displaying all types of machinery, vintage steam engines and organs, and vehicles from cars to tractors. Gymkhana runs all day. Open 1100 to 1800. Information Mr Bennett. Tel: 01946 832790.

West Cumbria Rose Society Show. Egremont. Week commencing 14th July.

Whitehaven.The Beacon. Exhibitions. Information : 01946 695678.

    Percy Kelly 1918-1993. 28th March to 27th June.

    Events for Museums Week. 17th-25th May.

    Bursting Stone, Ingrid Pollard. 1st July to 8th August.

    William Pit. Commemorating 50th Anniversary. 12th August to 5th September.

    Royal Photographic Society Creative Group Members Exhibition. 1997. 7th Sept to 12th October.

    Shepherds Well Pottery. 15th October to 30th November.

    December. Crafts for Christmas.

Whitehaven Civic Hall. Theatre Group 'Pajama Game' 5th-10th May.Info: 01946 63452.

    Whitehaven Male Voice Choir. 21st June.

    Cumbria Brass Ban Competition. Annual Open Contest. 2nd Nov.

Whitehaven.St James. West Cumbria Orchestra. Hugh Turpin. 28th June.

Whitehaven. Masonic Hall. Rambling Club. Talk. Mountain memories. 19th March.

    Masonic Hall. Rambling Club. Talk. 'Cumbrian Heritage'. 26th March.

Whitehaven.Rosehill Theatre. Exhibitions. Info: 01946 692422.

    Keith McLean. Lakeland Watercolours. 1st Feb to 16th March.

    Classical Music. Camerata Roman. 15th March.

    Tim Wood. Buildings in Acrylic. 17th March to 26th April.

    'The Owl who was afraid of the dark'. 17th & 18th March.

    Talk "Lakeland Aplhabet'. 20th March.

    China Crisis. Band. 22nd March.

    Irish Folk. Davey Arthur & Co. 23rd March.

    Folk Music. Brass Monkey. 28th March.

    'Half a Sixpence' April 4th-7th.

    Ivan Drever & Duncan Chisholm. Wolfstone. April 12th.

EVENTS

    The Wolves. Plaines Plough. 21st April.

    Patrick Street. 23rd April.

    Classical Music. Manchester Boys Choir. 26th April.

    Classical Music. Evelyn Glennie. 31st May.

    Classical Music. Nettle & Markham Pianos. 28th June.

Whitehaven. Rosehill. Every Wednesday. Film Matinee. Info: 01946 692422.

Whitehaven. URC Church. Wildlife Trust. 'Basker Makers Day'. 21st March.

Whitehaven. Y.M.C.A. Every Thursday. W I Market. Info: 01228 21774.

Whitehaven Carnival & Gala Fair. Civic Hall, Lowther Street Whitehaven. 5th July. Carnival parade, fun day in the park, sideshows, entertainments for children. Starts 1100. Informatiomn Mr Kelly. Tel: 01946 65202

Malcolm Wilson Rally. Main Street Cockermouth. 1st March. Car rally orgainsed jointly by West Cumbria Motorsports Club, Kirby Lonsdale Motor Club, and Morecambe Motor Club. Open 0900 to 1630 Information Mr Kenyon Tel: 01900 826604.

Windermere National Park Cruise. 4th August. Information 015394 46601.

Wordsworth House. Cockermouth. William Wordsworth Birthday. April 7th Poetry readings, music, birthday cake. National Trust event. Info 015394 35599.

    Trusty the hedgehog. Childrens afternoon events and activities with the National Trust's cuddly character. 28th may. National Trust event. Info: 015394. 35599.

    Summer Flower Festival. June 23-June 28. National Trust event. 015394 35599.

    Craft Demonstration. Throughout July. National Trust Event.

    The Wordsworth's at home. Aug 5th to Aug 7th. family sketch afternoons. National Trust event. Info. 015394 35599.

Workington. The Forum. Every Thursday & Saturday. Live Entertainment. Info: 01900 604544.

Workington Lonsdale Park. Every Saturday. Greyhound Racing. Info: 01900 602464.

Workington. Monroes. Every Friday. & Saturdays. Live Music. Info: 01900 602122.

Workington. New Westlands. Every Saturday. Live entertainment & dancing. 01900 604544.

Workington. Helena Thompson Museum. Spectacles in the 3rd World. 18th & 29th March.

Workington. Helena Thompson Museum. Local History. 'The Music Hall'. 2nd April.

Workington. Helena Thompson Museum. 7th April to 10th May. Workington Embroidery Group. Exhibition of textiles..

Workington. Helena Thompson Museum. 15th April. Paradise Island..Pocklington's Pleasure.

Workington. The Helena Thompson Museum. 7th May. Local History. 'Mountain Rescue'.

Workington. The Helena Thompson Museum. 20th May. Outing to Mellerstein.

Workington. The Helena Thompson Museum. 17th June. Carlisle at War..

Workington. The Helena Thompson Museum. 15th July. The Medieval Knight, His Life, Arms, Heraldry, & Chivalry.

Workington. The Helena Thompson Museum. 3rd Sept. Local History. Cross Canonby.

Workington. The Helena Thompson Museum. 16th September. Ladies of the Lakes, from St Bega to Beatrix.

Workington. The Helena Thompson Museum. 7th October. Local History. The Hapsbergs.

Workington. The Helena Thompson Museum. 5th November. Local History. 'Maryport harbour; Info: 01900 603517.

EVENTS

Workington. The Helena Thompson Museum. 3rd December. Local History. Christmas Event.

Workington. Day Centre. 26th March. Allerdale Model Railway Club. Info: 01900.64104.

Workington Christmas Lights. Switched on 7th December.

Workington Music Festival. October.

Workington. Carnegie Theatre & Arts Centre. European Ballet. 'Coppelia'. 30th March.

Workington. Carnegie Theatre & Arts Centre. Dance Festival. 5th-10th April.

Workington. Carnegie Theatre & Arts Centre. Sue Cunningham. Clairvoyant. 30th April.

Workington. Carnegie Theatre & Arts Centre. Tredegar Orpheus Male Voice Choir & Roslyn Singers. 4th May.

Workington. Carnegie Theatre & Arts Centre.. 16th-18th May. Keswick Jazz Festival. Info: 01900 602122.

Workington. Carnegie Theatre & Arts Centre. 19th-24th May. Annie Warbucks.

Workington. Carnegie Theatre & Arts Centre. 6th-11th Sept. 'Singing in the Rain.

Workington. Carnegie Theatre & Arts Centre. 21st November. 'Ga-Ga' Tribute to Queen.

Workington Carnegie Theatre & Arts Centre. 30th November. Raymond Froggatt.

Workington. Curwen Hall. Curwen Fair. Pageant & Country Fair. 24th May.

Workington. Theatre Royal. Playgoers 'Shadowlands'. 19th-25th March Info: 01900 603161.

Workington. Theatre Royal. Playgoers 'Ladies in Retirement'. 7th-13th May.

Workington. Trinity Methodist Church. The Carnegie Singers Carol Concert. 20th Dec.

Workington. Trinity Methodist Church. Carnegie Singers Annual Concert. 17th May.

Workington. Trinity Methodist Church. Carnegie Singers. Xmas

EVENTS
Music. 20th December.
Workington Town Firework Display. 9th November.
Workington. Trinity Methodist Church. The Carnegie Singers Annual Concert. 17th May.

196   *Travellers' Guide to Cumbria's Western Lakes & Coast*

ADVERTISERS ANNOUNCEMENTS

The Printing House Museum. Cockermouth.

The Working Museum of Printing is set in a building which dates back to the 16th Century. On display is a varied and interesting range of historical presses and equipment, the earliest, a Cogger press dated 1820.

The range of presses includes an Imperial press, two Colombians, two Albions, a Jones press, Cropper Minerva, an Arab, Heidleberg and Wharfedale. There is also a hot metal section with Linotype and Monotype. Visitors are offered the opportunity to gain 'hands on' experience by using some of the presses displayed, to produce cards or keepsakes. The Museum aims to cater for many tastes, the large varied and ever changing displays will appeal to both the young and old alike. Open Monday to Saturday 10. 11am to 4. 00pm. Admission charge.

St Bees School. St Bees.

St Bees School was founded in 1583 and occupies an extensive site in the village of St Bees. It is fully co-educational and has around 300 students aged 11-18 years, a high proportion of whom are boarders.

In addition to its historic buildings, St Bees has excellent modern teaching facilities. Languages and Information Technology are particularly well catered for in the Business Management Centre, which is available for use by students at the International Centre.

Opportunities exist to take part in almost all sports, team and individual. There is a heated indoor swimming pool, a sports hall, squash courts and the schools own golf course overlooks the sea. St Bees has welcomed overseas students for many years. Some of those attending the International Centre may choose to return home at the end of their course while others may use it as a preparation for further study in the United Kingdom.

The St Bees International Centre provides tuition in English so that students can enter the next stage of their education with confidence. All abilities can be catered for. Courses are intensive, but enjoyable and varied, and. at all times, relevant to each student's needs. Tuition is carried out both individually and in small groups using modern, purpose-built facilities. All teachers are experienced and fully qualified. The excellent teaching in the centre ensures that rapid progress is made. Students normally leave St Bees International Centre with qualifications which are internationally recognised, and appropriate to their individual requirements. St Bees is an accredited centre for the University of Oxford examinations in English as a Foreign Language, at all levels from Elementary to Advanced

The International Centre is part of St Bees School, one of the longest established and most successful schools in the north of England.

The St Bees Management Centre........... This was opened by H. R H. The Prince of Wales in 1993 and represents a unique initiative, linking the school with the educational needs of commerce and industry. The latest facilities for information technology and modern language teaching in the school are closely associated with a conference and management training centre for the business community.

Admission to the school is usually at the ages of 11, 13 and 16 and the Headmaster is always pleased to welcome parents who wish to visit St Bees and see the school in action. Scholarships are available for Academic Distinction, Music and Art. The school also offers Bursaries, Sixth Form Sports Bursaries and Government Assisted Places.

ADVERTISERS ANNOUNCEMENTS

Ulpha Post Office.

Ulpha Post Office and Craft Shop is situated in the Duddon Valley with its stunning fell scenery and easily accessible River Duddon.

Here you'll not only find one of the smallest Post Office and general stores, but also an original craft shop featuring local artists and craftspeople. A variety of wooden items from pine kitchen furniture and bookcases to letter racks are made in those premises.

The Stables. Bootle. Nr Millom.

The Stables at Bootle is a pleasant modern conversion of a former coach-house and stables for the neighbouring Cross House. The guest bedrooms are situated in the former hayloft, the double room has a full en-suite bathroom whilst the twin room has a bathroom next door. The views from these rooms are superb, the wide sweep of Corney Fell to the rear of the property and the impressive Black Combe to the south. Both rooms are comfortably furnished with duvets on the beds. Guests have the use of their own dining room and TV lounge, the dining room is in the former groom's room and retains old tack hooks and a former gun cupboard.

The gardens surrounding the house are particularly pretty, being bordered on two sides by rivers- to the south runs the fast and stony Kinmont Beck and to the west the River Annas a more gentle stream. We have extensive lawns and patio areas for relaxing or perhaps enjoying a cup of tea after a strenuous day out.

There is plenty to do in the area. Ther are many varied walks either from the house or within a short drive. The sea is only two miles away. The village of Bootle is quiet and pretty, and from Bootle station one may catch local trains to Millom and Barrow to the south or up the coast towards Whitehaven and eventually Carlisle. By car (5 miles) the visitor may travel up the coast to visit Muncaster Castle and Gardens (with owls), a little further north is the attractive estuary village of Ravenglass with quaint houses and the 'La'al Ratty' steam railway and further on again are Windscale and Sellafield with its fascinating visitor centre. Inland there is all the beauty of the Lake District's fells, valleys and lakes, from the wild rugged Wast Water to the beauty of the Dudden Valley, Coniston and Windermere.

A day's itinerary could start by waking up to views of the sun rising over Black Combe and sounds of Kinmont Beck rushing by your window. After a full English breakfast, a five mile drive brings you to Muncaster Castle, view the Pele Tower, take the free 'Walkman' tour, visit the 77 acres of gardens, a riot of colour in spring and early summer and then visit the Owl Centre to see owls ranging from the tiny Pygmy Owls to gigantic Eagle Owls. From here the enthusiast can drive another two miles to Ravenglass and take the spectacular 15 inch gauge steam railway up the River Mite Valley and on through Irton Road Station and The Green Station terminating at Eskdale (Dalegarth) Station. From these village stations numerous exploratory walks along Miterdale or the lovely River Esk or through woods to Dalegarth Falls described as Lakelands loveliest waterfall, can be taken. After a busy day the short drive back to Bootle can end with a full four course evening meal at 'The Stables', followed by coffee, a walk round the gardens and relaxing in the TV lounge.

ADVERTISERS ANNOUNCEMENTS

Kellet Country Guest House, Silecroft.

...... is a delightful Victorian property standing in its own extensive grounds of some two acres, close to the sea, yet still within the Lake District National Park, and all that the Lake District has to offer. Our home offers... large comfortable bedrooms each with either double or twin beds, attractively decorated, double glazed, cnetral heated, with hot and cold water to all rooms, plus tea and coffee making facilities, bedside radio, light and alarm, colour T.V, even electric blankets for when the cold weather demands it... PLUS from every room... delightful views of the mountains of Black Combe along with sight of our own beautifully laid out gardens.

Even our residents lounge is a delight for it offers comfortable settees and armchairs, colour TV and video, (together with extensive collection of films) books, magazines, stereo etc.. Coffee/tea is, of course, permanently 'on tap'.

Our lovely little village of Silecroft is located on a long road between the main coast road and the sea, just three miles from Millom. Cobble walls line the streets, and the village still has its own railway station with regular throughput of trains from the north and south daily. In the village there are two highly popular inns, together with a post office, general stores, village hall, and.... surprisingly, it's own 9 hole golf course.

Local sights within easy reach include The Lake District National Park and which includes the well known towns and villages of Coniston, Grasmere, Hawkshead, Windermere, Ambleside, Rydal, Ulverston, Cartmel, Eskdale, Boot etc, etc, not forgetting the Ravenglass and Eskdale Railway, Grizedale Forest, Muncaster Castle, Scafell Pike (England's highest peak) Hardknott Pass and Wrynose Pass (once atempted, never forgotten !!), Sellafield, various National Trust properties, Birds of Prey Centre, along with nature reserves and wild life parks. Bird lovers will be pleased to learn that the RSPB have a bird sanctuary just three miles from here...

.... oh, and less we forget Silecroft beach is officially one of the cleanest beaches in the north of England and boasts seven miles of beautiful sandy shores... So the sea and sand on one side, and the Lake District National Park on the other... what more could you wish for.

Oldbury Contract Services

was a family-run company which started distributing leaflets and other literature in the North East in 1987.

The proprietor, Leon Oldbury, had a background in sales and marketing for Granada as well as experience in making promotional videos. At the finish of a contract as Public Relations Manager of a stately home in Yorkshire, he entered the tourism market full time.

He was offered the opportunity to sell advertising space for a Lakeland magazine and for the Lake District National Park for which he also later did distribution.

The company grew in the early nineties until their vans could be seen all over the UK, distributing local tourism information to hotels, guest houses and attractions in Cumbria as well as main holiday guides to Information Centres and Libraries throughout the whole country, promoting local businesses nationwide.

In 1995, he was founder member of an organisation called the Info-net, a network of

ADVERTISERS' INDEX

literature distributors which covers the entire UK on a monthly basis, offering the very best service in visitor promotions. Current clients include Dove Cottage, World of Beatrix Potter, Lakeland Motor Museum and most of the local tourist authorities.

Mailshots are also undertaken on behalf of clients such as Cumbria Tec and Northern Development Company.

In 1994, they became members of Quality Guild in addition to already being members of Cumbria Tourist Board, Northumbria Tourist Board and Cumbria's Western Lakes and Coast Tourism Trade Association.

As from January of 1997, this company is now part of **RegentLane Ltd**, publishers and printers of guide books and other tourism literature. Regentlane recently bought out the rights to publish the *Towns and Villages of Britain* series of books from Messrs Village Publications Ltd. In addition to this range, they have now started a further range called the *Travellers' Guides*.

Being also book manufacturers, they can print and bind almost any kind of book or booklet. They have recently produced guide books on Broughton-in-Furness, Wasdale and other parts of the Lake District as well as the life stories of various fascinating characters who have lived in the area. Several authors either have or are about to have their work in print whether it be their auto-biography or simply their experiences in one field or another.

Ready for Easter is the humourous story of a couple who decided to give up life in the city and establish a bed and breakfast business in Hawkshead. Illustrated throughout, it gives an insight as to the trials and joys of such an undertaking.

Venus and Her Men resulted from the find of documents in Poland and details the true-life drama of a 14 year old young woman who took part in wars during the fifteenth century.

Two Wheels on a Tin Road follows a 700-mile cycle route across France, tracing the route of the ancient Tin Road when Cornwall supplied that metal to the Middle East during the Bronze Age.